D1601513

Myths, Models,
and U.S. Foreign Policy

MYTHS, MODELS & U.S. FOREIGN POLICY

The Cultural Shaping of Three Cold Warriors

STEPHEN W. TWING

LYNNE
RIENNER
PUBLISHERS

BOULDER
LONDON

Published in the United States of America in 1998 by
Lynne Rienner Publishers, Inc.
1800 30th Street, Boulder, Colorado 80301

and in the United Kingdom by
Lynne Rienner Publishers, Inc.
3 Henrietta Street, Covent Garden, London WC2E 8LU

Library of Congress Cataloging-in-Publication Data
Twing, Stephen W., 1961–
   Myths, models, and U.S. foreign policy : the cultural shaping of
three cold warriors / Stephen W. Twing.
      p.   cm.
   Includes bibliographical references and index.
   ISBN 1-55587-766-4 (hc : alk. paper)
      1. United States—Foreign relations administration—History.
2. International relations and culture—History. 3. Dulles, John
Foster, 1888–1959—Views on foreign relations. 4. Harriman, W.
Averell (William Averell), 1891–1986—Views on foreign relations.
5. McNamara, Robert S., 1916–   —Views on foreign relations.
I. Title.
JZ1479.T88   1998
306.2—dc21   98-3322
                                                                  CIP

British Cataloguing in Publication Data
A Cataloguing in Publication record for this book
is available from the British Library.

Printed and bound in the United States of America

      The paper used in this publication meets the requirements
 ⊗ of the American National Standard for Permanence of
      Paper for Printed Library Materials Z39.48-1984.

   5 4 3 2 1

For Christina

Contents

Preface

This work grew out of a strong conviction that ideas matter. It examines the shared meanings that members of U.S. society have imposed on the world. It also explores how those shared meanings helped to shape three important U.S. statesmen and their policy approaches to the Cold War. As such, it is a work of interpretation, seeking to examine individual worldviews and policymaking behavior in light of the shared meanings that have helped to define for Americans their society and its role in the world. In addition to closely examining three important myths and three important representative characters, the book also suggests a process by which those symbolic structures helped to influence U.S. Cold War–era foreign policy by shaping key policymakers.

* * *

During my work on this project, I have acquired many debts, both intellectual and personal. At the University of South Carolina I benefited tremendously from the guidance and intellectual encouragement of Donald Puchala, Daniel Sabia, and John Sproat. I also owe a special debt of gratitude to my adviser and friend Jerel Rosati for his guidance, encouragement, and friendship. I am extremely grateful to Jeanette Baker for reading the entire manuscript and providing insightful feedback. Completion of the book would never have been possible without the direct involvement, general patience, and encouragement of my wife, Christina. Lynne Rienner, Bridget Julian, and Shena Redmond of Lynne Rienner Publishers were extremely helpful throughout the publication process. Finally I am deeply indebted to my parents, Rhoda Ann and Al Twing, who always encouraged my curiosity.

1

Culture and U.S. Foreign Policy

In recent years there has been increased interest among scholars of U.S. foreign policy in cultural influences on the content of that policy. The problem with much of the existing work on this topic is that its authors simply assert that there is a connection between certain strands of U.S. culture and certain patterns of U.S. foreign policy behavior without examining how (or even whether) these cultural elements actually influence the behavior of individual policymakers. This book seeks to explore this cultural shaping process whereby particular symbolic structures influence the ways individual policymakers view themselves and view and act toward the world.

Scholars trying to explain the content of U.S. foreign policy often focus on two important questions: How do key policymakers view the world? and What are the key sources of these worldviews?[1] Although most scholars of foreign policy behavior would agree that policymaker worldviews are an important variable in the foreign policy making equation, there is no consensus as to the source of these worldviews.

Some scholars have used theoretical tools from the personality or cognitive fields of psychology.[2] Others have examined how policymakers' worldviews are shaped by their use (and misuse) of historical examples.[3] Although such psychological and historical approaches are useful and important, they do not directly address the important role of culture. Indeed, even with increased scholarly interest, the role of U.S. culture in shaping the worldviews of American foreign policy makers has remained underexplored. One reason is that there is so little agreement among scholars as to the definition of culture.

CULTURE AS MEANING

In the field of cultural anthropology, there are many broad definitions of culture. The nineteenth century British anthropologist

1

E. B. Tylor defined culture as "that complex whole which includes knowledge, belief, art, law, morals, custom, and habits acquired by man as a member of society."[4] This definition is all-encompassing, and since it includes both ideas and behaviors, it would be extremely unwieldy as a basis from which to do research on the relationship between culture and policymaker worldviews. This encompassing behavioral-ideational approach to defining culture is shared by American anthropologist A. L. Kroeber, who writes, "Culture is the mass of learned and transmitted motor reactions, habits, techniques, ideas, and values and the behavior they induce."[5]

Other anthropologists such as Ruth Benedict seem to focus solely on behavioral aspects, arguing, "Culture is that complex whole which includes all the habits acquired by man as a member of society."[6] Because this definition fails to address ideational components of culture, it does not provide a useful starting point for researching the culture-to-worldview connection. In fact, all three of these anthropological definitions of culture are unsuitable for this type of research. And there are hundreds more in the cultural anthropology literature that are equally unsuitable.[7]

This definitional pluralism within the field of cultural anthropology is not an insurmountable obstacle, however. There is a fairly rich tradition of sociological thinkers who theorize about culture and whose conceptualizations of it are useful for exploring the culture-worldview-behavior connection. The three classical sociologists whose works are most relevant for this purpose are Karl Marx, Émile Durkheim, and Max Weber. All three thought extensively about the role of culture in influencing human behavior. All three thinkers (albeit to differing degrees) approached the culture concept from the standpoint of the problem of meaning.[8] That is, all operated from the assumption that human beings have a basic need to make sense of the world and to feel connected to something larger than themselves. Conceptualizing culture as a system of meaning provides an excellent starting point to look for the behaviorally relevant linkage among cultural phenomena (i.e., myths, religions) and individual policymakers.

Of these three sociological thinkers, Karl Marx probably focused on the problem of meaning the least. In his theory of historical materialism, cultural phenomena such as religion and myths are a part of society's superstructure, which is powerfully determined by its economic base. Culture, therefore, is of secondary importance for Marx in his attempt to explain macrolevel social change. To the extent that Marx considered cultural phenomena, he tended to focus on religion.

Marx saw the need to conceptualize culture as a system of meaning but believed that the alienation brought on by capitalist relations of production created a void of meaning. For Marx, religion filled this void but was a form of false consciousness: It was created by humans to help dull the pain of their oppression and their alienation from themselves, their labor, and other human beings.[9] And at the same time that it dulled this sense of alienation—caused, he said, by the capitalist system—it obscured and perpetuated it. So Marx did approach culture as a system of meaning of sorts even as he downplayed its role in his social theory.

French sociologist Émile Durkheim tended to focus on religion as an important example of culture as a meaning system. He also held the notion that religion is (at least in part) a symbolic representation of social forces that act on the individual.[10]

In his study of primitive religious practices in Australia, *The Elementary Forms of the Religious Life,* Durkheim shows how religious symbolism serves to represent predominant social forces to individuals, thus helping them both make sense of and feel reverence for the society. In his analysis of the totem, he explains that a deity confronts the individual both as a constraint and as a source of strength and ennoblement.[11] He concludes that the forces of constraint and empowerment portrayed in religious symbolism are actually representative of social forces acting on the individual: Society presents itself as a deity through the symbolism of the totem. Thus for Durkheim, "Religion ceases to be an inexplicable hallucination and takes a foothold in reality. In fact we can say that the believer is not deceived when he believes in the existence of a moral power upon which he depends and from which he receives all that is best in himself: this power exists, it is society."[12]

In his definition of religion, Durkheim builds in the notion of religion as a system of meaning:

> Before all it is a system of ideas with which individuals represent to themselves the society of which they are members, and the obscure but intimate relations which they have with it. This is its primary function; and though metaphorical and symbolic, this representation is not unfaithful. Quite on the contrary, it translates everything essential in the relations which are to be explained: for it is an eternal truth that outside of us there exists something greater than us, with which we enter into communion.[13]

Thus for Durkheim, religion is a cultural phenomenon that supplies the individual with meaning in its most basic form: a sense of connectedness to something larger than ourselves.

Like Durkheim, Max Weber conceptualized culture generally and religion specifically as systems of meaning. In his essay "Methodology in Social Science and Social Policy," Weber summed up his argument that culture should be understood as a system of meaning. "The transcendental presupposition of every cultural science lies not in our finding a certain culture or any 'culture' in general as valuable but rather in the fact that we are cultural beings, endowed with the capacity and the will to take a deliberate attitude towards the world and to lend it significance."[14]

Like those of Durkheim, Weber's cultural studies involved the study of religion. In perhaps his most famous such study, *The Protestant Ethic and the Spirit of Capitalism*, Weber analyzed the connection between two Protestant doctrines (predestination and the theory of the elect) and the strong motivation among members of some Protestant sects to accumulate capital and succeed in business activities.[15] Weber did not argue that these ascetic Protestant beliefs were the sole factor responsible for the rise of capitalism in these societies, but he did make a persuasive case that they played an important role.

After showing that this Calvinist theodicy played a role in creating the rationalized and bureaucratized world of modern capitalism by imposing a set of meanings on believers' everyday lives, Weber went on to lament that the workers in the modern capitalist world were suffering from a shortage of meaning.[16] Thus like Durkheim and Marx, Weber highlighted the ubiquitous human need to feel connected to something larger than oneself, the need for meaning.

Following in the footsteps of Marx, Durkheim, and Weber, a new generation of sociologists approach culture as a system of meaning. In the works of Robert Bellah, Peter Berger and Thomas Luckmann, and Clifford Geertz, one finds an approach to culture that is, if anything, more focused on the central importance of meaning for the human condition than are the works of Marx, Durkheim, and Weber. By their own admission, all of these later sociologists build on and modify the works of the earlier theorists.[17]

In his work on the sociology of religion, Robert Bellah explicitly draws on the work of Marx, Durkheim, and Weber. At the same time he criticizes their work for being overly reductionist (i.e., for being too quick to reduce religious phenomena to material social forces).[18] In response to this problem, he proposes a doctrine he calls symbolic realism, which treats religious symbolism as an objective entity that cannot be reduced to material social forces.[19] In other words, Bellah sets out to study religious symbolism itself, because of the central importance of its meaning for human beings, not in an effort to find out what social forces lie at its foundation.

Particularly enlightening is Bellah's discussion of symbols and meaning.

> Symbols are cultural objects that serve to give meaning to acts or objects by classifying them in categories that include other acts or objects. They provide a context of meaning for discrete acts and objects. Meaning in this sense is location in a context, in a larger interrelated framework defined by values or norms of a more general order than the specific act or object. Human action is almost by definition symbolic action, which is another way of saying that it always involves culture.[20]

For Bellah, then, the problem of meaning must be central to a working conception of culture. Often he stresses the cognitive aspects of the human need for meaning (i.e., the need to make sense out of the world). But he does not ignore the human need for meaning in the noncognitive, more intuitive and affective sense (i.e., the need to feel connected to something larger than ourselves). In fact, he laments the lack of sources of this latter type of meaning in modern society.[21] Thus like Marx, Durkheim, and Weber before him, Bellah conceives of culture as a socially transmitted system of meaning, but he focuses more explicitly on two distinct senses in which humans need meaning.

Like Bellah, Peter Berger and Thomas Luckmann build on the thought of Marx, Durkheim, and Weber, although not exclusively.[22] They also share Bellah's conception of meaning as location within a context. Berger and Luckmann's classic 1966 *The Social Construction of Reality* is a powerful theoretical treatment of the dialectical process by which human subjective meanings become objectified into the reality that we experience as society and of how those objectifications allow individuals to live in and make sense of the world.[23] In their treatment of this dialectical process, they clearly emphasize the meaning-providing aspect of human culture.

> I apprehend the reality of everyday life as an ordered reality. Its phenomena are prearranged in patterns that seem to be independent of my apprehension of them and that impose themselves upon the latter. The reality of everyday life appears already objectified, that is constituted by an order of objects that have been designated as objects before my appearance on the scene. The language used in everyday life continuously provides me with the necessary objectifications and posits the order within which these make sense and within which everyday life has meaning for me.[24]

Besides this basic level of symbolic meanings found in the socially constructed reality of everyday life, Berger and Luckmann discuss four other levels of symbolic meaning frameworks. Although basic-level meanings are sufficient for helping individuals move through their everyday surroundings, there are times when more comprehensive meaning frameworks are needed. These frameworks range from simple explanations at the lowest level (perhaps further categorizations of objects encountered in everyday life) to symbolic universes at the highest level of inclusiveness (e.g., philosophical traditions or religious doctrines).[25] Symbolic universes represent the highest level of meaning integration.

Berger and Luckmann, then, provide a detailed conceptualization of culture as a source of meaning. Their scheme of ever-widening spheres of meaning is extremely useful because it allows the analyst of culture to locate particular cultural phenomena (i.e., myths, theodicies) within this range of widening comprehensiveness of context. And their systematic analysis of the dialectical culture production process is extremely important for providing an understanding of how humans impose meaning on their world, creating social reality and even, to some extent, themselves.

Perhaps the most significant cultural theorist of this era is Clifford Geertz. Like Bellah, Berger, and Luckmann, Geertz builds on the thought of Durkheim, Weber, and, to a lesser extent, Marx.[26] Geertz has probably contributed more than any other thinker to the development of the semiotic culture concept. He argues that human culture consists of socially transmitted symbolic structures that are intersubjectively shared by members of a society who use them to orient themselves to their physical and social world.[27] Since human beings, relative to other animals, are born with few genetically encoded instructions for behavior, their behavior is, as Geertz puts it, "guided predominantly by cultural rather than genetic templates."[28] According to Geertz, with no rigid genetic templates to orient them to their world, human beings use these socially transmitted symbolic structures as mental models that guide them through everyday life.[29]

In his study of religion, Geertz explores both the cognitive and the intuitive/affective dimensions of the human need for meaning and shows how religion (and culture more generally) connects our everyday lives with a much larger reality, within the context of which our everyday world makes sense.[30] In this sense religion is what Berger and Luckmann call a symbolic universe.[31] For Geertz, however, the affective aspects of symbolic universes are just as important as the cognitive aspects. Religious symbols may help us make sense of the world by connecting us to something larger, but the connection itself also fulfills an important need. Thus in Geertz's treatment of religion, these societally transmitted symbolic structures fulfill the most basic cognitive and affective human requirements.

U.S. FOREIGN POLICY AND SYMBOLIC STRUCTURES

Whereas religion is an important symbolic structure for fulfilling cognitive and affective requirements, it is not by any means the only one. The task for the cultural analyst studying U.S. foreign policy is to locate other such symbolic structures transmitted within U.S. society. Upon locating and examining these symbolic structures, the analyst must then attempt to determine how they have influenced the behavior of American policymakers. This is precisely the aim of this book.

Scholars of U.S. foreign policy have identified several interesting symbolic structures transmitted within U.S. society that serve as important sources of meaning for Americans and that have foreign policy relevance. Historian Michael Hunt argues that U.S. foreign policy has been guided by a three-pronged foreign affairs ideology based on liberal exceptionalism and racism.[32] Historian Loren Baritz argues that the U.S. Vietnam policy was heavily influenced by both a myth of U.S. technological invincibility and a Puritan-inspired "city on the hill" myth that portrays the United States as democratic example and savior for the world.[33]

Historian Arthur Schlesinger Jr. agrees that U.S. foreign policy has been significantly influenced by the city-on-the-hill myth. He sees historical phases where U.S. diplomacy was shaped first by the city-on-the-hill myth and then by an experimental or pragmatic myth that has a more realpolitik orientation.[34] Whereas the city-on-the-hill myth calls for the United States to stay true to its highest ideals in its dealings with the world, the pragmatic myth suggests that since the United States is an ongoing and vulnerable democratic experiment, it must doggedly pursue its interests in the world in the most effective way possible.

A third foreign policy–relevant myth, the market myth, has been identified by historian William Appleman Williams. Williams argues that since the turn of the century the United States has followed an economically exploitive "open door" approach to the rest of the world.[35] He argues that underlying this open-door approach has been a mythical conception of U.S. society as the idealized arena for economic competition.

So Baritz, Schlesinger, and Williams have identified three myths that not only serve as important sources of meaning and identity for Americans but also are relevant for U.S. foreign policy. These three scholars have identified an important connection between certain strands of American culture and the content of U.S. foreign policy. Their work suffers from a common shortcoming, however. Each scholar identifies a myth (or combination of myths), points to patterns in U.S. foreign policy behavior, and assumes that the myth (or myths) must have somehow shaped the policy, but none attempts to explain precisely how culture shapes policy. The key to understanding the relationship between U.S. culture and foreign policy lies in exploring and examining this mechanism of influence.

How does one make sense out of these different myths, two of which (the Puritan and pragmatic) seem to be quite contradictory in their substantive influence on U.S. foreign policy? Some scholars such as Schlesinger argue that these myths alternate over time in exercising the predominant influence over U.S. foreign policy with periods of Puritan crusading followed by periods of pragmatic experimentation.[36] Unfortunately, Schlesinger does not discuss just what determines whether the foreign policy of an era will be Puritan or pragmatic. Are changes in the cultural orientation of U.S. policy simply responses to changes in U.S. society or in the international environment, or can they be attributed merely to changes in the circulation of policymaking elites? Is it possible that these three cultural traditions could exercise influence over policy simultaneously in tension with each other? One way to answer this question is to examine the cultural shaping of individual policymakers.

Do individual statespersons suffer from a form of cultural schizophrenia, conceiving of themselves as Puritans today and pragmatists or entrepreneurs tomorrow? Or is it more likely that some policymakers identify consistently over time with the city-on-the-hill myth, others with the pragmatic myth, and still others, the market myth? After all, these three myths serve as important sources of not only collective identity in society but also individual identity; they help to answer the question What makes one an American? Thus it would seem that if an individual is influenced more by one myth than by the others, this identification would tend to be somewhat stable over time.

The only way to answer this question is to examine closely the biographies, and thereby the cultural shaping, of individual statespersons. This is also the only way to make the crucial two-part connection between these different societal-level symbolic structures and the worldviews and self-conceptions of leaders and between the worldviews and self-conceptions of leaders and their policy behavior.

In addition to these myths, there is another type of societal-level symbolic structure that warrants examination for its influence on U.S. foreign policy. Closely related to the three myths previously outlined are three representative characters. Alasdair MacIntyre first identified the representative character in his 1984 moral-philosophical treatise entitled *After Virtue;* Robert Bellah and his colleagues further developed the concept in *Habits of the Heart: Individualism and Commitment in American Life.* Whereas the three myths serve as idealized models of U.S. society, various representative characters within U.S. culture serve as idealized models for individual behavior.[37] The three representative characters within U.S. culture that correspond to the city-on-the-hill, pragmatic, and market myths are, respectively, the Puritan, the manager, and the entrepreneur.

These two sets of societal-level symbolic structures (the three myths and the three representative characters, all of which will be discussed in much more detail in Chapter 2) and their influence on individual worldviews, self-conceptions, and policymaking behavior are the focus of this book. The exploration of this cultural shaping process is conducted via three case studies. Each closely examines one statesman's formative experiences, his evolving worldview and self-conceptions, and finally his policy preferences and policymaking behavior in light of these societal-level symbolic structures.

The subjects are three important cold warriors: John Foster Dulles, Averell Harriman, and Robert McNamara. Analyzing the worldviews, self-conceptions, policy preferences, and policymaking behavior of three cold warriors provides a common substantive focus. All three of these men were faced, in their careers as policymakers, with the superpower confrontation that dominated the global political scene during the Cold War years. Focusing on the Cold War era thus allows one to compare and contrast the way they conceptualized the communist threat and the strategies and tactics they devised for dealing with that threat. Previous study of Cold War–era U.S. diplomatic history has suggested that these three statesmen differed significantly both in the ways they conceptualized the Cold War confrontation and in the strategies and approaches they proposed.

Perhaps these differences in worldview and approach can be partially explained by the fact that each individual was predominately influenced by a different set of myths and representative characters. Previous impressionistic study of the three suggests that John Foster Dulles may have been predominately influenced by the city-on-the-hill myth and the Puritan representative character, whereas Averell Harriman may have been influenced more by the market myth and the entrepreneur character, and Robert McNamara may have been more influenced by the pragmatic myth and the manager representative character. In order to get at the worldviews, self- and role conceptions, policy preferences, and policy behavior of these statesmen, I have made extensive use of their personal papers and correspondence.[38] A set of basic questions was designed and used to aid in identifying their basic normative and descriptive beliefs about world politics in general and about Cold War U.S. foreign policy in particular.[39]

In Chapter 2, I discuss the societal-level symbolic structures (i.e., the myths and representative characters). In addition to elaborating on them conceptually, I explore how they have been transmitted through American society and how they have informed the nation's political discourse.

NOTES

1. I am using the term *worldview* to denote the body of basic descriptive and normative beliefs a policymaker holds about world politics. Typical component beliefs in the worldview of a policymaker would address such basic issues as the structure of the international system, identification of the most threatening actors in the system, and the preferred role of the United States in the world.

2. For a classic example of the personality approach see Alexander George and Juliette George, *Woodrow Wilson and Colonel House: A Personality Study* (New York: Dover, 1956). For a classic example of the cognitive approach see Robert Jervis, *Perception and Misperception in World Politics* (Princeton: Princeton University Press, 1976).

3. See Richard Neustadt and Ernest May, *Thinking in Time: The Use of History for Decision Makers* (New York: Free Press, 1986).

4. A. L. Kroeber and Clyde Kluckhohn, *Culture: A Critical Review of Concepts and Definitions* (New York: Random House, 1952), 81.

5. Ibid., 84.

6. Ibid., 81.

7. Ibid.

8. Robert Wuthnow, *Meaning and Moral Order: Explorations in Cultural Analysis* (Berkeley: University of California Press), 35.

9. Karl Marx, "Contribution to a Critique of Hegel's Philosophy of Right," 43–44, reprinted in Neil Smelser, *Karl Marx on Society and Social Change* (Chicago: University of Chicago Press), 13–14.

10. Émile Durkheim, *The Elementary Forms of the Religious Life* (New York: Collier Books, 1961), 236.

11. Ibid., 240.

12. Ibid., 257.

13. Ibid.

14. Max Weber, "Objectivity in Social Science and Social Policy," in Max Weber, *The Methodology of the Social Sciences* (New York: Free Press, 1949), 81.

15. Max Weber, *The Protestant Ethic and the Spirit of Capitalism* (New York: Charles Scribner's Sons, 1958).

16. Ibid., 182.

17. For an excellent review of the influence of Marx, Durkheim, and Weber on these later theorists, see Wuthnow, 18–49.

18. Robert Bellah, *Beyond Belief: Essays on Religion in a Posttraditional World* (New York: Harper and Row, 1970), 248–250.

19. Ibid., 253.

20. Ibid., 261.

21. Ibid., 255.

22. Peter Berger and Thomas Luckmann, *The Social Construction of Reality: A Treatise in the Sociology of Knowledge* (New York: Anchor Press, 1966), 6–18.

23. Ibid., 18–22.

24. Ibid., 22.

25. Ibid., 94–97.

26. Clifford Geertz, *The Interpretation of Cultures* (New York: Harper-Collins, 1973), 405.

27. Ibid., 12.

28. Ibid., 75.

29. Ibid., 44.

30. Ibid., 108.

31. Berger and Luckmann, 95–97.

32. Michael Hunt, *Ideology and U.S. Foreign Policy* (New Haven: Yale University Press, 1987).

33. Loren Baritz, *Backfire: A History of How American Culture Led Us into Vietnam and Made Us Fight the Way We Did* (New York: Morrow, 1985).

34. Arthur Schlesinger Jr., *The Cycles of American History* (New York: Houghton Mifflin, 1986).

35. See William Appleman Williams, *The Contours of American History* (Chicago: Quadrangle Press, 1966). See also William Appleman Williams, *The Tragedy of American Diplomacy* (New York: Dell, 1962).

36. Schlesinger, 16–17.

37. See Alasdair MacIntyre, *After Virtue* (South Bend: University of Notre Dame Press, 1984), 25–31. See also Robert Bellah et al., *Habits of the Heart: Individualism and Commitment in American Life* (New York: Harper and Row, 1985), 39–41.

38. The Dulles case study is the only one that makes extensive use of speeches to tap into the policymaker's worldview. Speeches could be viewed as less than ideal windows into an official's worldview, since in the modern era they are increasingly written by professional speechwriters. Dulles, however, consistently refused the services of speechwriters, preferring to draft his own speeches, albeit with occasional feedback from colleagues. See Townsend Hoopes, *The Devil and John Foster Dulles* (Boston: Little, Brown, 1973), 149.

39. The questions were as follows:

1.a. What is the relationship between morality and international relations?

1.b. How much weight should moral considerations carry in the formulation and conduct of U.S. foreign policy?

1.c. To what extent should the Cold War be viewed in moral terms?

2.a. What is the role of power in international relations?

2.b. How should U.S. power best be used in the Cold War? What forms should it take (i.e., military, diplomatic, economic, ideological/cultural)?

2.c. What are the most worrisome sources of Soviet power in the Cold War (i.e., military, diplomatic, economic, ideological/cultural)?

2.d. What is the best strategy for dealing with the Soviets in the Cold War context? Can they be bargained with?

2.e. Should U.S. foreign policy be strictly guided by a set of overarching principles (moral or geostrategic) or should policymakers leave themselves free to react to the global environment as it changes?

2

Myths and Representative Characters in U.S. Culture

U.S. society, like any other, has been held together in part by certain symbolic structures that have provided its citizens with meaning and identity. This chapter is an exploration of the two types of societal-level symbolic structures described in Chapter 1: the "city on the hill," market, and pragmatic myths about U.S. society and the Puritan, entrepreneur, and manager representative character types.[1] The idea is to faithfully capture the meaning inherent in the stories that Americans have told about themselves for more than 350 years.

The first type of symbolic structure that we will explore is the myth. The *American Heritage Dictionary* provides a definition of myth as "a real or fictional story, recurring theme or character type that appeals to the consciousness of a people by embodying its cultural ideals or by giving expression to deep, commonly felt emotions."[2]

This definition presents a notion of myth that is applicable to modern industrial societies.[3] It represents a tradition of thinking about myth that is best exemplified by Émile Durkheim.[4] For Durkheim, myth serves to provide collective identity and an emotional bond among a people. As myths in this Durkheimian sense, the city-on-the-hill, pragmatic, and market myths each tell a particular kind of story about America and each embody a particular notion of what it means to be an American.

For Durkheim, myths fall into a larger category of socially transmitted symbolic structures that he calls collective representations.[5] Members of a society use collective representations to conceptualize their society and those things that affect it.[6] Durkheim argues that in addition to serving as cognitive heuristic models, collective representations also serve important affective, social-solidarity-enhancing aspects. He argues that through these collective representations society is infused with value (and indeed in some cases, sacred qualities).

Durkheim's notion of myth flows neatly from his discussion of the collective representation concept: "The mythology of a group is the system of beliefs common to this group. The traditions whose memory it perpetuates express the way in which society represents man and the world; it is a moral system and a cosmology as well as a history. . . . Through it the group periodically renews the sentiment which it has of itself and of its unity."[7] Thus for Durkheim, the myth/ritual complex is crucial for creating individual respect and reverence for the society as well as collective identity.[8] The city-on-the-hill, market, and pragmatic myths have served to infuse U.S. society with value, and this fact is vitally important for understanding any human social behavior in that context, including U.S. foreign policymaking behavior.

THE REPRESENTATIVE CHARACTER CONCEPT

The other key concept at the societal level of analysis is the representative character. This concept was first developed by Alasdair MacIntyre and later adapted by Robert Bellah and his colleagues.[9]

MacIntyre presents the representative character as a hybrid between the sociological concept of role and the concept of a cultural ideal. He describes it in terms of the following dramatic metaphor:

> There is a type of dramatic tradition—Japanese Noh plays and English medieval morality plays are examples—which possesses a stock set of characters immediately recognizable to the audience. Such characters partially define the possibilities of plot and action. To understand them is to be provided with a means of interpreting the behavior of the actors who play them, just because a similar understanding informs the intentions of the actors themselves; and other actors may define their parts with special reference to these central characters. So it is with certain kinds of social roles specific to particular cultures. They furnish recognizable characters and the ability to recognize them is socially crucial because a knowledge of the character provides an interpretation of the actions of those individuals who have assumed the character. It does so precisely because those individuals have used the same knowledge to guide and structure their behavior.[10]

To the extent that an individual is influenced by one of these culturally generated representative characters, he or she takes on certain values and patterns of social behavior. As MacIntyre argues, armed with knowledge of this character-based template, an outside observer is capable of interpreting the individual's actions in their proper cultural context. MacIntyre argues that a representative character within a culture serves as a sort of ideational funnel that captures broad moral or social ideals and focuses them into models of social behavior for individuals to follow. "They are, so to speak," he writes, "the moral representatives of their culture, and they are so because of the way in which moral and metaphysical ideas and theories assume through them an embodied existence in the social world."[11] Thus the notion of a culturally generated representative character provides a useful conceptual linkage between cultural traditions at the societal level and policymaker self-conceptions. The crucial task for the cultural analyst of U.S. foreign policy is to determine whether (and how) these representative characters (and myths) color the worldviews and self-conceptions of these statesmen and influence their policymaking behavior.

Several of the representative characters in U.S. culture have already been identified in contemporary scholarly works. In their 1985 study entitled *Habits of the Heart: Individualism and Commitment in American Life,* Robert Bellah, Richard Madsen, William Sullivan, Ann Swidler, and Steven Tipton take MacIntyre's representative character concept and apply it to U.S. culture. They identify five major representative characters; among them are the Puritan, the entrepreneur, and the manager. Bellah and his colleagues reiterate MacIntyre's claim for the power of the representative character concept to illustrate how cultural ideals and traditions are channeled into modes of individual behavior. "A representative character is a kind of symbol," they write, "a public image that helps define, for a group of people, just what kinds of personality traits it is good and legitimate to develop."[12]

According to Bellah and his colleagues, the Puritan representative character flows from the city-on-the-hill myth, first developed by John Winthrop.[13] The Puritan is characterized by a burning drive to obey the word of God and to set up and maintain a community of God's chosen people.[14] The paradigmatic mode of social action for the Puritan is conversion and mobilization of followers to fight against evil in the world. The implicit epistemology of the Puritan is that truth and the good are revealed by the Bible—an infallible source. The Puritan views his community as the locus of good and sees the rest of the world as evil. Latter-day Puritans have viewed the United States in the same terms and have seen it as the nation's duty to recreate the world in its (and therefore God's) image.

The entrepreneur representative character flows directly from an understanding of U.S. culture that arose with the development of a national market during the mid-to-late 1800s.[15] At the core of the moral personality of the entrepreneur is a powerful competitive individualism.[16] To the entrepreneur, power means the ability to drive competitors out of the marketplace or at least to drive a hard bargain in a business deal. The paradigmatic mode of social action for the entrepreneur is head-to-head competition and negotiation in a market context. The entrepreneur is unfettered by the Puritan's biblical morality and epistemology of revelation and subscribes instead to the morality (or lack thereof) of laissez-faire and the epistemology of social Darwinism. Thus as the market myth provides a particular model for understanding U.S. society, the entrepreneur character provides a model for understanding how an individual should behave in such a society.

Although the entrepreneur character continues to be a powerful model, Bellah and his colleagues argue that the dominant representative character in twentieth-century U.S. society is the manager.[17] They note the irony in the fact that it was the American entrepreneurs or robber barons who created the modern context within which the corporate manager operates.[18] And whereas both the entrepreneur and the manager characters operate in a business context, there are distinct differences between the two. Direct competition with other entrepreneurs is the paradigmatic mode of social action for the entrepreneur; administration of human and material resources and social engineering is the manager's primary mode. In other words, the manager's primary role "is to persuade, inspire, cajole, and intimidate those he manages so that his organization measures up to the criteria of effectiveness shaped ultimately by the market, but specifically by those in control of his organization—finally, its owners."[19] The job of the manager is to experiment with patterns of employee and resource manipulation until one that maximizes corporate profit is found. Thus the manager adopts the morality and the epistemology of a vulgarized pragmatism— whatever works best is good and whatever is borne out by experience (or experiment) is true. For the manager, power means the ability to experiment with human and nonhuman resources and the ability to manipulate them in ways that will maximize organizational efficiency.

Each of these representative characters (the Puritan, the entrepreneur, and the manager) is a symbolic structure transmitted within U.S. society that serves as a model for individual behavior. The task for the cultural analyst studying U.S. foreign policy is to determine to what extent important policymakers embody these representative characters. This is accomplished by looking for self-conceptions and patterns of behavior that are consistent with the paradigmatic modes of social action and with moral and epistemological profiles of the various representative characters.[20]

THE MEANING AND IDENTITY GAP IN EARLY AMERICA

When the first European settlers arrived in America, there was a significant need for new symbolic structures that would provide new constitutive meanings and a collective identity that fitted the settlers' new situation. The myths and representative characters discussed previously helped fill these meaning and identity needs quite well.

Throughout *Democracy in America*, Alexis de Tocqueville describes and explains the emergence of a democratic society in the United States by comparing its features with aristocratic societies in Europe. However, de Tocqueville does not limit himself to describing the political-structural differences between a democratic society and an aristocratic society. Upon reading *Democracy in America* one is struck by the extent to which he renders intelligible the complex economic, social, and cultural forces at work at the birth of the American republic. In fact, what de Tocqueville does is provide a "thick description" (to borrow Clifford Geertz's phrase) of the birth of a modern society in America.[21]

One of the first things that jumps out at the cultural analyst reading de Tocqueville's work is the meaning and identity vacuum that faced the members of the emerging American society. Again and again de Tocqueville describes the stark contrast between the constricting, convention-laden social milieu of the aristocratic societies in Europe and the extremely egalitarian, indeed nearly chaotic, social milieu of the emerging democratic society in America. This contrast is illuminated nicely in the following quotation:

> In democracies men are never stationary; a thousand chances waft them to and fro, and their life is always the sport of unforeseen or (so to speak) extemporaneous circumstances, thus they are obliged to do things which they have imperfectly learned, to say things which they imperfectly understand, and to devote themselves to work for which they are unprepared by long apprenticeships. In aristocracies every man has one sole object, which he unceasingly pursues; but among democratic nations the existence of man is more complex; the same mind will almost always embrace several objects at once, and these objects are frequently wholly

foreign to each other. As it cannot know them all well the mind is readily satisfied with imperfect notions of each.[22]

The settlers had left a society in which identity and everyday reality were tightly defined by rigid hierarchical social structures and found themselves in a society that was relatively free of such structures.[23] And yet every society has a need for legitimation. Peter Berger and Thomas Luckmann, in *The Social Construction of Reality*, define legitimation as the creation of new symbolic structures whose crucial function is to allow individuals to make sense of the social order.[24] There was also a need for symbolic structures to provide sources of identity for the citizens of the emerging American republic. The problem of national identity takes a unique form in America as compared to many European countries where national identity is developed organically from centuries of common history as well as ethnic, linguistic, and religious homogeneity. In his *American Politics: The Promise of Disharmony*, Samuel Huntington captures the essence of the Americans' unique identity problem: "For most peoples, national identity is the product of a long process of historical evolution involving common ancestors, common experiences, common ethnic background, common language, common culture, and usually common religion. National identity is thus organic in character. Such is not the case in the United States. American nationalism has been defined in political rather than organic terms."[25]

Huntington argues that the primary sources of American national identity are the foundational liberal democratic ideas embodied in the Declaration of Independence and the Constitution. He calls this corpus of political ideas the "American Creed."[26] Whereas Huntington's diagnosis of the American identity problem is essentially persuasive, his solution to the problem is incomplete. This "American Creed" is certainly an important source of identity for Americans, but it is not the only source.

Indeed, the very same symbolic structures that served to legitimate the social order in the emerging American society de Tocqueville described were also important sources of identity for Americans. The city-on-the-hill, market, and pragmatic myths and the Puritan, entrepreneur, and manager representative characters helped Americans make sense of their society and provided them with sources of collective identity.[27]

THE CITY-ON-THE-HILL MYTH

Wee shall find that the God of Israel is among us, when tenn of us shall be able to resist a thousand of our enemies, when he shall

make us a praise and glory, that men shall say of succeeding plan-
tations: the lord make it like that of New England: for wee must
Consider that wee shall be as a citty upon a Hill, the eies of all
people are upon us: so that if wee shall deale falsely with our god
in this worke wee have undertaken and soe cause him to withdraw
his present help from us, wee shall shame the faces of many of
God's worthy servants, and cause their prayers to be turned into
curses upon us till wee be consumed out of the good land whither
we are going.[28]

This quotation is taken from John Winthrop's sermon entitled
"A Modell of Christian Charity." He presented this sermon to the
founding members of the Massachusetts Bay Company on board
the *Arbella*, which was taking them to the New World in 1630. In this
sermon we find the genesis of the first myth of origin of American
society. The city-on-the-hill myth embodied in Winthrop's sermon
provided an important source of identity for the Puritans who
would people the New England settlement—it dubbed them the
new Israelites, God's chosen people. It also served to legitimate—
that is, explain and justify—the new social order.

This myth told them that they were bound individually to each
other as a church and polity, and collectively to God, by a holy
covenant.[29] They were on a divine mission to set up the perfect
Christian society as an example to the rest of the world, and everything they would be asked to do by their leaders flowed from this
premise.[30] God was watching closely and would help them as long
as they didn't stray from their mission, but if they failed, He would
surely desert them in the wilderness.[31] It is hard to imagine a symbolic structure with more legitimating force or one that would provide as much identity as the city-on-the-hill myth first put forth by
Winthrop in that 1630 shipboard sermon.[32] This myth gave the Puritan settlers a perfect blueprint of the social order they were to
build, explained to them why they must do it, and in the process
told them exactly who they were.

The influence of the city-on-the-hill myth and the underlying
covenant theology remained very strong in the minds of the first
generation of Puritan New Englanders. But by the second and third
generations, church leaders began to warn that the Puritans were
becoming too interested in material concerns, were ignoring their
covenant with God, and would surely suffer divine punishment for
this.[33]

By the 1660s there existed what might be called a generational
crisis of faith in the Puritan church and polity. Many of the second-
generation Puritans were failing to have the (episodic emotional)
conversion experience, which was a requirement of full admission

into the church covenant.[34] In 1661, the church leaders held a special conference and altered the covenant doctrine to allow these technically "unsaved" individuals partial admittance.[35] This doctrinal innovation became known as the "halfway covenant," and as Perry Miller points out, it started a process of gradually expanding the membership to the point that the covenant idea lost its meaning and its ability to legitimate the rigid Puritan church and political hierarchy.[36] This expansion process was completed in the Great Awakening of 1740, in which revival leaders such as Jonathan Edwards extended membership in the covenant to all who would hear them.[37]

Although the Great Awakening of 1740 fatally sapped the power of covenant theory to legitimate the rigid church hierarchy in New England, it did serve to spread the influence of the city-on-the-hill myth beyond New England into the other colonies.[38] Indeed, during the decades following the Great Awakening, the city-on-the-hill myth underwent a significant transformation that would enhance its influence both intensively and extensively. As Nathan Hatch concludes from his survey of New England sermons of the era in *The Sacred Cause of Liberty*, by the 1750s this Puritan-inspired myth began to be infused with Whig political values by influential clergymen. As Hatch points out, this merging of powerful political values into the city-on-the-hill myth only enhanced its legitimation and identity-forming potential at a time when the colonies were faced with the French and Indian War and a gradually developing confrontation with Great Britain.[39] New England clergymen achieved this grafting of Whig political values onto the city-on-the-hill myth by imparting to Puritan settlers a tremendous thirst for liberty.[40] This injection of the cause of liberty into the founding myth provided extremely inspirational imagery for colonists entering into a confrontation with the mother country.

Indeed, during the Revolutionary War the city-on-the-hill myth (infused with images of a struggle for liberty) was evoked with great frequency, according to Hatch.[41] Thus the founding myth began to be used by religious and political elites to mobilize citizens of the colonies against Great Britain in the run-up to the Revolutionary War.

We see in this politicization of the myth an important tendency to demonize the adversary (in this case it was Great Britain, but during the French and Indian War it was France) and to canonize America.[42] Hatch shows how this demonization of Europe and self-canonization continued after the revolution and into the Napoleonic era. His survey of sermons during this period shows that influential clergymen saw the world as a confrontation between the young American republic, representing God and liberty, and the nations of Europe, which represented tyranny and the Antichrist.[43] As we will see, this mirror-imaging effect is an important by-product of the city-on-the-hill myth and significantly affects the way Americans under its influence react to international conflict.[44]

Another important development in this stage of the evolution of the city-on-the-hill myth is the fact that influential clergymen began to think that before the kingdom of God would come on earth, America would first have to spread liberty and the republican form of government throughout the world.[45] This new democratic aspect of America's mission is significant because prior to the Revolutionary War, the focus of the mission was solely on spreading the true (read "the Protestant") gospel to the rest of the world. This obligation to become a democratic as well as an evangelical missionary to the world would become a very important ideational force driving U.S. foreign policy during the late nineteenth and twentieth centuries.[46]

In the first decades of the nineteenth century, when revivalism spread over the entire country, the idea of a U.S. mission to improve the rest of the world became institutionalized in interdenominational missionary associations whose twofold purpose was to "save" the inhabitants of the American frontier and then to "save" the rest of the world.[47] As Perry Miller argues, the idea that the United States had a God-given mission that drove this intense and geographically widespread missionary effort became the basis for a powerful vision of the U.S. community.[48] The sermons and other writings that Miller cites from the leaders of these missionary associations came from many different denominations and from all over the country, which is a good indicator of how thoroughly the city-on-the-hill myth had spread by the early nineteenth century.[49]

Nor was the spread of this myth confined to formal religious circles or clergy. Indeed, Herman Melville, one of the brightest lights in nineteenth-century American literature, helped to strengthen and perpetuate the myth. In *White Jacket,* he writes:

> And we Americans are the peculiar, chosen people—the Israel of our time; we bear the ark of the liberties of the world. . . . God has predestined, mankind expects, great things from our race; and great things we feel in our souls. The rest of nations must soon be in our rear. We are the pioneers of the world; the advance guard, sent on through the wilderness of untried things, to break a new path in the New World that is ours. . . . Long enough have we been skeptics with regard to ourselves, and doubted whether,

indeed the political Messiah had come. But he has come in us, if
we would but give utterance to his promptings.[50]

Later in 1876 in a poem entitled *Clarel*, Melville would accuse
America of abandoning its covenant with God and would warn of
the consequences.[51] Thus he provided strong literary support for
the maintenance of the city-on-the-hill myth even when he felt that
America was not living up to it.

In the late-nineteenth and early-twentieth centuries we find political leaders using the city-on-the-hill myth to praise America and
to encourage Americans to follow through on their God-given mission to improve the world. In 1898 during the Spanish-American
War, Indiana senator Albert Beveridge exhorted Americans to fulfill
their obligations as the people chosen by God to save the world:

> He has made us the master organizers of the world to establish sys-
> tem where chaos reigns. He has given us the spirit of progress to
> overwhelm the forces of reaction throughout the earth. He has
> made us adepts in government that we may administer govern-
> ment among savage and senile peoples. . . . He has marked the
> American people as His Chosen Nation finally to lead in the re-
> generation of the world. This is the divine mission of America,
> and it holds for us all profit, glory, happiness possible to man. We
> are trustees of the world's progress, guardians of its righteous
> peace. The judgment of the Master is upon us: "Ye have been
> faithful over a few things; I will make you ruler over many
> things."[52]

Beveridge's remarks during and after the Spanish-American
War represent a new kind of politicization of the city-on-the-hill
myth. Here we see an important political leader using the myth to
mobilize the American people for war. Beveridge redefines America's divine mission. It is no longer enough to serve as a shining example or to Christianize the rest of the world; now God wishes the
United States to provide all other societies with good (meaning
U.S.-style democratic) government. The city-on-the-hill myth in the
hands of Beveridge becomes an American obligation to rule the
world. Perhaps, as some have argued, the dramatic expansion of
America's obligations inherent in this myth merely reflects a recognition of the growth of American power by those who perpetuated
the myth during this period.[53] At any rate, America's God-given
mission as presented by this myth would continue to expand during
the twentieth century.

Perhaps the most famous twentieth century American statesman to invoke the city-on-the-hill myth in relation to foreign policy

was Woodrow Wilson. During a 1919 trip around the country to offer and explain the Treaty of Versailles and the League of Nations to the American people, Wilson gave speeches in which he clearly laid out America's God-given mission in the world. In Salt Lake City, he proclaimed:

> I for my part want to go in and accept what is offered to us, the leadership of the world. A leadership of what sort, my fellow citizens? Not a leadership that leads men along the lines by which great nations can profit out of weak nations, not an exploiting power, but a liberating power, a power to show the world that when America was born it was indeed a finger pointed toward those lands into which men could deploy some of these days and live in happy freedom, look each other in the eyes as equals, see that no man was put upon, that no people were forced to accept authority which was not of their own choice, and that out of the general generous impulse of the human genius and the human spirit, we were lifted along the levels of civilization to days when there should be wars no more, but men should govern themselves in peace and amity and quiet. That is the leadership we said we wanted and now the world offers it to us.[54]

This millennialist vision has the United States responsible for no less than creating a democratic utopia throughout the entire world and is a continuation of the Beveridge theme of providing good government for the world. Wilson believed very strongly that America—and he personally—had a very special God-given mission to save the world from war and repression. This belief was clearly reflected in his behavior at the end of the war during the peace negotiations and during his attempts to get the treaty ratified by Congress.[55]

With Wilson, then, we have a very powerful and influential policymaker who embellishes the city-on-the-hill myth with rhetoric and who seems to be very strongly influenced by the myth in his conduct of U.S. foreign policy.

Thus over time we can discern a clear developmental pattern with regard to this founding myth. From its genesis in John Winthrop's speech on the *Arbella* in 1630, the myth has evolved even as it has spread from the Massachusetts Bay settlement throughout the expanding American republic.

For the first Puritans, the mission was simply to be a shining example of a godly community. Later generations of Puritan mythmakers expanded the mission to include Puritanizing (not just Christianizing) first England and then the rest of the world. As the myth spread throughout the growing republic, the mission began to

include spreading democracy as well as the true religion throughout the world. As America began to grow in power during the late-
nineteenth and early-twentieth centuries, new mythmakers such as
Beveridge and Wilson began to give the myth a much more aggressive and militant tone. The divine mission in the twentieth-century
version of the city-on-the-hill myth made America responsible for
bringing about a utopian democratic millennium throughout the
world. And twentieth-century mythmakers like Wilson wanted the
United States to pursue aggressively this millennial vision with all
the power at its command.

THE PURITAN REPRESENTATIVE CHARACTER

Closely related to the city-on-the-hill myth is the Puritan representative character. Like the entrepreneur and manager representative
characters, the Puritan is characterized by three basic elements: a
distinct epistemological stance, a distinct moral stance, and a distinct paradigmatic mode of social action. The elements of the Puritan representative character emerged from the telling and retelling
(in histories and novels about Puritan New England) of the life stories of Puritan political and religious leaders and from intellectual
histories of the era.[56] These elements came together to form the
idealized model for individual behavior that is the Puritan representative character.

The Puritan representative character is unusual in that both its
epistemological stance and its moral stance have a biblical source.
Put simply, the Puritans believed that the Bible was the only source
for conceptions of the true and the good. In fact, as Perry Miller
and Thomas Johnson explain in the introduction to *The Puritans,*
the Puritans' strict and literal use of the Bible as a moral and epistemological guide was the main issue dividing them from the An-
glicans, whose interpretations of the Bible were much less strict and
literal. As Miller and Johnson argue,

> The difference between the Anglican and the Puritan, then, was
> that the Puritan thought the Bible, the revealed word of God, was
> the word of God from one end to the other, a complete body of
> laws, an absolute code in everything it touched upon; the Angli-
> can thought this a rigid, doctrinaire and utterly unjustifiable ex-
> tension of the authority of scripture. The Puritan held that the
> Bible was sufficiently plain and explicit so that men with the
> proper learning, following the proper rules of deduction and in-
> terpretation, could establish its meaning and intention on every
> subject, not only in theology, but in ethics, costume, diplomacy,

military tactics, inheritances, profits, marriages, and judicial procedure.[57]

The Puritan believed that only the regenerate souls who had received the grace of God were capable of properly interpreting God's word in the scripture and His order throughout the universe. Since only a small number of people in each congregation were considered regenerate or true members, an elite group in the Massachusetts Bay Colony was in charge of determining what constituted the true, the good, and the just for the rest of the colony.[58] As Miller points out in *Errand in the Wilderness,* this led to a very authoritarian church and polity during the first hundred years of the Massachusetts Bay Settlement, or until the Great Awakening of 1740.[59]

Puritan religious and political leaders took their responsibility as interpreters of God's will very seriously, and they saw themselves as chosen by God for this crucial role.[60] This led to a double sense of "chosenness" on the part of Puritan leaders such as John Winthrop; he was the chosen leader of God's chosen people.[61] This sense of chosenness and destiny is an important characteristic of Puritan leadership because it tends to be accompanied by an unwillingness to compromise, especially when the leader perceives sacred principles to be at stake. Also, in conjunction with the Puritan's revelation-based moral and epistemological stances, this sense of chosenness gives the Puritan leader a distinct paradigmatic mode of social action: conversion and mobilization of followers to carry out God's will in the world.

The first and most powerful example of this Puritan mode of social action may be found in John Winthrop's famous shipboard "model of Christian charity" sermon to the first settlers of the Massachusetts Bay Colony. In this sermon, which contains the seeds of the city-on-the-hill myth, Governor Winthrop exhorted his fellow colonists to give their all so that their divine mission to the new world would succeed.[62] The sermon is full of Old Testament imagery, which Winthrop used to strengthen the sense that these Puritan settlers were in fact the new Israel and as such were tightly bound to each other and to God in a holy covenant.[63] He told his fellow settlers that even as the *Arbella* carried them to their destination, the eyes of God and the Christian world were on them and they must not fail.[64]

Later generations of Puritan leaders in New England continued to use this style of mobilization. Indeed, the second generation of Puritan religious leaders relied on it heavily in the 1660s and 1670s as they fought to keep the New England Puritans true to their covenant with God by preaching fiery jeremiads.[65]

Increase Mather, one of the more famous of the second generation Puritan religious leaders, was a master of the jeremiad. In one entitled "The Day of Trouble Is Near," he wove imagery from the Old and New Testaments to reinforce the covenant identity of the Puritan settlers, remind them of their divine mission, and give an exhaustive list of the ways they were failing that mission. He finally warned them of the divine punishment they would suffer if they did not mend their ways.[66]

We find another example of this Puritan style of persuasion and mobilization in the Reverend Arthur Dimmesdale in Nathaniel Hawthorne's classic novel about the New England Puritans, *The Scarlet Letter.* Early in the novel, we find Reverend Dimmesdale pleading with the leaders of the settlement to allow Hester Prynne to keep her (and unbeknownst to the leaders, his) illegitimate child, Pearl. Dimmesdale argues powerfully that it is God's will that Hester should raise the child both as punishment for her sin of adultery and as a safeguard to keep her from returning to her sinful ways:

> This child of the father's guilt and the mother's shame hath come from the hand of God, to work in many ways upon her heart, who pleads so earnestly . . . to keep her. It was meant for a blessing; for the one blessing of her life! It was meant, doubtless, as the mother herself hath told us for a retribution too; a torture, to be felt at many an unthought of moment; a pang, a sting, an ever recurring agony, in the midst of troubled joy! . . . Therefore it is good for this poor, sinful woman that she hath an infant immortality, a being capable of eternal joy or sorrow, confided to her care—to be trained up by her to righteousness—to remind her, at every moment, of her fall—but yet to teach her, as it were by the Creator's sacred pledge, that, if she bring the child to heaven, the child will also bring its parent thither.[67]

In this passage, the Reverend Dimmesdale illustrates the paradigmatic Puritan style of persuasion and mobilization. First he claims persuasively to know what God's will is in the matter, thereby establishing his knowledge of the true and the good. Once he has persuaded the town leaders that it is God's will that Hester Prynne raise the child, they are left no choice but to grant her parental rights and to do so without further discussion.[68] Thus (his own sin notwithstanding) he shows all three elements of the Puritan representative character: the revelation-based moral and epistemological stances and the paradigmatic mode of social action.

The manifestation of elements of the Puritan representative character has not been limited to Puritan political and religious leaders, be they figures historical or literary. Indeed, in the diplomatic behavior of Woodrow Wilson during and after World War I, we can see all three elements. In *Woodrow Wilson and Colonel House: A Personality Study,* Alexander and Juliette George present British prime minister Lloyd George's recollections of Wilson's arrival at the Versailles conference. According to Prime Minister Lloyd George, Wilson attempted to persuade the gathered leaders to support the idea of a League of Nations by arguing that it was God's will: "Why has Jesus Christ so far not succeeded in inducing the world to follow His teaching in these matters? It is because He taught the ideal without devising any practical means of attaining it. That is the reason why I am proposing a practical scheme to carry out His aims."[69]

Here Wilson manifests all three elements of the Puritan representative character. His epistemological and moral claims are based on revelation—he knows what God's will in this matter is. He presents himself as the one who is chosen to bring about the implementation of God's will in the form of the League of Nations. He uses his privileged moral and epistemological stance—his knowledge of God's will—to attempt to persuade the other leaders. Thus Wilson at Versailles provides a good early-twentieth-century example of a statesman who embodied the Puritan representative character.

THE MARKET MYTH

The market myth of American society provides an alternative to the city-on-the-hill myth as a source of collective identity and legitimation for members of society. Whereas the founding myth endows American society with a sacred and biblical meaning, the market myth endows it with a much more worldly, even profane, meaning. The city-on-the-hill myth legitimates U.S. society by linking Americans transcendently to the creator of the universe; the market myth legitimates U.S. society by glorifying the worldly rewards that come from hard work and successful enterprise in this world. According to the market myth, what makes America special is that it is ostensibly the only place where a person can start from a position of abject poverty and little education and through hard work, constant self-improvement, and the courage to take risks in "the market" end up the owner of a huge commercial enterprise with all the attendant power, status, and worldly comforts.

Unlike with the city-on-the-hill myth, it is impossible to pinpoint precisely the origins of the market myth. One problem is that many of the economic ideas that underlie the myth, such as those of Adam Smith and others, had their origins in Europe. There is evidence, however, that long before the classical liberal economic ideas of Adam Smith and others arrived, people began to think about U.S. society in terms that were consistent with the market myth.

In fact, during the early eighteenth century, Puritan religious leaders in New England began to warn that citizens were worrying too much about their individual business concerns to the detriment of their sacred obligations as members of a covenant with God.[70] Puritan ministers did, however, stress to their congregations that their salvation depended upon their having an earthly (i.e., occupational) calling in addition to their all-important, covenant-derived religious calling.[71] As Irvin G. Wyllie points out in *The Self-Made Man in America*, analysis of the early-eighteenth-century sermons of leading Puritan ministers such as Cotton Mather shows the interweaving of a budding market ethos and the traditional covenant ethos.[72] Cotton Mather's famous 1710 sermon entitled "Essays to Do Good" is perhaps the most widely read example of this Puritan synthesis of a market ethos and the covenant ethos.[73]

Thus we find some of the seeds of an embryonic market ethos coming from the same Puritan tradition that brought us the city-on-the-hill myth. However, within the Puritan tradition, pursuit of an earthly calling was absolutely subordinate to the all-important religious calling inherent to the covenant with God. It is only later, in the early nineteenth century, that we see a completely secular market ethos beginning to take hold.[74]

Many scholars of American culture point to Benjamin Franklin as something of a transitional figure between the Puritan-based covenant ethos and the developing secular market ethos.[75] As Wyllie points out, Franklin grew up in Puritan Boston, read Cotton Mather's "Essays to Do Good" as a child, and later would admit that they had a strong influence on him.[76] In Franklin's many writings on how to succeed, he provided young Americans with a set of secular commercial virtues that would help them build their fortunes in the proper way.[77] Like the Puritans, Franklin stressed the need to work hard in developing a successful commercial enterprise.[78] However, unlike the Puritans Franklin did not subordinate commercial activity to an overarching covenant obligation. For him, hard work in the pursuit of business success was important because it developed the proper sort of individual and contributed to the public good. It was not a means to salvation.[79]

In the early nineteenth century, after his death, Benjamin Franklin was a central figure in the rags-to-riches theme that was so prominent a part of the larger market mythology rapidly developing during this time.[80] This theme—constantly repeated in thousands of self-help books, articles, speeches, and sermons—formed the core of the emerging market myth during the second half of the nineteenth century.[81] As Wyllie demonstrates, spreading the "self-help gospel" became a huge business after the Civil War. Self-help books were published and distributed all over the country, and self-help lectures were very heavily attended.[82]

Another important medium for the theme was the rags-to-riches novel. The most famous author of this genre was undoubtably Horatio Alger. The heroes of his novels had names like Ragged Dick and Tattered Tom and started out as poor city boys. The young hero would raise himself up by cultivating in himself the proper commercial virtues, working extra hard, and staying alert for business opportunities (there was also usually a little luck involved).[83] The Alger novels sold over 50 million copies during the late nineteenth and early twentieth centuries and as such were an incredibly powerful carrier of the rags-to-riches theme and the market myth.[84] These were also sustained in grade school classrooms by the *McGuffey Reader* textbook, which was used throughout the country for the final three-quarters of the nineteenth century.[85]

The central idea of the rags-to-riches theme was that any young man (women were excluded) in the United States who cultivated the proper virtues and worked hard could build up a substantial business enterprise with all the attendant rewards of material success.[86] America was thus presented as a unique land of economic opportunity where there were no rigid class distinctions.

The central principles of the market myth are individualism and competition. For all of the central mythical figures, whether they were Horatio Alger's fictional heroes or real people like Benjamin Franklin and Andrew Carnegie, the journey from poverty to business success was a lonely one. First the hero struggled to cultivate in himself the proper commercial virtues; then to scrimp, save, and gain access to capital; and then, after he had built up a successful business or (in the case of Alger's boys) achieved a lofty position in someone else's firm, to maintain what he had achieved. Even the great robber barons like Carnegie, Rockefeller, Morgan, and Harriman all continued to struggle to fight off competitors and expand market share. In all of these success stories that are the stuff of the market myth, the moral of the story was the same: Success is achieved through devoting one's life to it.

This theme of individual struggle in the market myth power-fully explained and legitimated the American free enterprise sys-tem. As Wyllie argues, the myth "callously condemned the majority who failed and charged them with delinquency [while] reserv[ing] the halo of merit for those who succeeded."[87] According to the logic of the myth, business success is solely a product of intense in-dividual effort; therefore, those who do not succeed must be lazy. Also, the successful businessman is entitled to his wealth because he has earned it. Thus the market myth was a powerful ideational force for preserving the economic status quo in U.S. society during the Gilded Age.

Another related theme in the market myth is the jealous pro-tection of individual economic striving from governmental inter-ference. The market myth holds that a large part of the economic developmental success of U.S. society has been the direct result of a strictly enforced hands-off attitude on the part of government to-ward competition in the free market.[88] This idea that America achieved its economic success as a result of faithful worship at the temple of laissez-faire lends an added air of historical uniqueness to the American economic success story. It also becomes the basis for a quasi-messianic tendency to offer the American economic experi-ence as a model for the rest of the world.[89] During the Progressive Era the self-made-man theme of the market myth was used in the arguments of reformers who were trying to establish more govern-ment control over big business and break up the giant trusts. They argued that these trusts so dominated the market that they left no room for individuals to create their own businesses.[90] Thus when the huge firms set up by the heroes of the market myth began to re-strict the opportunities for up-and-coming entrepreneurs, reform-ers began to use some of the imagery of the market myth to argue for increased government control over those businesses.

THE ENTREPRENEUR REPRESENTATIVE CHARACTER

During the late nineteenth century, when the market myth was per-haps at the peak of its influence, a new representative character arose in American culture that nicely complemented it. This repre-sentative character was described variously as the "robber baron," the "mogul," or the "titan" in U.S. fiction and journalism, but fol-lowing Bellah, I shall call this new character the entrepreneur.[91] The entrepreneur was the self-made business magnate who was, at once, both producer and product of the Gilded Age. Bellah and his colleagues describe the great American entrepreneurs as "captains of industry who could ignore the clamor of public opinion and rise to truly national power through economic means alone."[92] The great entrepreneur has often been the target of intense criticism by liberal and reformist social observers (including Bellah et al.). Nonetheless, this representative character has been a powerful part of U.S. culture since its advent during the Gilded Age.

In *America as a Civilization,* Max Lerner describes the tremendous power with which the entrepreneur character captured the imagination of the American people.

> Every civilization has its characteristic flowering in some civilization type, the persona of the social mask on which the ordinary man in the civilization models himself. . . . The persona of the American civilization has been the businessman—the "Titan," as Dreiser called him; the "Tycoon" as *Fortune* called him. Where other civilization types have pursued wisdom, beauty, sanctity, military glory, predacity, asceticism, the businessman pursues the magnitudes of profit with a similar single-minded drive. . . . The survivors in the fierce competitive struggle were those who most clearly embodied the businessman's single mindedness of purpose.[93]

Lerner notes that the great entrepreneur was often attacked by muckrakers in the media, but he argues that the impact of this new character on the popular imagination was not dampened by these attacks.

> By the time of the first World War, the Titan had caught the imagination of the novelists as well as the populace. . . . Americans needed no fire breathing imperialist swaggers to express their sense of national importance. The Titan was all the symbol they needed. . . . Even when the muckrakers excoriated him . . . they left little doubt their target was indeed a Titan. The magazine readers glimpsed the outlines of the heroic in the subjects of the biographical exposes and felt more envy than indignation.[94]

Thus as Lerner argues, the entrepreneur character was embraced, warts and all, by many Americans.

But what was the essence of this entrepreneur character? It is perhaps best found in the works of those American fiction writers who focused on the entrepreneur as their central character. One of the best known portrayals appeared in W. D. Howells's *The Rise of Silas Lapham,* first published in 1885. Howells's Silas Lapham was not a business hero on the magnitude of the real-life robber barons, men such as Carnegie, Gould, Hill, and Rockefeller.

Lapham's mineral paint business was very successful both nationally and internationally, but his notoriety was mostly limited to the Boston area, where his business was located.[95]

Nonetheless, we see much of the essence of the entrepreneur representative character in Lapham. While developing his paint business, he manifested a single-minded determination to maintain control over and to expand the business and his profits as far as possible.[96] In the course of these efforts, he forced out a partner whose infusion of capital during an earlier downturn had kept the business from going under.[97] The reader is led to suspect, via Lapham's wife's moral criticism, that Lapham had fully intended to force the partner out when profits were again realized.[98] This kind of cutthroat tactic in business dealings (often with accompanying social Darwinistic justifications) is very much a prominent behavioral aspect of the entrepreneur representative character. Eventually, Lapham showed remorse over this earlier harsh treatment of his partner and made loans to him, an action that indirectly led to the bankruptcy of his paint business.

Howells reveals the fiercely competitive and shrewd nature of the entrepreneur involved in business dealings in a later passage in the book wherein he describes Lapham trying to negotiate with a competing paint manufacturer whose operation threatens the success of his own.

> He found the West Virginians full of zeal and hope, but in ten minutes he knew that they had not tested their strength in the money market, and had not yet ascertained how much or how little capital they could command. Lapham himself, if he had so much would not have hesitated to put a million dollars into their business. He saw, as they did not see, that they had the game in their own hands, and that if they could raise the money to extend their business, they could ruin him. It was only a question of time, and he was on the ground first. He frankly proposed a union of their interests. He admitted that they had a good thing, and that he should have to fight them hard; but he meant to fight them to the death unless they could come to some terms. Now the question was whether they had better go on and make a heavy loss for both sides by competition, or whether they had better form a partnership to run both paints and command the whole market.[99]

This passage illustrates perfectly the fierce "survival of the fittest" milieu of the competing entrepreneurs and the hardball approach to business negotiations that are the essence of the paradigmatic mode of social action of the entrepreneur.

In the real-world struggles between the great U.S. entrepreneurs, or robber barons, during the Gilded Age, some of these businessmen and their apologists even used the Spencerian theories of social Darwinism that were coming into fashion to justify their fiercely competitive business methods. Leland Baldwin describes this phenomenon in *The Meaning of America.*

> The Great Entrepreneurs could scarcely avoid the knowledge that their actions were violating even the harsh tenets of Calvinism by ignoring its injunction to social responsibility. What was needed was a philosophical justification of their course. It was the mission of Herbert Spencer to provide this. . . . Darwinism's triumph in the United States was delayed by the Civil War, but soon thereafter it was put to use, under the name of Social Darwinism, to explain and justify the methods of the Great Entrepreneurs and the Finance Capitalists.[100]

The Darwinistic and naturalistic theme of "survival of the fittest" finds its way into one of the best-known fictional portrayals of the American entrepreneur. In Theodore Dreiser's *The Financier* and *The Titan,* we find perhaps the most famous fictional portrayal of an American entrepreneur in the character of Frank Algernon Cowperwood. Young Cowperwood realizes at a very young age that he wants to create a business empire rivaling that of any of the robber barons.[101]

There is a scene very early in *The Financier* in which the young Cowperwood is trying to figure out the natural order of the world, and he stumbles upon a fish tank in a local market wherein a lobster gradually wears down a squid over a couple of days and eventually devours it.[102] Dreiser describes how the drama in the fish tank helps Cowperwood.

> "That's the way it has to be I guess" he commented to himself. That squid wasn't quick enough. . . . It made a great impression on him. It answered in a rough way that riddle that had been annoying him so much in the past: "How is life organized?" Things lived on each other—that was it. . . . For days and weeks Frank thought of this and of the life he was tossed into, for he was already thinking of what he should be in this world, and how he should get along.[103]

Thus Cowperwood internalizes at a very young age the "law of the jungle" that he eventually comes to live by during his business career.

Throughout the rest of *The Financier* and into its sequel, *The Titan,* the reader is brought along on Frank Cowperwood's very successful business career (which does have some fits and starts on the way). Cowperwood never attains the magnitude of business empire of the robber barons, a goal for which he desperately and ruthlessly strives. Nonetheless, he does become one of the richest and most powerful businessmen in Chicago, and he does so by opposing anyone who gets in his way.

All through these two novels, Dreiser treats the reader to in-depth explorations of Cowperwood's philosophy of business and life. The tenets of Cowperwood's personal philosophy reveal the moral essence of the entrepreneur character. Here is a sample from Cowperwood's earlier years in business.

> The moral nature of Frank Cowperwood may at this juncture be said to have had no material or spiritual existence. He had never had, so far as he had reasoned at all, a fixed attitude in regard to anything except preserving himself intact and succeeding. His father talked . . . of business honor, commercial integrity, and so forth. Frank thought of this a long time at moments. What was honor? . . . Men seemed to think it referred to some state of mind which would not allow a man to take undue advantage of another; but life experience taught, and was teaching him something different. Honor was almost, he thought, a figment of the brain. If it referred to anything, it referred to force, generosity, power. . . . So far as he could see, force governed this world—hard cold force and quickness of brain. If one had force, plenty of it, quickness of wit, and subtlety there was no need for anything else. Some people might be pretending to be guided by other principles—ethical and religious, for instance; they might actually be so guided—he could not tell. If they were they were following false or silly standards.[104]

Dreiser's Cowperwood provides an extreme example of the "ruin or be ruined" social Darwinistic moral stance of the entrepreneur character. The only principle of concern is self-survival and prosperity. Howells's Silas Lapham was not nearly as morally bankrupt as Dreiser's Frank Cowperwood, but both exhibit the same amoral obsession with building their business empires.

THE PRAGMATIC MYTH

The pragmatic myth of the United States is perhaps best understood by contrasting it with the city-on-the-hill myth. Whereas the founding myth derives the central meaning of America in an a priori fashion from revelations of the will of God, the pragmatic myth derives the central meaning of America in an a postiori fashion from the concrete political institutions that have flourished in the United States. America's greatness and uniqueness stem not from divine election or chosenness but rather from the remarkable success of the political institutions set up by the founding fathers. Seen through the lens of the pragmatic myth, the American experience has been a grand experiment in which the social and political ideas of the founding fathers (as embodied in the institutions they designed) have been tested constantly and have proven themselves valid.

The most thorough treatment of the pragmatic myth can be found in Daniel Boorstin's *The Genius of American Politics*. He states: "The marvelous success and vitality of our institutions is equaled by the amazing poverty and inarticulateness of our theorizing about politics. No nation has ever believed more firmly that its political life was based on a perfect theory. And yet no nation has ever been less interested in political philosophy or produced less in the way of theory."[105] Boorstin argues that Americans have come to believe that "the Founding Fathers equipped our nation at its birth with a perfect and complete political theory, adequate to all our future needs." He argues further that Americans believe this doctrinal "gift" from the past is kept alive and embodied in the American "way of life," even though they never feel the need to make the theory explicit.[106] To illustrate the unique way Americans mythologize history to clarify their national identity, he examines the American political hagiography in which the Founding Fathers—who supposedly infused American institutions with their guiding values—are in turn infused with mythical significance.[107] He then goes on to describe the essence of the pragmatic myth:

> The facts of our history have thus made it easy for us to assume that our national life, as distinguished from that of the European peoples who trace their identity to a remote era, has had a clear purpose. Life in America—appropriately called "The American Experiment"—has again and again been described as the test or the proof of values supposed to have been clearly in the minds of the Founders. While as we shall see, the temper of much of our thought has been antihistorical, it is nevertheless true that we have leaned heavily on history to clarify our image of ourselves.[108]

Indeed, as Arthur Schlesinger points out in *The Cycles of American History*, many of the Founding Fathers and early presidents contributed to the development of the pragmatic myth by describing the American experience as a political experiment of epic proportions.[109] In *The Federalist Papers*, Alexander Hamilton evoked experimental imagery when he wrote, "It has been frequently remarked, that it seems to have been reserved to the people of this country, by their conduct and example, to decide the important question, whether societies of men are really capable or not, of establishing good government from reflection and choice, or whether they are forever destined to depend, for their political constitutions, on accident and force."[110] In his attempt to persuade the people of New York to support the proposed constitution, Hamilton tried to infuse the decision with extra significance by making it a part of a grand American experiment on behalf of all mankind.

George Washington echoed this experimental theme in his first inaugural address: "The preservation of the sacred fire of liberty and the destiny of the republican model of government are justly considered, perhaps, as deeply, as finally, staked on the experiment intrusted to the American people."[111]

Like Hamilton, Washington burdened the American people with being involved in a grand experiment on which the political fate of mankind hinged. The experimental theme was later picked up by Thomas Jefferson in his first inaugural address.

> I know indeed that some honest men fear that a republic can not be strong, that this Government is not strong enough; but would the honest patriot, in the full tide of successful experiment, abandon a government that has so far kept us free and firm on the theoretic and visionary fear that this government, the world's best hope, may by possibility want energy to preserve itself. I trust not. . . . Sometimes it is said that man cannot be trusted with the government of himself. Can he, then, be trusted with the government of others? Or have we found angels in the form of kings to govern him? Let history answer this question.[112]

We see not only clear America-as-experiment imagery in this address but also an interesting preference for the value of experience over the value of a priori theory. In rebuttal to those who, based on their readings of the classical theorists, believed that republican government could not long survive, Jefferson pointed to the actual experience and success of the American political experiment. If there were any doubts about the new system, Jefferson seemed to be arguing, let the test of experience decide its merits and not some abstract theory.

This preference for a postiori knowledge over a priori knowledge is an important element of the collective self-understanding that the pragmatic myth provides for the American people. Through the lens of the pragmatic myth, they come to see themselves as a people who arrive at the true and the good through experience. The American political system is good because experience has proven it to work.

In *Democracy in America,* Alexis de Tocqueville discusses Americans' preference for a postiori knowledge.

> I think that in no country in the civilized world is less attention paid to philosophy than in the United States. . . . Yet it is easy to perceive that almost all of the inhabitants of the United States use their minds in the same manner, and direct them according to the same rules; that is to say, without ever having taken the trouble to define the rules, they have a philosophical method common to the whole people. To evade the bondage of system and habit, of family maxims, class opinions, and, in some degree, of national prejudices; to accept tradition only as a means of information, and existing facts only as a lesson to be used in doing otherwise and doing better . . . to tend to results without being bound to means, and to strike though the form to the substance—such are the principle characteristics of what I shall call the philosophical method of the Americans.[113]

De Tocqueville's Americans were inclined to "accept . . . existing facts only as a lesson to be used in doing otherwise and doing better." This is the essence of the collective identity that Americans acquire when they view themselves through the lens of the pragmatic myth.

During the 1830s the public political discourse was still full of the imagery of the pragmatic myth. In his farewell address in March 1837, Andrew Jackson referred to the "American experiment" in the same terms in which George Washington had decades before.

> The lessons contained in this valuable legacy of Washington to his countrymen should be cherished in the heart of every citizen to the latest generation. . . . Forty years have passed since this imperishable document was given to his countrymen. The Federal Constitution was then regarded by him as an experiment—and he so speaks of it in his address—but an experiment upon the success of which the best hopes of his country depended; and we all know that he was prepared to lay down his life, if necessary, to secure it a full and fair trial. The trial has been made. It has succeeded beyond the proudest hopes of those who framed it.[114]

Jackson went on to warn that the experiment that had thus far gone so well could still be undone and therefore had to be considered as ongoing.[115] Nonetheless, his assessment of the "state of the experiment" was much more optimistic than those of the earlier presidents.

Use of the experimental imagery of the pragmatic myth was not limited to only presidential addresses. As Rush Welter points out in his *The Mind of America: 1820–1860,* the idea of the United States as an experiment was very widely seized upon in political discourse. In his book, Welter samples the speeches of clergymen, business leaders, and civic leaders to show that the experimental imagery of the pragmatic myth was widely used during this period.[116] By the mid-1800s, success had made Americans more confident in the outcome of their national experiment than the founding fathers had been.[117]

This confidence in the original "experiment" did not detract from an ongoing interest in experimenting further; the pragmatic myth continued as an influence on the collective identity of the American people. Writing about the character of late-nineteenth-century Americans, cultural historian Henry Steele Commager sums up the extent to which Americans identified with the pragmatic myth: "The inclination to experiment was deeply ingrained in the American character and fortified by American experience. America itself had been the greatest of experiments, one renewed by each generation of pioneers and each wave of immigrants, and, where every community was a gamble and an opportunity, the American was a gambler and an opportunist."[118]

A good indicator of the extent to which Americans still identified with the pragmatic myth at the end of the nineteenth century is the warm reception they gave to the emerging American philosophical method known as pragmatism. The best-known and most widely read pragmatists during the late-nineteenth and early-twentieth centuries were William James and John Dewey.[119] Pragmatism eschewed attempts to arrive at truth via abstract or a priori reasoning, instead asserting that truth, or, more precisely, pluralistic truths, are arrived at through the interaction of human intelligence with concrete experience.

This new American philosophical method of pragmatism was perfectly suited to the American-as-experimenter portrayed by the pragmatic myth. Commager captures this fit better than anyone.

> These qualities in pragmatism reflected qualities in the American character. . . . It cleared away the jungle of theology and metaphysics and deterministic science and allowed the warm sun of common sense to quicken the American spirit as the pioneer cleared the forests and the underbrush and allowed the sun to quicken the soil of the American West. In a sense, the whole of American experience had prepared for it and now seemed to validate and justify it. For America had been a gamble that had paid off, an experiment that had succeeded. . . . Pragmatism's willingness to break with the past, reject traditional habits, try new methods, put beliefs to a vote, make a future to order, excited not only sympathy but a feeling of familiarity. No wonder . . . pragmatism

caught on until it came to be almost the official philosophy of America.[120]

Thus going into the twentieth century, Americans had a native philosophical method that suited their image of themselves as experimenters.

PIONEERS AND MANAGERS
AS REPRESENTATIVE CHARACTERS

The pragmatic myth has been complemented by two distinct and context-bound representative characters. The first, dominant during the nineteenth century, was the frontiersman. Later, when the industrial/bureaucratic social milieu of twentieth-century America relegated this representative character to a quaint and distant past, the frontiersman was displaced by the manager.

During the early nineteenth century, when Americans were pressing steadily into the western frontier, American authors such as James Fenimore Cooper and Washington Irving produced a significant body of fiction that chronicled the conquest of the continent and produced a new representative character: the frontiersman.[121] As developed in these frontier novels, the frontiersman embodied the qualities of the American as experimenter and used them to conquer the wilderness. James Oliver Robertson shows the significance of the frontiersman representative character by juxtaposing it with the Puritan character.

> The great, gray Puritan is Christian civilization on its mission to the New World. . . . The bronzed, buckskinned Frontiersman is the New World and its wildness. The Frontiersman is the discoverer, the pathfinder, who adapts to whatever he finds and who lives in the wilderness. . . . The Frontiersman is the heroic survivor, the adaptor . . . the jack of all trades. . . . These two figures are archetypes of American experience, celebrated in American myth and ritual, widely available to Americans as models, explanations, and rationales of themselves and their universe.[122]

Robertson goes on to stress the pragmatic qualities of the frontiersman character. He writes of the frontiersman that "above all he was convinced that diversified, non specialized, jack-of-all trades adaptability was a positive virtue, the only possible way to be in an American community."[123]

This representative character was the perfect complement to the pragmatic myth. But by the twentieth century the frontier was a distant memory, and the American social landscape had been radically changed by industrialization and bureaucratization. In this modern context, the frontiersman character lost much of its meaning.

The rise of the corporation as the predominant pattern of business organization has dramatically changed U.S. society (and indeed all industrialized societies). Within this new social landscape, a new representative character has emerged—the manager. As Bellah and his colleagues argue in *Habits of the Heart,* "The bureaucratic organization of the business corporation has been the dominant force in this century. Within the corporation, the crucial character has been the professional manager. . . . Although the manager in effect builds upon the work of the entrepreneur and shares with him the drive to achieve and problem solving activism that are old American traits, the social positions and outlooks of the two types differ importantly."[124]

Whereas the entrepreneur's drive to achieve is actualized through creating a business empire by fierce bargaining and competition with other empire builders, the manager's drive to achieve is actualized by controlling and manipulating the resources of the corporation in an effort to find the most profitable resource combination.[125] The manager's manipulation of these corporate resources may be seen as an ongoing experiment that is deemed successful when corporate profits are increased. In this quest for effectiveness as defined by profit, the manager is very much a technician. As Bellah and his colleagues put it, "The manager's view of things is akin to that of the technician of industrial society par excellence, the engineer, except that the manager must admit interpersonal responses and personalities, including his own into the calculation of effectiveness."[126]

In *After Virtue,* Alisdair MacIntyre follows Max Weber in examining how the appeal to effectiveness and scientific objectivity provides the modern bureaucratic manager with his authority.[127] In an effort to show how the premises of the moral-philosophical school of emotivism have penetrated (in his view, infected) modern society, he points out that the character of the manager embodies a key premise of emotivism, namely the "obliteration of the distinction between manipulative and non-manipulative social relations."[128] He goes on to argue that the effectiveness criterion from which the manager derives his or her authority is really a moral fiction.[129]

MacIntyre concludes that the effectiveness criterion is merely "part of a masquerade of social control" because the real-life manager cannot possibly achieve the level of effectiveness that is imputed to the manager representative character.[130]

We shall also have to conclude that another moral fiction—and perhaps the most culturally powerful of them all—is embodied in the claims to effectiveness and hence to authority made by the central character of the modern social drama, the bureaucratic manager. . . . The claim that the manager makes to effectiveness rests of course on the further claim to possess a stock of knowledge by means of which organizations and social structures can be molded. Such knowledge would have to include factual, law-like generalizations which would enable the manager to predict that, if a state of affairs of a certain type were to occur or be brought about, some other state of affairs of some specific kind would result. For only such law-like generalizations could yield those particular causal explanations and predictions by means of which the manager could mold, influence and control the social environment.[131]

Although MacIntyre challenges the effectiveness-based claims to authority of real-life managers, at the same time he illustrates the tremendous legitimating power of the manager representative character. The salient question becomes, How did the manager representative character in American culture acquire this aura of effectiveness with its attendant authority to manipulate?

The manager's status as high priest in the cult of effectiveness began to develop with the management-efficiency theories of Frederick Taylor and the subsequent emergence of the field of scientific management during the Progressive Era.[132] The theories that emerged from this field placed upon the corporate manager the burden of maximizing the efficiency of the industrial operation.[133]

Taylor himself was the prototype for the initial version of the modern manager character—the efficiency expert. Writing in the 1930s, American author John Dos Passos captured the essence of the efficiency expert in his novel *The Big Money*.[134] In an introduction to the book Dos Passos drew a character profile of the young Frederick Taylor during the days he was developing his efficiency theories.

Production went to his head and thrilled his sleepless nerves like liquor or women on a Saturday night. He never loafed and he'd be damned if anybody else would. Production was an itch under his skin. . . . That was the beginning of the Taylor System of Scientific Management. He was impatient of explanations, he didn't care whose hide he took off in enforcing the laws he believed inherent in the production process. . . . He filled the shop with college students with stopwatches and diagrams, tabulating, standardizing. "There's the right way of doing a thing and the wrong way of doing it; the right way means increased production, lower costs, higher wages, bigger profits": the American plan.[135]

Later in *The Big Money,* Dos Passos described an efficiency expert at an airplane engine plant whose efforts to increase production were driving the production workers so hard that they were unable to have sex with their wives when they went home at night.[136] In a scene designed to convey the Marxist theme of the industrial workplace squeezing the life forces out of the alienated worker, the novel's protagonist, engineer and part owner of the plant Charley Anderson, listened to one of his foremen, Bill, complaining about the efficiency expert. "Bill wasn't laughing anymore. 'Honestly, no kiddin'. That damn squarehead make the boys work so hard they can't get a hard on when they go to bed, an' their wives raise hell with 'em.' . . . Charley was laughing. 'You're a squarehead yourself, Bill and I don't know what I can do about it, I'm just an employee of the company myself. . . . We got to have efficient production, or they'll wipe us out of business. Ford's buildin' planes now.'"[137]

With his discussion of the young Taylor in his introduction and his brief description of the efficiency expert in the novel itself, Dos Passos made it clear that he thought Taylorism and the rise of the industrial efficiency expert were having a significant (albeit damaging in human terms) impact on the U.S. industrial workplace. For Dos Passos with his socialist agenda, the rise of the efficiency expert was a decidedly negative development. For people who aspired to run profitable industrial enterprises, however, the efficiency expert was viewed as the prophet of profits.

It seems fitting that Frederick Taylor, the original industrial efficiency expert, should have been an American. His constant experimentation and implicit moral stance (whatever works best is good) were quite consistent with the pragmatic myth of America. Whereas the frontiersman served as the representative character for the pragmatic myth during the nineteenth century, the efficiency expert (later fully developed into the manager) served that role during the industrialized twentieth century.

Scientific management placed the burden of efficiency on the manager, but it also conferred upon him the authority and legitimation that only science can give in the modern world. As Samuel Haber argues, the Taylorites' use of the term *scientific* to describe the field of management was very much a semiotic power play. "The adjective 'scientific' strengthened its appeal further by suggesting disinterestedness, rigor, and a method employing the power of laws of nature."[138] The emergence of the field of scientific management also gave rise to the creation of graduate schools of business and to the professionalization of the field of management.[139]

By the 1940s and 1950s the dominant image of the manager was no longer of the efficiency expert standing over the assembly line with a stopwatch and a slide rule. The new manager could be found in a plush top-floor office controlling a huge, complex, bureaucratic organization with the help of such modern management tools as control accounting and operations research.[140] During the 1950s and 1960s a substantial literature appeared in which management consultants and business school professors sought to define the essential intellectual and leadership qualities of the modern manager.[141] In many of these works, the manager's actions are seen as based on the kind of science and rationality-based authority that is so effectively questioned by MacIntyre in *After Virtue*.

The best example of this is in Charles Sumner's "The Managerial Mind." In describing a "factual attitude" as one necessary attribute of the managerial mind, Sumner illustrates what MacIntyre calls the "moral fiction" of managerial effectiveness. "The first empirical quality, which might be called the factual attitude, is particularly valuable in the world of managerial action, where the manager has to cause or control specific events in his problem situation."[142]

Another important intellectual quality of the modern manager, according to Sumner, is the "quantitative attitude." In describing this attitude, Sumner explicitly provides the manager with an authority boost by comparing the manager's use of quantitative methods with the use of such methods in the world of science.

> The quantitative attitude satisfies two needs of the scientist. It helps him to be objective, and it enables him to "prove" his relationships or laws. . . . This mathematical predisposition can also be of value to the executive. It can result in improved ways of doing things. . . . Operations research, digital computers, probability and game theory, systems theory, automation, and such social sciences as applied anthropology are all adding to the possibilities for being "scientific" in the sense of measuring the consequences of managerial decisions.[143]

Thus the modern manager is presented as having the same strong empirical and quantitative orientation toward the world as the scientist. This image of the new American manager wielding the empiricism and quantitative methodology of science also showed up in the American business fiction of the day. In his 1952 novel *Executive Suite*, Cameron Hawley described the advent of this new type of manager. "The world was changing. The Bullards were defeated, and the Shaws were inheriting the earth. The accountants and the calculators had risen to power. The slide rule had become the scepter. The world was overrun with the ever-spawning swarm of figure-jugglers who were fly specking the earth with their decimal points, proving over and over again what could be proved true by a clerk with a Comptometer."[144] In addition to having these scientific qualities (and the authority that comes with them), the manager was also often presented as having a powerful predisposition toward problem solving. A good illustration of this attribute may be found in the following quote from David Ewing in *The Managerial Mind:*

> Possibly no aspect of the managerial mind is more baffling and frustrating to the nonmanager than this attitude toward problems and difficulties. It is an attitude characterized by a willingness to disturb, to probe, to "look for trouble" and even to "make trouble." He is like the engineer who is never satisfied with his work, however perfect it may seem to others, but is always tinkering with it, stopping the machine to see if he can find a trouble spot or a way of making it run better.[145]

Ewing captured the essence of the modern American manager-as-experimenter. His portrayal was echoed by Herrymon Maurer.[146]

Maurer argued that the modern American manager still exhibited some of the psychological characteristics of the American frontiersman even as he functioned within the context of the modern corporation.

> The large U.S. corporation is indeed new. Compared with older forms of American enterprise, it is new in appearance. But its motivations are not new to American history. In the large corporation there is the optimism of settlers in a new land who saw bounty instead of scarcity. . . . There are the boyish enthusiasm for growing things where things never grew before, and the zest for surmounting obstacles. There are the frank indifference to abstract theory and the ready urge to experiment. There is in short, a continuity of psychological motives that have helped to make the large corporation a genuinely and uniquely American creation.[147]

Thus in its evolution from the efficiency expert of the late Progressive Era to the modern corporate head of the 1950s and 1960s, the American manager representative character acquired more science-based authority while still retaining the aura of the restless and pragmatic American experimenter.

Having outlined the development of the city-on-the-hill, market, and pragmatic myths and the Puritan, entrepreneur, and manager representative characters in American culture, I now turn to the Dulles, Harriman, and McNamara case studies to examine the extent to which these symbolic structures influenced the world-views, self-conceptions, policy preferences, and policy behavior of these three important cold warriors.

NOTES

1. This is achieved through a survey of important cultural histories and U.S. character studies as well as important works of U.S. literature and other forms of cultural artifacts.

2. *American Heritage Dictionary,* 2nd college ed. (Boston: Houghton Mifflin, 1985), 827.

3. There is a tradition of thinking about myth, best exemplified by Ernst Cassirer, that focuses on the penetration of the supernatural into the everyday world and refers to a type of explanatory heuristic mostly found in primitive societies. For a good discussion of the various traditions of thought about myth see Henry Tudor, *Political Myth* (New York: Praeger, 1972).

4. Ibid., 46–47.

5. For a detailed discussion by Durkheim of the collective represen-tation concept, see his 1898 essay "Individual and Collective Representa-tions," reprinted in Émile Durkheim, *Sociology and Philosophy,* translated by D. F. Pocock (Glencoe, IL: Free Press, 1953), 1–35. See also Durkheim, *The Elementary Forms of the Religious Life,* translated by Joseph Swain (New York: Collier Books, 1961), 480–486.

6. Durkheim, *The Rules of the Sociological Method,* 8th ed., translated by Sarah Solajay and John Mueller (Glencoe, IL: Free Press, 1966), xlix.

7. Durkheim, *Elementary Forms,* 419–420.

8. Much of Durkheim's discussion of the myth concept is found in his studies of primitive societies. This does not mean that this concept is not valid for the study of modern societies, however. Durkheim himself argued that the main purpose of his study of primitive religions was to develop an understanding of the basic human symbolic value–infusion process, which, he argued, operated in modern secular societies no less than in primitive ones. See Durkheim, *Elementary Forms,* 15.

9. Alasdair MacIntyre, *After Virtue* (South Bend: Notre Dame Press, 1981). Robert Bellah, Richard Madsen, William Sullivan, Ann Swidler, and Stephen Tipton, *Habits of the Heart: Individualism and Commitment in Ameri-can Life* (New York: Harper and Row, 1985).

10. MacIntyre, 27.

11. Ibid., 28.

12. Bellah et al., 39.

13. Ibid.

14. Ibid., 29.

15. Ibid., 42.

16. Ibid., 43.

17. Ibid., 45.

18. Ibid., 44–45.

19. Ibid., 45.

20. There is a great deal of overlap between the types of self-concep-tion and behavior patterns highlighted by the representative character con-cept and those highlighted by the personality approach to analyzing poli-cymaking behavior. The main difference between the cultural approach and the personality approach is one of purpose. The personality approach focuses on explaining idiosyncracies in individual self-conceptions and be-havior and seeks to explain as much as possible about unique individuals.

The cultural approach seeks to highlight sources of self-conceptions and behavior that are shared to some extent by members of a society.

21. For a discussion of Geertz's "thick description" concept, see his *The Interpretation of Cultures* (New York: HarperCollins, 1973), ch. 1.

22. Alexis de Tocqueville, *Democracy in America* (New York: Vintage Books, 1990), vol. 2, 223.

23. Of course, there were exceptions to this generalization about the lack of hierarchical structures that rigidly defined identity and social reality in America, the most notable being the Puritan settlements in New England.

24. Peter Berger and Thomas Luckmann, *The Social Construction of Reality: A Treatise on the Sociology of Knowledge* (New York: Anchor Press, 1966), 92–93.

25. Samuel Huntington, *American Politics: The Promise of Disharmony* (Cambridge: Harvard University Press, 1981), 23.

26. Ibid., 14.

27. It is not my intention to imply that these particular symbolic structures are the only ones to have served these functions in U.S. society; they are merely the most relevant for understanding U.S. foreign policy.

28. John Winthrop, quoted in Robert Bellah, *The Broken Covenant: American Civil Religion in Time of Trial* (Chicago: University of Chicago Press, 1992), 14–15.

29. Loren Baritz, *City on a Hill: A History of Ideas and Myths in America* (New York: John Wiley, 1964), 17–19.

30. Perry Miller argues that the primary intended audience for this model Christian society was in fact England and that the Puritans hoped eventually to return to England and set up the same kind of theocracy there. See his *Errand in the Wilderness* (Cambridge: Harvard University Press, 1964), 12–13.

31. Baritz, 16–17.

32. Indeed, as Perry Miller points out, the entire covenant theology that the Puritans brought with them from England was a much more powerful doctrine, in terms of legitimation potential, than the Calvinist doctrine from which it evolved. Miller describes it as an effort to render Calvin's god "less inscrutable, less mysterious, [and] less unpredictable" in an effort to provide a more coherent moral code and to link that code to the means of attaining salvation. See Miller, 55.

33. Ibid., 6–7.

34. Ibid., 158.

35. Ibid., 159.

36. Ibid., 159–160.

37. Ibid., 160–161.

38. Bellah, 177.

39. Nathan Hatch, *The Sacred Cause of Liberty* (New Haven: Yale University Press, 1977), 46–47.

40. Ibid., 76–78.

41. Ibid., 60–61.

42. Ibid., 84–86.

43. Ibid., 152–153.

44. For a good discussion of the effect of mirror imaging on international conflict in general and on the U.S. conduct of the Vietnam War, see Ralph K. White, *Nobody Wanted War* (New York: Doubleday, 1968); see also

John Dower, *War Without Mercy: Race and Power in the Pacific War* (New York: Pantheon, 1986).

45. Hatch, 156.

46. During the mid-1840s the doctrine of manifest destiny with its notion of a God-given expansionist mission met with widespread popularity. See Frederick Merk, *Manifest Destiny and Mission in American History: A Reinterpretation* (New York: Alfred A. Knopf, 1963).

47. Perry Miller, *The Life of the Mind in America: From the Revolution to the Civil War* (New York: Harcourt Brace, 1965), chs. 1–2.

48. Ibid., 48.

49. Ibid., chs. 1–2.

50. Ibid.

51. Bellah, 58–59.

52. Albert Beveridge speech, quoted in Edward M. Burns, *The American Idea of Mission: Concepts of National Purpose and Destiny* (New Brunswick: Rutgers University Press, 1957), 16.

53. Arthur Schlesinger Jr., *The Cycles of American History* (New York: Houghton Mifflin, 1986), 17.

54. Woodrow Wilson speech in Salt Lake City, September 23, 1919, in Ray S. Baker and William E. Dodd, eds., *The Public Papers of Woodrow Wilson (1917–1924)* (New York: Harper, 1970), vol. 2, *War and Peace,* 355.

55. See Alexander George and Juliette George, *Woodrow Wilson and Colonel House: A Personality Study* (New York: Dover, 1956). See also John G. Stoessinger, *Crusaders and Pragmatists: Movers of Modern American Foreign Policy* (New York: W. W. Norton, 1985), ch. 1.

56. The best intellectual histories of Puritan New England include Miller's *Errand in the Wilderness* and *The Life of the Mind in America.* See also Ralph Barton Perry, *Puritanism and Democracy* (New York: Vanguard Press, 1944), and Baritz, *City on a Hill.* For an excellent collection of Puritan writings on such various subjects as politics, literature, science, and so on see Perry Miller and Thomas H. Johnson, eds., *The Puritans* (New York: American Book Company, 1938).

57. Miller and Johnson, 43.

58. Miller, *Errand in the Wilderness,* 162–163.

59. Ibid.

60. Edmond Morgan, *The Puritan Dilemma: The Story of John Winthrop* (Boston: Little, Brown, 1958), 86–89.

61. Ibid., 69–71.

62. Bellah, 13–15.

63. Ibid., 14–15.

64. Ibid.

65. Miller, *Errand in the Wilderness,* 6–9.

66. Michael G. Hall, *The Last American Puritan: The Life of Increase Mather* (Middletown: Wesleyan University Press, 1988), 96–99.

67. Nathaniel Hawthorne, *The Scarlet Letter* (New York: W. W. Norton, 1978), 84–85.

68. Ibid., 85–86.

69. George and George, 230.

70. Miller, *Errand in the Wilderness,* 159.

71. This is the theme of Cotton Mather's famous 1701 sermon entitled "A Christian at His Calling," a reprint of which may be found in Moses Rischen, ed., *The American Gospel of Success* (New York: Quadrangle Books, 1965).

72. Irvin G. Wyllie, *The Self-Made Man in America: The Myth of Rags to Riches* (New York: Free Press, 1954), 12.

73. Ibid.

74. Apparently this transition began sooner in other areas of the country. As Perry Miller discovered in his analysis of colonial literature in Virginia, religious leaders in that colony had reconciled themselves to the deemphasis of a covenant understanding of society and the ascendance of a market understanding as far back as the early seventeenth century. See Miller, *Errand in the Wilderness*, 139–140.

75. See Wyllie, 12, and Bellah, 69–71.

76. Wyllie, 12.

77. Examples of these writings include *The Autobiography, Poor Richard's Almanack,* and "The Way to Wealth." For *The Autobiography* and other essays such as "The Way to Wealth" see Benjamin Franklin, *The Autobiography and Other Writings* (New York: Penguin Books, 1986).

78. Wyllie, 13.

79. Bellah, 69–70.

80. Wyllie, 13–14.

81. Ibid., 116–133.

82. Ibid., 116–122.

83. James Oliver Robertson, *American Myth, American Reality* (New York: Hill and Wang, 1980), 167–168.

84. Ibid., 169.

85. Wyllie, 126.

86. In his analysis of the self-help works in *The Self-Made Man in America,* Irvin Wyllie found they prescribed most frequently the virtues of industry, frugality, sobriety, perseverance, punctuality, loyalty, obedience, and initiative. See especially ch. 3 in Wyllie.

87. Wyllie, 151.

88. Edward McNall Burns, *The American Idea of Mission: Concepts of National Purpose and Identity* (New Brunswick: Rutgers University Press, 1957), 162–165.

89. Ibid., 161.

90. See Richard Hofstadler, *The Age of Reform* (New York: Vintage Books, 1955), 215–227.

91. Bellah et al., 41–44.

92. Ibid., 43.

93. Max Lerner, *America as a Civilization* (New York: Simon and Schuster, 1957), 274.

94. Ibid., 276.

95. W. D. Howells, *The Rise of Silas Lapham* (Bloomington: Indiana University Press, 1971).

96. Ibid.; see especially ch. 1.

97. Ibid., 45–48.

98. Ibid., 43–45.

99. Ibid., 317.

100. Leland Dewitt Baldwin, *The Meaning of America: Essays Toward an Understanding of the American Spirit* (Pittsburgh: University of Pittsburgh Press, 1976), 176–177.

101. Theodore Dreiser, *The Financier* (New York: Harper, 1912), chs. 1–4.

102. Ibid., 10–15.
103. Ibid., 13–15.
104. Ibid., 102–103.
105. Daniel Boorstin, *The Genius of American Politics* (Chicago: University of Chicago Press, 1953), 8.
106. Ibid., 9.
107. Ibid., 11–19.
108. Ibid., 11.
109. Arthur Schlesinger Jr., "The Theory of America: Experiment or Destiny?" in *The Cycles of American History*, 10–12.
110. Alexander Hamilton, James Madison, and John Jay, *The Federalist Papers* (New York: Bantam Books, 1982), 2.
111. Washington's first inaugural address, April 30, 1789, in J. D. Richardson, *A Compilation of the Messages and Papers of the Presidents: 1789–1902* (Washington, DC: Bureau of National Literature and Art, 1903), vol. 1, 53.
112. Ibid., 322.
113. De Tocqueville, vol. 2, 3.
114. Richardson, vol. 3, 295.
115. Ibid., 295–296.
116. Rush Welter, *The Mind of America: 1820–1860* (New York: Columbia University Press, 1975), 22–25.
117. Ibid., 23.
118. Henry Commager, *The American Mind: An Interpretation of American Thought and Character Since the 1880s* (New Haven: Yale University Press, 1950), 12.
119. For James on pragmatism see *The Will to Believe* (New York: Longmans, Green, 1896) and *A Pluralistic Universe* (New York: Longmans, Green, 1909). For Dewey on pragmatism see *Reconstruction in Philosophy* (Boston: Beacon Press, 1920) and *Human Nature and Conduct* (New York: Henry Holt, 1922). For an excellent overview of pragmatism see John P. Diggins, *The Promise of Pragmatism: Modernism and the Crisis of Knowledge and Authority* (Chicago: University of Chicago Press, 1994).
120. Commager, 97.
121. Cooper's best-known works during this period include *The Pioneers* (1823), *The Last of the Mohicans* (1826), *The Prairie* (1827), *The Pathfinder* (1840), and *The Deerslayer* (1841). Irving's best-known frontier works are *The Adventures of Captain Bonneville* (1837) and *A Tour of the Prairie* (1835). For an excellent analysis of the development of the frontiersman character in Cooper and Irving see Lucy L. Hazard, *The Frontier in American Character* (New York: Thomas Y. Crowell, 1927), ch. 3.
122. James O. Robertson, *American Myth, American Reality* (New York: Hill and Wang, 1980), 135–136.
123. Ibid., 144.
124. Bellah et al., 45.
125. Ibid., 42–45.
126. Ibid., 45.
127. MacIntyre, 26–27.
128. Ibid., 30.
129. Ibid., 74.
130. Ibid., 77.

131. Ibid.

132. Samuel Haber, *Efficiency and Uplift: Scientific Management in the Progressive Era, 1890–1920* (Chicago: University of Chicago Press, 1964).

133. Ibid., 44.

134. John Dos Passos, *The Big Money*, book 3 of *U.S.A. Trilogy* (New York: Random House, 1937).

135. Ibid., 22.

136. Ibid., 309.

137. Ibid., 309–310.

138. Ibid., 55.

139. Ibid., 94–95.

140. Charles E. Sumner, "The Managerial Mind," in Robert Manley and Sean Manley, eds., *The Age of the Manager* (New York: Macmillan, 1962).

141. For example, see ibid. See also David Ewing, *The Managerial Mind* (New York: Free Press, 1962), and Peter F. Drucker, *The Effective Executive* (New York: Harper and Row, 1966).

142. Sumner, 153.

143. Ibid., 154.

144. Cameron Hawley, *Executive Suite,* excerpted in Manley and Manley, 189.

145. Ewing, 64.

146. Herrymon Maurer, *Great Enterprise: Growth and Behavior of the Big Corporation* (New York: Macmillan, 1955).

147. Ibid., 103.

3

The Cold War Evangelism of John Foster Dulles

There is considerable disagreement among scholars as to how engaged Eisenhower was in the foreign policy making process, but most will agree John Foster Dulles (1888–1959) was a very important adviser to the president on foreign policy matters.[1] Dulles brought considerable knowledge about the world to the Eisenhower administration, and he was highly trusted and respected by the president.[2]

The conventional wisdom regarding Dulles tends toward a portrayal of him as simplistic, self-righteous, and not overly intelligent. He was, however, a very complex and sophisticated individual. He was full of contradictions and possessed a powerful intellect. Throughout his careers as international lawyer, leader of national and international church organizations, and finally as civil servant and diplomat, Dulles never stopped thinking and writing about the world and international relations. Consequently, tracing the evolution of Dulles's complex worldview and pinpointing its sources (cultural or otherwise) is a very difficult task.

Specifically, I seek to determine to what extent Dulles's worldview was influenced by any of the three myths and three representative characters discussed in Chapters 1 and 2. The task then is to examine his policy preferences and policymaking behavior as secretary of state to determine the extent to which they were consistent with his worldview.

THE EARLY YEARS

One of the most significant aspects of Dulles's childhood for the shaping of his worldview was his extremely religious upbringing.[3] His father, Allen Macy Dulles, was pastor of the First Presbyterian Church in Watertown, New York. John Foster and his four siblings were brought up in a very strict environment.[4] They were expected to attend all church functions and participated in rigorous Bible study at home.[5] Interestingly, the effects of this strict religious up-bringing do not show up in Dulles's writings or speeches until the late 1930s. Dulles himself reflected on its importance in a speech given before his hometown Chamber of Commerce in 1952: "It is not surprising that it made an impression. It was an impression that was not always enjoyable at the time, but the older I have grown and the wider has been my experience, the more I have appreciated that early religious upbringing and have seen how relevant it is to the far-flung and changing scenes of life."[6]

Also significant for Dulles's developing worldview was his exposure to a world much larger than Watertown.[7] Both his parents were well educated and well traveled, and they took John Foster and his siblings on many trips to Europe while they were children.[8] More important, Dulles's mother, Edith Foster Dulles, was the daughter of John Watson Foster, a successful international lawyer and diplomat whose career included ministerial appointments to Mexico, Spain, and Russia and culminated in his serving as secretary of state under Benjamin Harrison.[9] As young children, John Foster and his siblings spent a great deal of time at their maternal grandparents' home in Washington, D.C., where they were exposed to their grandfather's political and diplomatic milieu.[10] The Washington diplomatic setting was a fitting nursery for a boy who would spend his life thinking and writing about world politics and eventually occupy his grandfather's office at the State Department.

Another experience that significantly influenced Dulles's worldview was his undergraduate career at Princeton University. Dulles entered Princeton at the tender age of sixteen in 1904, and while there he was awarded many honors for academic achievements in his philosophy and government majors.[11] He studied extensively in philosophy, wrote a prize-winning senior thesis in logic, and upon graduation was awarded a one-year fellowship to the Sorbonne, where he studied under Henri Bergson.[12] Just as the influence of his strong religious upbringing remained buried for decades, so too did the influence of this early exposure to philosophy.

Dulles's studies in government at Princeton seem to have had a much more immediate impact on his worldview and life. The main reason was that one of Dulles's professors in government was Woodrow Wilson, also the university president.[13] Dulles would later credit Wilson's influence, saying, "The major benefit I got from Princeton was participating in Woodrow Wilson's courses where I gained my interest in public affairs."[14] This interest was enhanced while Dulles was still at Princeton when his grandfather, John Watson Foster, took him to the Second Hague Conference in May 1907 and gave him a role as a secretary to the Chinese delegation.[15]

Woodrow Wilson's influence on the young John Foster Dulles would continue long past their classroom relationship at Princeton. As Ronald Pruessen shows throughout *The Road to Power,* in later years, Dulles would frequently point to Woodrow Wilson as an important role model and source for ideas.[16] Dulles borrowed substantially from Wilson's Fourteen Points in putting together his own program for reforming the international system and to a large extent adopted Wilson's crusading style of diplomacy.

After Princeton, Dulles's next contact with Woodrow Wilson was at the Versailles peace conference in 1919. On leave from his partnership at the prestigious Sullivan and Cromwell law firm, Dulles went to the conference in the capacity of legal counsel to the U.S. delegation.[17] There he was directly involved in the negotiation and drafting of important parts of the reparations agreements, and he was a central participant in the argument with the Allies over the question of including war costs in the reparations package.[18] As Pruessen points out, Dulles's in-depth involvement with the reparations negotiations at Versailles was important in shaping his worldview.[19] Dulles shared with Wilson and his senior colleagues on the Reparations Commission a concern that any heavy reparations burden placed on the Germans would create economic and political instability throughout Europe and the world.[20] This concern is consistent with the somewhat narrow economic focus that came to characterize Dulles's early analyses of international relations.

Throughout the 1920s and early 1930s, Dulles's thinking and writing about international relations focused almost exclusively on economic issues such as international trade, finance, and currency exchange. This is not surprising, since during this period, Dulles was back at Sullivan and Cromwell, where he was involved in the legal affairs of huge commercial and financial firms that were conducting business internationally.[21]

During the 1920s he focused on how international trade, finance, and currency exchange were being adversely affected by war-related debt and reparations problems.[22] He constantly stressed the need for a rational resolution of the war debt in Europe.[23] He urged the Allies to be realistic about Germany's ability to pay its debts, and in turn he urged the United States to be realistic about the Allies' ability to pay their U.S. war debts.[24] In the conclusion of a 1922 *Foreign Affairs* article, he warned the U.S. leadership of the economic and political consequences of not dealing with the debt problem.[25]

The underlying assumption both here and in Dulles's other writings during this period was that free-flowing trade and capital and stable currency exchange were the primary requirements for a peaceful world. This assumption may be interpreted as being consistent with the market myth, that is, the free market is the superior organizing principle for society and U.S. society comes closest to achieving the free market ideal.

Dulles's international analyses of the early years of the Great Depression also reflect the market myth in their strong antipathy toward government interference with market forces.[26] In 1932 he wrote, "the existing system of currency controls, quotas, clearings, etc. is more and more throttling international trade and commerce. Each new restriction by one state has been met by a counter-restriction by another state. The result is a virtual elimination of triangular operations and the reduction of trade to isolated barter transactions."[27] He went on to call such government controls "an intolerable interference with and stifling of individual initiative and enterprise."[28] This abhorrence of governmental interference with business, whether at home or abroad, and the reverence for "individual initiative" is very consistent with the market myth of America and with the extension of its tenets into the international realm.

Thus an examination of Dulles's earliest writings on international relations shows that his early thinking on the subject was primarily focused on economic concerns. It also reveals that his worldview during this period was more consistent with the market myth than with the city-on-the-hill or pragmatic myths.

PHILOSOPHICAL WRITINGS—1934–1940

In *The Road to Power*, Pruessen characterizes 1934–1940 as Dulles's philosophical period; this is an apt description of his thinking during these years.[29] In 1934, Dulles's writings on international relations turned from a focus on specific economic problems to more abstract theorizing about world politics. The predominant theme in these writings was the inevitability of change in world politics and the absence of an alternative to force as a vehicle for change.

He constantly criticized formal peace instruments (i.e., the League of Nations, Kellogg-Briand Pact) for not recognizing the inevitability of change in the international arena and for not creating alternatives to war as a change agent. As he put it in his 1935 "The Road to Peace" in the *Atlantic Monthly*, "Peace plans, if they are to be effective, must be constructed so as to take into account these two fundamental facts—namely, the inevitability of change, and the present lack of any adequate substitute for force as an inducement to change."[30]

For Dulles, there were two kinds of forces active in world politics, those states that were content with their material position and status in the world, or the status quo powers, and those states that were not, the dynamic powers. Dulles argued that the status quo powers were always the sponsors of peace instruments or treaties such as the League of Nations and the Kellogg-Briand Pact, which were based on the assumption of indefinitely freezing the status quo. Such plans were doomed to fail because they did not create mechanisms that would prevent pressures for change in the dynamic states (i.e., Germany, Japan, and Italy) from building to the point of general war.[31]

Dulles developed these themes much further in a series of articles and speeches from 1934 to 1939 that culminated in the publication of his first book in 1939.[32] In *War, Peace, and Change,* he built on his portrayal of international relations as constant conflict between status quo and dynamic forces and did so on a very abstract level. There he identified the status quo–dynamic conflict as a fundamental problem in all human societies.[33] To prevent this conflict from constantly resulting in violence, human societies had come up with solutions he categorized as either ethical or political in nature.[34] Ethical solutions sought "to mould the human spirit so that desires will either be so diluted in intensity or so metamorphasized in character that conflicts in desire will be minimized." He categorized as political those "efforts which are primarily directed to creating a scheme of society which provides substitutes for force as the solvent of conflicting desires."[35] The rest of the book is an effort to determine the extent to which these kinds of solutions could be used at the level of international relations to solve the ever-present conflict between status quo and dynamic forces. It is in these solutions that we are given a good look at his worldview at the time.

Dulles's worldview in *War, Peace, and Change* still showed signs of having been significantly influenced by the market myth, representing continuity with his earlier political-economic analysis. There is also, however, evidence of a developing religious stream of thought that is more consistent with the city-on-the-hill myth. Dulles continued to develop this religious pattern of thought throughout the rest of his life, and it shows prominently in his public statements and correspondence. It is at this stage of Dulles's intellectual development that we begin to see the layered structure of a very complex worldview.

It is clear throughout *War, Peace, and Change* that Dulles still viewed a healthy international economy as a fundamental condition for peace. He argued there and in other writings that a fluid international economy could provide a peaceful outlet for the acquisitive energies that drive dynamic states from the inside.[36] He was very critical of the way national boundaries act to contain the acquisitive energies that build up inside dynamic states, often to the point that they lead to war. He wrote:

> Partly as a result of conscious decision, partly in consequence of policies adopted for other reasons, national boundaries have come to be barriers substantially barring those without from availing of opportunities within. Deliberate measures designed to effect this result are, typically, restrictions on immigration and even on temporary visits; restrictions on imports through tariffs, quotas and embargoes; restrictions on exports; restrictions on alien ownership of real estate and upon alien investment in many types of enterprises. Such measures, which are manifold, are deliberately designed to prevent aliens from sharing in domestic opportunities and to conserve them for the national group.[37]

A liberalized international economy would also minimize the extent to which citizens came to deify their own state as an economic protector and benefactor and demonize other states as hoarders of economic opportunity.[38]

Dulles used the early history of the United States as a model for preventing the buildup of dynamic energies inside states and reducing the tendency to deify one's own state and demonize others.[39] He argued that with the (admittedly substantial) exception of the American Civil War, the free flow of interstate commerce in the United States reduced drastically the incidence of violent conflict between the states.[40] He did admit that whereas citizens ceased to personify their individual states, they transferred this personification/deification to the national state as it solidified.[41]

Here again, Dulles's arguments were consistent with the market myth of America and its premise that the free market is the superior way to organize a society and that the United States is the perfect realization of the free market ideal. Dulles sought to persuade his readers that if the entire world were organized around the same free market principles, it would be safer and much more prosperous. This view highlights a crusading strain within the market myth that holds up the United States as the ideal model of a market society.

We also see in Dulles's worldview the market myth's stress on individualism. The assumption underlying his analysis was that if governments would stop putting obstacles in the way of individuals trying to improve their situation through commerce, the world would be much more peaceful.

This stress on keeping individuals free from government inter-ference is found in the conclusion to *War, Peace, and Change,* where Dulles wrote:

> We should not accept the increasing tendency of the group au-thority [i.e., government] to destroy individual freedom and ini-tiative. It is particularly important that the intellectual freedom of the individual be preserved. Only from such a source can we ex-pect the originality of thought necessary to cope with those crises which successively arise as social concepts, useful in their origin, are carried to dangerous extremes.[42]

This concern for protecting the enterprising individual from government interference would remain a prominent theme in Dulles's writings for the rest of his life. This may be partly explained by the fact that Dulles spent the greater part of his adult life as an international lawyer, trying to remove obstacles (governmental and otherwise) in the way of large business concerns engaged in inter-national commerce.

Whereas certain patterns of Dulles's thinking in *War, Peace, and Change* show market myth influence, others are inconsistent with the market myth and may be seen as transitional to more of a city-on-the-hill orientation. This view is most evident in his discussion of the ethical solution to war. As was noted earlier, Dulles argued that the tendency of citizens to deify their own state and demonize oth-ers was a significant cause of war. He suggested that this phenome-non could be reduced if people substituted a universal religion and deity as an object of adulation.[43]

He noted that there was a time when religions had this kind of spiritual grip on populations but that as that grip weakened, the personified state filled the vacuum.[44] He then called for a reversal of that trend:

> Devotion to an ideal and willingness to sacrifice therefor are among the finest of human traits. Also, they are among the most dangerous. It is indispensable to our well-being that they be in-voked only in a truly worthy cause. It has now become indispens-able to international peace that they be inculcated on a basis which transcends that of nationality. Such broad causes have been revealed and can again become vital. They can absorb that will-ingness to sacrifice which demands an outlet. Only if this occurs can we expect the personified state to shrink to a diminished role in human imagination. Only if this occurs can we release spiritual forces into a sphere of greater universality.[45]

He went on to call for a "form of spiritual revival" and suggested that the universal religion should stress "the concept of a duty to fellow man" and should "promote the welfare of the human race." He noted that these were central objectives of Christianity, perhaps suggesting it as the best candidate.[46]

As we will see, this pattern of religious thinking, which first manifested in *War, Peace, and Change,* continued to develop throughout the 1940s and eventually coalesced into a distinct vision of a preferred world order where states patterned their behavior (to the extent possible) according to moral law. Throughout his later writings and speeches, Dulles strongly adhered to this vision while also remaining committed to an international free market economy.[47]

Dulles's views on the economy were more or less fully developed by the time he wrote *War, Peace, and Change.* As Mark Toulouse chronicles in *The Transformation of John Foster Dulles,* from 1937 to 1945, Dulles devoted much of his thinking and writing to exploring and promoting an active role for religion in creating a peaceful world.[48] During this period, Dulles was heavily involved with the Federal Council of Churches, an involvement that culminated in his being named the chairman of that organization's Commission on a Just and Durable Peace in 1940.[49]

THE QUEST FOR A SPIRITUAL BASIS FOR WORLD ORDER

Dulles's involvement with the Federal Council of Churches profoundly affected his personal normative beliefs about how to achieve a more peaceful world. He described this influence in a 1949 church address.

> I began to understand the profound significance of the spiritual values that my father and mother had taught. . . . Serving at the same time in both religious and political groups made ever clearer the relationship between the two. I saw that there could be no just and durable peace except as men held in common simple and elementary religious beliefs: belief that there is a God, that he is the author of a moral law which they can know, and that he imparts to each human being a spiritual dignity and worth which all others should respect. Wherever these elementary truths are widely rejected, there is both spiritual and social disorder.[50]

Not only did his work with the Federal Council of Churches revitalize his attachment to the religious values he was taught while growing up in a Presbyterian manse, he also became convinced that church organizations could play a vital role in creating a "just and durable" postwar peace. Later in the same address he described this role.

> It is the churches that dependably keep alive and pass on, from generation to generation, belief in God, in moral law, and in the spiritual nature of man. . . . It is the churches that have missionary affiliations that spread great spiritual truths throughout the world. They have central agencies . . . that provide studies of world problems by qualified Christian statesmen. These if used, can create an enlightened public opinion that will directly influence the acts of government and of the United Nations.[51]

The self-defined mission of the Commission on a Just and Durable Peace was to educate Christians about world problems, to convince them that Christian principles could help shape a more peaceful postwar world, and to mobilize public opinion in order to push government leaders to take steps that would create a postwar order that reflected these Christian principles.[52] This mission reflected very closely Dulles's strong belief in the power of Christian ideas and public opinion. In fact, he was the driving intellectual force behind many of the commission's ideas and programs.[53]

It is during the period of his involvement with the Commission on a Just and Durable Peace that we first see Dulles taking on certain aspects of the Puritan representative character. He shared the Puritan's revelation-based epistemological and moral orientation: He held the Bible to be the definitive source of both truth and the moral law, and he believed that the Christian church had the responsibility to spread "these great truths." More important for our purposes, Dulles exhibited during this period the Puritan's paradigmatic mode of social action. He (along with the rest of the commission) was primarily engaged in attempting to mobilize people to do God's work by showing them a divine blueprint for a peaceful world. This is illustrated by the following passage from the introduction (written by Dulles) to the commission's statement of guiding principles.

> As members of the Christian church, we seek to view all problems of world order in the light of the truth concerning God, man, and God's purpose for the world made known in Jesus Christ. We believe that the eternal God revealed in Christ is the ruler of men, and of nations and that his purpose in history will be realized. For us he is the source of all moral law and the power to make it effective. From this faith, Christians derive the ethical principles upon which world order must be based.[54]

Some of Dulles's writings during this period also contain passages that are versions of the city-on-the-hill myth. One good example comes from a 1942 essay entitled "A Righteous Faith": "We in the United States became conscious of 'a manifest destiny' and 'American Dream.' . . . We saw that we might fashion here a state of ordered freedom that would be a beacon to the world."[55] Another good example comes from a 1944 speech entitled "A Nation's Foreign Policy": "The American people, from the beginning, charted for themselves a clear-cut course. They dedicated themselves to finding as a nation economic, intellectual, and spiritual institutions which would advance the welfare of their own people. By that conduct and example, they felt, they could best aid mankind and as a by-product of that endeavor assure for themselves the good-will of people everywhere."[56]

Both of these passages contain what might be called a secular version of the city-on-the-hill myth. It is secular because it does not stipulate that America's mission comes from God. It is interesting that Dulles would evoke a secular version of this myth during what might be called his most religious period. The refusal to identify the United States with a higher religious cause is, however, consistent with some of his other writings of this period, many of which warned against the tendency to identify one's own nation with some higher cause.[57]

Also, Dulles and the commission were not trying to directly mobilize the United States as an international actor but rather to mobilize members of Christian churches everywhere to pressure their governments to create international structures (such as the UN and World Bank) that would facilitate just and peaceful change in the international system. However, since the Federal Council of Churches was concerned primarily with churches in the United States and since Dulles and other commission members recognized how important U.S. leadership would be in the postwar era, they did focus on mobilizing public opinion in the United States to steer policymakers toward creating international structures that were consistent with Christian principles. They were pushing especially for a global forum in which nations' actions would be governed by concern for adherence to moral law and not by power-political considerations. They very much hoped that the UN General Assembly would provide such a forum.[58]

Neither Dulles nor the other members of the commission were naive enough to think that nations would completely abandon power-political considerations in an effort to adhere to the moral law. Thus the commission urged concerned Christian citizens to temper their quest for a more moral international order with a realistic sense of what was actually achievable.[59]

It is important to understand that the Dulles commission did not seek directly to influence policymakers but to influence them indirectly by enlightening and mobilizing public opinion. As Toulouse points out,

> Dulles often emphasized that the nature of the politician's job required both a quest for power and a concern for the national interest. Dedication to the universal welfare of humankind strikes most politicians as an intrusion from the outside. . . . However, the task of the individual citizen is different from that of the political leader. The American people—especially the Christian audiences he addressed—should, according to Dulles, try to press universal concerns on their political leaders. Thus, out of their mandate to serve the expressed needs of the people, political leaders might occasionally transcend normal behavior by including other than merely national concerns in their policy decisions.[60]

Dulles consistently posited such a dichotomy between national interests on the one hand and Christian concern for the universal interests of humankind on the other.[61] As Toulouse also shows, Dulles often warned against the tendency of governmental leaders to identify their own national interests with a universal religious cause.[62] This warning is particularly interesting in light of the fact that when Dulles was secretary of state he would frequently identify the interests and policies of the United States with universal religious concerns.

Analysis of Dulles's worldview during the period (1937–1945) of his involvement with these religious organizations shows that he had developed a distinctly religious vision of a preferred world order. In developing this religious vision of world order, however, he built on his earlier thinking about how to create a more peaceful world. Specifically, he continued to stress the need to create vehicles for peaceful change in the international system that would accommodate pressures for change from the dynamic states. He continued to believe that a liberalized international economic order was the most important element of such a system. He also continued to believe that the deification/demonization of states was a huge obstacle to peace, and he argued that a spiritual revitalization of universal religion (he seemed to prefer Christianity) could best erode this phenomenon.

As World War II was coming to a close, the core of Dulles's normative worldview was his vision of a world where change could occur peacefully because national boundaries would not hamper international commerce and national leaders would be forced by enlightened citizenries to consider the moral law in their foreign policy making. With the end of World War II and the beginning of the Cold War, Dulles would come to feel this vision was increasingly threatened by what he conceptualized as the forces of international communism. Increasingly he would come to identify the United States and the Western alliance as the only defenders of this vision of world order in which he believed so strongly. As he came to identify the United States more and more with his vision of a moral and liberal world order, he began to infuse more and more city-on-the-hill (and to a lesser extent, market) mythical imagery into his rhetoric. In doing so, he would frequently violate his own earlier warnings against the tendency of leaders to identify their own nations with the forces of righteousness and opposing nations with the forces of evil. Having examined the biography and development of Dulles's worldview up to the point in the mid-1940s when he began to become involved extensively in the making of U.S. foreign policy, I now turn to his late-life career as a full-time policymaker.

THE PURITAN EMERGES

In his biography of Dulles, Toulouse argues that during the early years of the Cold War, Dulles experienced a dramatic transformation, changing from a "prophet of realism" to a "priest of nationalism."[63] According to Toulouse, the pre–Cold War Dulles was a "prophet of realism, because while he worked for a more moral world order, he nonetheless recognized that, for the most part, individual states could not act morally, and that states' claims to moral righteousness were merely used to cloak the self-interest behind their actions in the world."[64] With the advent of the Cold War, Dulles was becoming a "priest of nationalism," arguing with increasing fervor that the United States and the Western alliance were fighting for morality and righteousness against the immoral forces of international communism.[65]

This transformation from prophet of realism to priest of nationalism took place during 1945–1950.[66] Dulles was a delegate to the 1945 UN conference in San Francisco and was a regular delegate to the General Assembly from 1946 to 1950. He also attended the foreign minister councils in 1945, 1947, and 1949 and negotiated the Japanese peace treaty in 1950.[67] As Toulouse chronicles, these meetings provided Dulles with face-to-face contact with the Soviets, and he began to note what he believed was a pattern of increasing Soviet intransigence at every meeting.[68]

As World War II was coming to a close, Dulles still held out hopes for maintaining a constructive postwar relationship with the Soviets. He expressed the need for such a relationship in a 1945 speech to the Economic Club of Detroit.

> Another overriding task of the next few years will be to develop more friendly relations with the Soviet Union. To us the Soviet governing class seems atheistic and materialistic. The Soviets on their side have little reason to trust us. . . . For many years we sought to prevent their having economic and diplomatic discourse with the rest of the world. Our public leaders denounced them up to the moment when Germany's attack made us perforce comrades in arms. What will happen when the fighting stops? Will our relations revert to what they were when war came? That would be a major disaster for us, for them, and for the world; but it is a disaster that stares us in the face.[69]

Dulles did mention the philosophical and ideological obstacles to a solid postwar U.S.-Soviet relationship. More important, though, he went out of his way to give the Soviets the benefit of the doubt, actually condemning prewar U.S. policy toward the Soviets for creating distrust. His portrayal here of the U.S.-Soviet relationship is consistent with the philosophy of the early Dulles (Toulouse's "prophet of realism") in that it legitimated the security concerns of the Soviets and did not seek to wrap U.S. interests and actions in a cloak of righteousness. This is in stark contrast to the tone of his writings on the Soviets just one year later.

In a manuscript for a 1946 article for *Life* magazine, Dulles wrote:

> The most urgent task of American statesmanship is to find the policies that will avoid a serious clash with the Soviet Union. . . . Indeed the more closely Soviet policies are studied, and the more intimately they are known, the greater does that danger appear. Soviet leaders assume that peace and security depend upon quickly achieving world-wide acceptance of Soviet political philosophy, which suppresses certain personal freedoms in the interest of achieving social harmony. The personal freedoms they would take away constitute our most cherished political and religious heritage. We have in the past fought to defend them when they seemed in jeopardy. The methods which Soviet leaders use are repugnant to our ideas of humanity and fair play. It would be foolish to rest our hope of peace on any genuine reconciliation of our faith with that now held by Soviet leadership.[70]

Here Dulles's portrayal of the U.S.-Soviet relationship is much more consistent with Toulouse's "prophet of nationalism." The United

States is now portrayed as the champion of human freedom, fighting against an aggressive Soviet campaign to destroy human freedom worldwide. Before the U.S. and the Soviet Union were portrayed as two states seeking to achieve security; now there is a confrontation of two "irreconcilable" rival "faiths," one good and one evil. Gone is Dulles's own earlier concern about the danger of wrapping one's own nation's cause in a cloak of righteousness while branding other nations as evil. It is important to remember that between early 1945 and mid-1946 there were developments that began to strain seriously the U.S.-Soviet relationship, and these developments were creating a great deal of pessimism throughout the U.S. foreign policy making elite as to the future of the Grand Alliance.[71]

During this period we begin to see vivid city-on-the-hill mythical imagery in Dulles's speeches and writings. In a 1946 speech at Princeton, he proclaimed that the history of the American people was the story of a great mission. He spoke longingly of the early years of the American republic:

> The American people were imbued with a great faith. We acted under a sense of moral compulsion, as a people who had a mission to perform in the world. Our conduct was largely determined by a religious belief that every human being had a God-given possibility of spiritual development and that to realize this was man's chief earthly aim. Accordingly we sought to organize a society which would promote the spiritual development of the individual. We wanted him to have not only spiritual freedom, but the surrounding conditions of intellectual and economic opportunity without which spiritual growth is seldom realized. . . . We sought through conduct, example and influence to promote everywhere the cause of human freedom. We availed of every opportunity to spread our gospel throughout the world.[72]

Dulles went on to lament that the American people seemed to have lost some of this great faith, but he argued that it could and had to be regained.[73] The city-on-the-hill imagery is unmistakable in this speech, and it is stronger here than in any previous speeches or writings, one reason being that Dulles added a very powerful theme—the quest for human freedom. There is also for the first time here an implicit notion that the American people's mission was God-given. In his earlier uses of city-on-the-hill imagery, there was no mention of God in connection with this mission.[74]

This more religious version of the city-on-the-hill myth clearly evoked the image of an American people divinely destined to be a force for human freedom in the world. Dulles developed this theme much further in a 1947 speech in Chicago, where he explicitly identified past U.S. foreign policy with this divine mission:

United States foreign policy is made at home. It is the projection
abroad of our national will. . . . Our will flows from the funda-
mentals of our faith. Our founders believed that there was a moral
law which gave reality to such concepts as justice and righteousness. They believed that all men are endowed by their creator with
certain inalienable rights. . . . They believed that men not only
had rights but also duties, to God and to each other. They felt a
sense of mission in the world . . . . Such basic beliefs have fixed
the course of our nation in history. They will continue to fix our
course, so long as Americans are true to their tradition.[75]

Dulles went on to list examples of past U.S. foreign policies that he
argued were "external manifestation[s] of American will" to promote liberty in the world. These policies included the Monroe Doctrine, the open-door doctrine, U.S. entry into World Wars I and II,
and U.S. leadership in the creation of the UN.[76] Dulles concluded
that these policies were shining examples of enlightened self-interest on the part of the United States.

The four foreign policies I have described reflect the practical ide-
alism of America. They are idealistic because inspired by a desire
to promote justice, as we see it, and to preserve human liberty.
They are practical because they recognize that our own freedom
would be imperiled if there were only wind and water between us
and militant dictatorship. . . . Today these policies face a serious
challenge from the Soviet Union. The professed social goals of Soviet Communism are not unlike our own; but Marxian communism is atheistic in conception and materialistic in its view of man.
It does not admit of a Creator who establishes eternal principles
of right and justice or who endows his creatures with inalienable
rights. It denies the sacredness of the human personality and
would force human beings into spiritual straitjackets.[77]

This passage is significant because in it Dulles explained nearly
two centuries of U.S. diplomatic history using the city-on-the-hill
myth. All of these historical watersheds, from the Monroe Doctrine
to the creation of the UN, were, according to Dulles, manifestations
of America's divine mission to promote liberty in the world. He was
thus arguing that U.S. foreign policy behavior had been and should
continue to be guided by this divine mission. At the same time,
however, Dulles argued that adherence to this divine mission and
these lofty principles had historically been consistent with U.S. national interest. Gone is the uneasy tension that Dulles the "prophet
of realism" once perceived between national interest and adherence to the moral law. Now we see the easy equation of national interest and moral imperative that Toulouse notes is characteristic of
the "priest of nationalism."

This newfound congruence between national interest and moral imperative facilitated painting the emerging Cold War confrontation between the United States and the Soviet Union in broad moral strokes. It represents a dramatic change in Dulles's views regarding the philosophical question of the relationship between morality and statesmanship. This new stance is quite consistent with a city-on-the-hill orientation. Indeed, by the early 1950s Dulles's entire worldview showed significant city-on-the-hill influence at both the philosophical and instrumental levels.

In 1945, Dulles had proclaimed to the Economic Club of Detroit that in its conduct of foreign policy, "our government should adopt and publicly proclaim long-range goals which reflect our high ideals."[78] Into the early 1950s, he continued to develop his argument for the importance of moral principle as a guide to U.S. foreign policy. In a 1952 speech to the Missouri Bar Association, he made it the central theme when he argued that "of course, moral principles do not alone provide all the practical answers that men need. . . . But few would doubt that the past dynamism of our nation has genuinely stemmed from a profound popular faith in such concepts as justice and righteousness and from the sense that our nation had a mission to promote these ideals by every peaceful means."[79] Dulles went on to argue that nonmoral diplomacy was unhealthy because "it inevitably makes for a break between our government and our people. Whether we like it or not—and I like it—our people are predominantly a moral people, who believe that our nation has a great spiritual heritage to be preserved. We do not feel happy to be identified with foreign policies which run counter to what we have been taught in our churches and synagogues and in our classrooms in American history."[80]

Against this moral U.S. mission in the world, Dulles counterposed the agenda of Soviet-led international communism: "Soviet Communism reflects a view totally different from the U.S. historic view. Its creed is materialistic and atheistic. It does not admit of any moral law."[81] This passage is consistent with the tendency on Dulles's part to portray the Cold War as a global moral confrontation between the forces of good and evil. This Manichaean vision of the world is also consistent with the various historical variations of the city-on-the-hill myth, especially the original seventeenth-century Puritan version (see Chapter 2). In a 1953 speech at the National War College, Dulles portrayed the Cold War in the simplest of moral terms.

> We have a world that is—for the most part—split between two huge combinations. . . . These huge concentrations are in conflict

because each reflects differing aims, aspirations and social, political, and economic philosophies. We must assume that they will continue to remain in basic conflict—in one way or another—until such time as the communists so change their nature as to admit that those who wish to live by the moral law are free to do so without coercion by those who believe in enforced conformity to a materialistic standard.[82]

Thus Dulles portrayed the Cold War as a battle between those who would live by the moral law (the United States and its Western allies) and those who would prevent this (the Soviets and the rest of the communist world).

Analysis of Dulles's early Cold War speeches and writings indicates that he took consistent stands on philosophical questions regarding the relationship of morality and diplomacy, the degree to which U.S. foreign policy should be guided by moral principles, and the extent to which the Cold War should be viewed in moral terms. His consistent moralism regarding these philosophical questions would lead us to expect him to take certain stands on more instrumental, policy-relevant questions about how to deal with the Soviets and the communist bloc.

More specifically, we would expect that given his belief in the inherent goodness of the U.S. mission in the world and the evil inherent in the communist agenda, he would be wary of policies that sought to negotiate or compromise with the communists. Analysis of his early Cold War statements on the subject of negotiating do in fact reflect such a wariness. In a 1950 speech at Vanderbilt University, Dulles argued strongly against relying on the ability to negotiate differences with the Soviets and the communist bloc:

Let us take first the question of negotiating and compromising with the Russian leaders. At first glance that seems a normal thing to do . . . that is what men of good will have been, for many years, urging that nations should do. The obstacle now is that our present differences relate primarily to beliefs, that can't be compromised. . . . I do not see how this issue is going to be compromised. Certainly we are not going to compromise, by one iota, our belief in the spiritual nature of man and our insistence that political institutions must respect that belief. . . . If we ever seemed ready to sacrifice human freedom in an effort to bring "peace" that would merely make the Russian communists even more confident that they are right and that their materialism is indeed the wave of the future. . . . That doesn't mean that nothing can be negotiated. . . . But don't let us delude ourselves into thinking the basic differences are of a kind that can be resolved by Truman and Stalin chatting together over a cup of tea.[83]

Thus Dulles posited that the main differences between the United States and the Soviets were at the level of basic beliefs and principles and were therefore irreconcilable. Indeed, for Dulles, for the United States to compromise these beliefs and principles would be to negate what he saw as the core of America's identity as a people. From Dulles's standpoint, failure by Americans to remain true to these principles constituted a failure to remain true to themselves.

Dulles was not, however, arguing against any and all negotiations with the Soviets. In fact, in the same speech he cited the negotiations that ended the 1949 blockade of Berlin as an instance where negotiations with the Soviets bore real fruit.[84] In this speech and others, however, he did manifest a basic belief that until the Soviets abandoned their basic philosophy, there would be very little room for negotiation or compromise on a general level. In this and other speeches he also argued that the Soviets had a history of going back on their agreements with the United States, a behavior pattern that he argued stemmed from their basic philosophy.[85]

If Dulles was wary of negotiation as a method for meeting the Soviet challenge, the question then became how U.S. power should best be used in dealing with the Soviets and what forms it should take. To a large extent, Dulles's answer to this question may be found in his 1952 critiques of the Truman administration's containment policy. These critiques were written as Dulles was actively campaigning for Eisenhower for the upcoming 1952 presidential election, and as such they were partially politically motivated. As we will see, however, there were enough substantial strands of continuity with Dulles's earlier writings about world politics and U.S. foreign policy (and indeed with his later writings) in these critiques to indicate that they were not merely cynical political attacks.

Dulles's fundamental criticism of the existing containment strategy was that (in addition to being too expensive) it was purely reactive and defensive and gave the Soviets complete initiative.[86] He argued that such a strategy was giving the Soviets time to consolidate their postwar acquisitions while using political subversion tactics to gain more influence around the world. Such a defensive and reactive posture sought only to contain the communist threat but did nothing to actually diminish it and as such was a perpetual drain on U.S. resources. He summed up this criticism when he wrote, "Our present negative policies will never end the type of sustained offensive which Soviet Communism is mounting; they will never end the peril nor bring relief from the exertions which devour our economic, political, and moral vitals. Ours are treadmill policies which, at best might perhaps keep us in the same place until we drop exhausted."[87]

Dulles went on to argue that whereas the United States should continue to maintain enough military power to be able to resist open communist aggression, it should also begin a political and spiritual offensive to liberate "captive peoples" held behind the iron curtain and to win newly independent peoples over by showing the superiority of the ideals and institutions of the "free world."[88]

Dulles based his argument for this political and spiritual offensive on three principles from his previous philosophical and religious writings:

> There are three truths which we need to recall in these times:
>
> 1) The Dynamic always prevails over the static; the active over the passive. We were from the beginning a vigorous, confident people born with a sense of destiny and mission. . . .
> 2) Nonmaterial forces are more powerful than those that are merely material. Our dynamism has always been moral and intellectual rather than military or material. . . . We always generated political, social and industrial ideas and projected them abroad where they were more explosive than dynamite.
> 3) There is a moral or natural law not made by man which determines right and wrong, and in the long run only those who conform to that law escape disaster. This law has been trampled by the Soviet rulers, and for that violation they can and should be made to pay. This will happen when we ourselves keep faith with that law in our practical decisions of policy.[89]

Here we see vivid city-on-the-hill imagery interwoven with the core principles of Dulles's earlier philosophical and religious writings about world politics. Dulles wove all of this into an urgent call for Americans to go forth and "liberate" the world from communist despotism.

His style here is very consistent with the Puritan representative character. He revealed to his American readers that it was their duty to follow God's moral law and carry out God's will that the communist transgressors against this moral law be punished. These passages are also very revealing as to his vision of how the Cold War should be fought by the American people. He believed that the "moral and intellectual dynamism" of the American people would be their most potent weapon against communism. He told Americans that it was their duty to spread their moral principles and political ideals in order to bring the captive and newly independent peoples into the "free world" by conversion.

Thus Dulles's policy of liberation was not (as some feared at the time) primarily military in nature. It was based on maintaining a stalemate militarily (including the use of threats of massive nuclear retaliation) while conducting a political, psychological, and spiritual offensive designed to weaken the Soviets from within and inoculate the developing world against their influence. As Dulles himself concluded, "We should let these truths work in and through us. We should be dynamic, we should use our ideas as weapons; and these ideas should conform to moral principles. That we do this is right . . . but it is also expedient in defending ourselves against an aggressive imperialist despotism. For even the present lines will not hold unless our purpose goes beyond confining Soviet Communism within its present orbit."[90]

Dulles's strong belief in the power of ideas as evidenced in his portrayal of the Cold War as a moral and spiritual battle was just short of Hegelian. It was also quite consistent with major themes from his philosophical and religious writings of the 1930s and 1940s.[91] His principle of the dynamic prevailing over the static comes straight from the pages of *War, Peace, and Change,* and his belief in the power of spiritual forces and the applicability of the moral law in world politics came from his work with the Federal Council of Churches. Given this thematic continuity, it is very difficult to dismiss his critique of containment policy as merely a cynical political attack on the Democrats.

In addition to the thematic continuity between Dulles's earlier writings and his Cold War writings, there is also a deeper element of continuity in terms of his basic approach to influencing international relations. Both during his work with the Federal Council of Churches and during his official involvement with the making of U.S. foreign policy (both before and after he became secretary of state), Dulles placed a great deal of stock in the power of moral principles and political ideals to mobilize people across state boundaries and thereby alter the course of world politics.

This pattern of continuity in his basic approach to influencing world politics is doubly significant because it is remarkably consistent with the Puritan representative character. This use of ideas to "convert and mobilize" people in order to change the world is the Puritan's paradigmatic mode of social action. The fact that Dulles continued to adhere to this basic approach to influencing world politics even as the world and his official roles changed is extremely significant.

The previous examination of Dulles's worldview in the early 1950s in the period right before he became secretary of state clearly reveals his views on such questions as the relationship between morality and diplomacy, the extent to which U.S. foreign policy should be guided by moral principles, and how to deal with the global communist threat. It is also clear from his writings and speeches that his worldview was significantly colored by the city-on-the-hill myth. There is also significant evidence in Dulles's worldview of a basic approach to influencing world politics that is remarkably consistent with the Puritan representative character. But how did these elements of his worldview influence his policy preferences and actual policymaking behavior as secretary of state? It is to this last, very complex step in this analysis that we now turn.

THE FOGGY BOTTOM YEARS

After Dulles took office as secretary of state in January 1953, it didn't take long for events to force the new administration to undertake a significant reappraisal of U.S. policy toward the Soviets. Joseph Stalin died unexpectedly on March 4, 1953.[92] After a funeral speech by new Soviet premier Georgi Malenkov that was surprisingly conciliatory toward the West, Eisenhower and others within the administration began to see an opportunity for a lessening of Cold War tensions. Dulles, however, saw the speech as a sign of Soviet weakening and argued that it was a time to turn up the pressure on the Soviets.[93] In a meeting of the National Security Council on March 12, 1953, Dulles argued that the death of Stalin created the possibility of nationalist discontent within the satellite states and that the United States should take steps to capitalize on this opportunity to weaken Soviet control in the satellites.[94] He was unable to dissuade Eisenhower from his optimistic interpretation of Stalin's death and the subsequent Malenkov speech, however, and the president instructed his speechwriters to prepare an address in which he could reach out to the new Soviet leadership.[95]

Hoopes argues, in *The Devil and John Foster Dulles,* that Dulles objected strongly to this movement toward détente but did not feel confident enough in the strength of his relationship with Eisenhower to directly confront him on the issue; he confined his efforts to trying to influence those in charge of drafting the speech.[96] In his memoirs, Eisenhower's speechwriter Emmett John Hughes describes Dulles's opposition to the speech as follows:

> Only obliquely to the president, but plainly to me, Dulles murmured his distrust and dislike for the whole project, almost to the end. Initially he voiced concern on the basis of some new signs of a communist "peace offensive," such as Chou En-lai's initiative for a Korean prisoner-exchange and Soviet agreement with the West to support Dag Hammarskjold's nomination at the United Nations

as Secretary-General. "I grow less keen about this speech," Dulles cautioned, "because I think there's some real danger of our just seeming to fall in with these Soviet overtures. It's obvious that what they are doing is because of outside pressures, and I don't know anything better we can do than to keep up those pressures right now."[97]

Eisenhower eventually delivered the speech (with its conciliatory tone intact) on April 16, 1953, and it was almost universally lauded by the media. Thus Dulles's opposition to the speech, and the softer line toward the Soviets that it symbolized, was virtually without effect.

Dulles's stated policy preference for taking advantage of the Soviet leadership transition by trying to exploit nationalist unrest in the satellite states was quite consistent with his belief that the United States should pursue a dynamic political and psychological campaign of "liberation" to undermine the Soviets from within. His aversion to Eisenhower's efforts to reach out to the new Soviet leadership was consistent with his belief in the basic irreconcilability of the differences between the United States and the Soviets. His policymaking behavior (i.e., arguing in the National Security Council meeting for efforts to exploit nationalism in the satellites and trying to dissuade the speechwriters from making the speech too conciliatory) were also consistent with his worldview. Even though Dulles's policy preferences and policymaking behavior did not ultimately shape the policy outcome in any significant way, this episode does establish marked consistency between particular city-on-the-hill–influenced beliefs on the one hand and his policy preferences and policymaking behavior on the other.

AVOIDING A DEAL WITH THE DEVIL IN GENEVA

Dulles's handling of the 1954 Geneva conference on Korea and Indochina provides another example of strong consistency between the elements of his worldview that were colored by the city-on-the-hill myth and his policy preferences and policymaking behavior. In this case, however, his preferences and behavior did strongly influence the policy outcome (an almost complete lack of U.S. support of both the negotiations and the resulting agreements regarding Indochina). Hoopes dramatically sums up Dulles's impact on the U.S. position: "None of Dulles' actions was to bring forth a darker harvest than his refusal to allow United States policy to support or even countenance a diplomatic settlement of the French colonial war in Indochina in the period from 1954 to 1956."[98]

As Hoopes's narrative makes clear, from the very start Dulles was opposed to negotiating with the communists to end the first Indochina War, and he was very effective at making sure that the United States would give as little support as possible to the negotiations and the agreements they produced.[99] Dulles had hoped, as late as fall 1953, that the French, with substantial U.S. financial assistance, could defeat the Vietminh if they followed the plan of General Henri Navarre to increase their troops by 68,000 men by the beginning of 1954.[100] By January 1954, however, the French government of Premier Joseph Laniel was very near collapse, and Laniel realized that he had to push for negotiations to end the war or his government would not survive.[101] The Berlin Conference of Foreign Ministers in late January 1954 provided the opportunity for the French to set up such negotiations.

Dulles realized that the French government would not survive if its delegation left Berlin without an agreement to discuss the Indochina War at the upcoming Geneva conference. He begrudgingly accepted the idea of holding talks on Indochina at the Geneva conference, but not without making it explicit in the communiqué that the presence of communist Chinese at the Geneva negotiations did not in any way constitute U.S. recognition of the People's Republic of China.[102] He reiterated the U.S. policy of nonrecognition of the Chinese in a televised address to the nation after the conference.

> Some profess to fear that the holding of this conference will imply U.S. recognition of Communist China. That fear is without basis. . . . The United States will not agree to join in a five-power conference with the Chinese aggressors for the purpose of dealing with the peace of the world. The United States refuses not because, as is suggested, it denies that the regime exists or that it has power. We in the United States well know that it exists and has power because its aggressive armies joined with the North Korean aggressors to kill and wound 150,000 Americans. . . . We do not refuse to deal with it where occasion requires. It is, however, one thing to recognize evil as a fact. It is another thing to take evil to one's breast and call it good. That explains our non-recognition of the Chinese regime. It is that position which is reflected in the final Berlin Conference Resolution. Under that resolution, the communist regime will not come to Geneva to be honored by us, but rather to account before the bar of world opinion.[103]

This is not a statement that would be made by someone who expected or wanted fruitful negotiations with the communists at Geneva. In fact, Dulles made it sound as though the Geneva conference would serve as a court in which to try the communist Chinese for "crimes against the moral law." It is all very consistent with Dulles's beliefs about the relationship between morality and diplomacy and the moral nature of the Cold War confrontation.

However, as Hoopes points out, Dulles and the Eisenhower administration as a whole were under a great deal of pressure from the congressional "China lobby" to take the hardest line possible against communist China.[104] In agreeing to allow the communist Chinese to sit at the table for the Indochina phase of the Geneva conference, therefore, Dulles exposed the administration to criticism from the China lobby. His concern about this could partially explain the severe tone of the previous statement. However, it would be a gross oversimplification to say that Dulles's strong advocacy of the nonrecognition policy was solely politically motivated. There is simply too much consistency with his previously stated beliefs about the importance of moral law (as represented by "the bar of world opinion") and about the irreconcilable philosophical differences that make it very difficult to negotiate with communists. There was little need here for Dulles to be cynical because he was protecting his political flank against people with whom he shared many very basic beliefs about the nature of the Cold War confrontation. It is hard to imagine that any member of the China lobby could have seen more "evil" in the Chinese communists than did Dulles himself.

Even as he was attempting to poison the atmosphere for negotiations at the Geneva conference, Dulles was still hoping that the French would not go into the conference feeling as though they had to come away with a negotiated settlement. At a February 26 meeting of the National Security Council, he held out hope that the French would not "push too hard for a negotiated settlement provided there was no real military disaster in Indochina prior to and during the conference."[105] Unfortunately for the French, and for Dulles, this "real military disaster" began to unfold just two weeks later in a place called Dien Bien Phu.

Dulles realized that because of the deteriorating French military position, the Laniel government would be forced to pursue aggressively a negotiated settlement with the communists at the upcoming Geneva conference.[106] At this point Dulles and Eisenhower found themselves in a very difficult position. Neither was happy about the prospect of the French negotiating with the communists over Indochina. At the same time they were being asked by the French for U.S. military intervention in the form of airstrikes to relieve the besieged fortress at Dien Bien Phu, an action that both felt they must resist.[107] Wanting to avoid both the prospect of a French "sellout" at Geneva and actual U.S. military intervention in Vietnam, Dulles came up with a concept he called united action.[108] The plan consisted of a coalition of states (the United States, Britain, France, Australia, New Zealand, Thailand, the Philippines, and the associated states of Indochina) banding together to form a regional security organization to defend against any further spread of communism into Southeast Asia. Dulles hoped that the organization could be set up before the Geneva conference began so that it would bolster the French negotiating position and keep the French from giving away too much.[109] He set out in late March to promote his united-action plan both at home and to the European Allies. Much to his dismay, the Allies balked at the plan. Both the British and the French feared that setting up such an organization before the Geneva conference would tend to make the Vietminh and the Chinese communists more intransigent and thus ruin the chances for fruitful negotiations, negotiations they both saw as the best solution to the Indochina problem.[110] With the failure to get his united-action plan implemented before the conference, Dulles resigned himself to the unpleasant reality of the Geneva negotiations on Indochina.

Dulles attended the Geneva conference reluctantly and for only one week, and his behavior there clearly reflected his disdain for the entire enterprise. His displeasure is summed up well by Hoopes. While at Geneva, Dulles "conducted himself with the pinched distaste of a Puritan in a house of ill-repute, quite brusquely refusing to shake hands with Chou En-Lai and instructing the American delegation to ignore at all times the presence and existence of the Chinese delegation."[111]

Dulles did not want the United States to be closely identified with any of the agreements produced at Geneva that legitimized communist territorial gains, and in this he was fully supported by Eisenhower.[112] To achieve this goal symbolically, Dulles made sure that after he left during the first week of the conference, the U.S. delegation would have no member at cabinet rank; all of the other delegations were led by foreign ministers. At the end of the conference, the U.S. delegation, under orders from Dulles, refused to sign the agreements and merely wrote a unilateral declaration stating that the United States "took note" of the agreements, "agreed to refrain from using force to disturb them," and stated that it would "view any renewal of aggression in violation of the agreements with grave concern."[113] In response to European criticism of the lukewarm U.S. support for the final Geneva agreements, Dulles proclaimed, "The United States has been concerned to find a way whereby it could help France, Viet-nam, Laos, and Cambodia find acceptable settlements without in any way prejudicing basic principles to which the United States must adhere if it is to be true to itself, and if the captured and endangered peoples of the world are to feel that the United States really believes in liberty."[114] Dulles clearly thought that the Geneva negotiations had produced an agreement legitimizing communist gains in northern Vietnam, something he had feared all along. Thus he felt that the United States could not accept this agreement "without prejudicing basic principles."

Dulles's belief about the moral nature of the Cold War confrontation and the resulting moral obstacles to negotiating with the communists are clearly reflected in his policy preferences and his policymaking behavior in this episode. In the face of a rapidly deteriorating French military position and irresistible political pressure on the French government to negotiate, Dulles poisoned the atmosphere by insulting the Chinese and actively sought alternatives to negotiating with the communists. When it became obvious that the French would negotiate, Dulles introduced his united-action plan in an attempt to undermine the negotiations. When this plan failed to short-circuit the Geneva negotiations, he attended the negotiations for just long enough to insult the Chinese again and instruct his delegation on how to distance themselves from the proceedings. When the negotiations finally produced an agreement, he was quick to show his distaste for it, saying in a post-conference statement that "the important thing from now on is not to mourn the past, but to seize the future opportunity to prevent the loss in Northern Vietnam from leading to the extension of communism throughout Southeast Asia."[115] The lack of U.S. support for the Geneva Accords was a central reason for their eventual collapse with the start of the Second Indochina War in 1958.

RELUCTANT SUMMITEER

Dulles's consistent opposition to negotiations with communist leaders continued into 1955. During spring of that year, many European leaders were calling for a four-power summit conference with the Soviet leadership.[116] Several positive Soviet moves during spring 1955 (most notably the signing of the Austrian State Treaty) persuaded Eisenhower that the time was indeed right for a summit meeting.[117] Prior to the completion of the Austrian treaty, Dulles had strongly and consistently advised Eisenhower against any summit meetings with the Soviets, using past instances of Soviet intransigence and dishonesty to buttress his argument.[118] However, with the completion of the Austrian treaty and with Eisenhower's resolve to go forward with the Geneva summit, Dulles reluctantly realized that the tide was against him, and he began to work with the president on an agenda for the meeting.[119]

In preparing Eisenhower for the summit, however, Dulles went to great lengths to warn him about the dangers that he felt were inherent in such a meeting.[120] In a presummit briefing memorandum, he warned Eisenhower that the Soviets would try to exploit world opinion to trap the United States into a bad disarmament agreement: "Undoubtedly, one of the major Soviet desires is to relieve itself of the economic burden of the present arms race. . . . Probably the Soviet Union will propose again, as it did in Berlin, a world disarmament conference. They believe that if world opinion can be aroused and focused upon us, we may accept disarmament under hastily devised and perhaps imprudent conditions."[121]

Apparently, Dulles had made up his mind that if the meeting were going to go forward, he would at least make sure that Eisenhower went in with his eyes open. He also wanted Eisenhower to confront the Soviets on the issue of the captive peoples behind the iron curtain. He suggested that Eisenhower should privately "raise the question [and] emphasize that if in fact the Soviets wish to reduce tension with the United States, they must deal with this problem which our people feel is covered by war agreements which have been violated."[122] Finally, Dulles argued that Eisenhower should be ready to use trade as a bargaining chip, but only after the Soviets had given substantial ground on other important issues: "the Soviet bloc is a deficit area and the free world is now a surplus area. No doubt the deficit countries would like to get our surplus. This may be the highest card we have to play. We should not give it away until we know that we are getting what we want in relation to Germany, the satellites, and international Communism."[123]

This last bit of presummit advice to Eisenhower is the most surprising of the three. Dulles's earlier suggestions for Eisenhower to watch out for Soviet manipulation and to privately confront the Soviet leaders on the issue of the captive peoples were in keeping with his well-documented distrust of the Soviets and his moral outrage over the people trapped behind the iron curtain. However, Dulles's suggestion that Eisenhower should use trade as a classical carrot-and-stick diplomatic maneuver was quite a departure from all of his previous writings on Cold War diplomacy. It was certainly not in keeping with his previous Puritan style of diplomacy. Perhaps for

Dulles, if such diplomatic "dealing" with the Soviets could produce the liberation of people behind the iron curtain, the ends would justify the means.

It is not clear from the record of the conference just how much Eisenhower followed Dulles's advice. Eisenhower did make quite an impression on the world by taking the initiative with his "open skies" proposal, and at the end of the conference popular expectations of improved East-West relations were at an all-time high. After the conference, Dulles set out immediately to keep these popular expectations under control.[124]

As was the case with the 1954 Geneva conference, Dulles's policy preferences were against negotiating with the communists, and his policymaking behavior consisted of trying to persuade Eisenhower against agreeing to the summit meeting. Thus both his policy preferences and policymaking behavior were consistent with his beliefs regarding the moral nature of the Cold War conflict. This time, however, he was unable to prevent the United States from being intimately involved in the talks. Once his initial policy preference was overridden by the president, his policymaking behavior (i.e., his presummit briefings of President Eisenhower) still reflected discomfort with the summit meeting and reflected his belief in the need to take a hard line with the Soviets and to confront them morally.[125] His efforts to lower public expectations about the summit were consistent with his belief in the ultimate irreconcilability of the basic issues separating East and West.

In a postsummit policy statement written for Eisenhower, Dulles argued that the "new Soviet attitude," as reflected in the Austrian treaty and other actions leading up to the Geneva summit, was merely a Soviet adjustment to the tough Cold War policies of the United States.[126] He also warned that "Geneva has certainly created problems for the free nations. For eight years they have been held together by a cement compounded of fear and a sense of moral superiority. Now the fear is diminished and the moral demarcation is somewhat blurred."[127] He closed by adding that if the Soviets followed Geneva with tangible actions such as loosening their hold in East Germany and the rest of Eastern Europe, the United States would continue to work to maintain the current state of relaxed tensions; but if the Soviets did not follow up with positive actions, the United States would be forced to revert to "the old state of distrust and tension."[128] Thus Dulles took quite a hardened view of the state of minidétente that was hailed by hopeful observers as the "spirit of Geneva."

CONSISTENT SINOPHOBIA

With regard to communists, especially the Chinese communists, Dulles would remain steadfast in his opposition to direct dealings with them. By 1957, most of the other industrialized nations were moving toward normalization of economic relations with China, but Dulles held firm in his opposition to any such action on the part of the United States, and Eisenhower supported his stand. At a March meeting in Bermuda Dulles tried unsuccessfully to convince British foreign secretary Selwyn Lloyd that the British should join the United States in its China policy of nonrecognition and nonadmittance to the UN.[129] In a June speech in San Francisco, Dulles defended his policy of political and economic isolation of communist China:

> Internationally the Chinese communist regime does not conform to the practices of civilized nations. . . . Its foreign policies are hostile to us and our Asian allies. Under these circumstances it would be folly for us to establish relations with the Chinese communists which would enhance their ability to hurt us and our friends. . . . Nothing could be more dangerous than for the United States to operate on the theory that if hostile and evil forces do not quickly or readily change, then it is we who must change to meet them.[130]

Thus at a time when the Western allies were beginning to normalize their relations with the People's Republic of China, and when there was beginning to be noticeable support in Congress for the United States to do so, Dulles maintained an unwavering opposition to any such action.[131] The fact that congressional opposition to normalizing relations with China was weakening at this point is especially significant because it provides evidence that goes against some Dulles biographers who argue that his hard-line stance against the Soviets and China can be explained almost entirely by his need to placate a harshly anticommunist public and Congress.[132]

BUILDING SPIRITUAL UNITY

The foregoing analysis of Dulles's policy preferences and policy-making behavior shows him to be fairly consistently opposed to negotiating with communist leaders whether they were Soviet or Chinese. And yet Dulles was noted for being an extremely active cold warrior and well-traveled secretary of state. If Dulles was so reluctant to negotiate with communist leaders, what was his preferred mode of Cold War diplomacy? The answer is largely that Dulles devoted much of his energy to building and maintaining unity among the global noncommunist coalition of nations.

Beginning even before he became secretary of state, Dulles filled his speeches and writings with warnings about the importance of unity in anticommunist alliances. Taken at face value, such behavior would hardly distinguish Dulles from any other Cold War secretary of state. What sets Dulles apart is the nature of the unity that he sought to build in the noncommunist world. From almost the beginning of the Cold War he spoke and wrote about the need for a spiritual unity based on common adherence to universal moral principles that could bind the anticommunist nations together in opposition to the forces of "godless communism."

In fact, Dulles's convictions about the power of a universal moral law as a binding and guiding force in international relations were first manifest in his writings during his World War II involvement with the Federal Council of Churches. With the advent of the Cold War, Dulles began to argue that the universal moral law should bind the noncommunist nations against the forces of communism and that part of the mission of the United States was to mobilize a noncommunist coalition around these moral principles. It is also true, however, that with the advent of the Cold War Dulles began to combine adherence to the religious-based moral law with adherence to liberal-democratic principles such as individual liberty. Nonetheless, by the early 1950s Dulles put a great deal of stock in the potency of these moral principles as a unifying force in the noncommunist world.

In a May 1952 speech in France, Dulles argued for the importance of building a bond between the noncommunist West and the noncommunist East around these shared moral principles.

> The people of the West believe basically in the equal rights and equal dignity of all men and in the sacredness of the individual personality of all. That faith had its beginning in Judea, where east and west met, and it held that all men, without regard to race and color, were the creation and concern of a universal God. That western belief in the nature of man is what has made western colonialism a self-liquidating affair. The political independence and new dignity that other races have won in recent years is not a frustration of western goals, but their fulfillment. Surely we can find ways to make that clear and, in so doing, create, between the free East and the free West, a sense of common destiny.[133]

In addition to showing Dulles's belief in the power of ideals as a binding and guiding force in international relations, this also illustrates his blending of Judeo-Christian principles with Western liberal democratic principles.

Dulles believed in these ideals and principles as a powerful psychological weapon for uniting the developing world against communist expansion. In another 1952 speech, Dulles argued that until then the communists had been more successful than the noncommunists in using their ideas to instill a strong sense of purpose in their followers in the Third World.

> Those dictators keep their grasp on captive peoples partly by force but also by providing a sense of momentous revolutionary movement. The very violence of their claim carries a conviction of sincerity and purpose which the free world lacks. The attraction of that is great. . . . There are many who acquiesce because they gain the satisfaction which comes from sharing in strong purposes of world-wide scope. They do not feel attracted by freedom which seems barren of purpose and which, as they see it, survives strongly only where it has past accumulations on which to feed. The situation will be totally different when our own conduct and example again brilliantly illumine the truth that men do not have to choose between freedom which is sterile and captivity which is purposeful.[134]

In another speech during the same period, Dulles argued that it was the responsibility of the United States to play the role of moral and spiritual leader in order to maintain morale within the noncommunist coalition.

> A second reason against divorcing diplomacy from morality is that this strikes at the heart of free world unity. Today, the United States has an inescapable responsibility for leadership. Only leadership that inspires confidence will prevent the free world from falling apart and being picked up, piece by piece by Soviet Communism. United States foreign policies today represent the core of potential unity and that core is rotten unless it is a core of moral principle. . . . Throughout the ages men have experimented with artificial means for binding nations into common action for a common cause. They have experimented with military alliances, with subsidies, with coercion. None of these methods has stood the stress and strain of fluctuating danger. The only tie which dependably unites free peoples is awareness of common dedication to moral principles.[135]

In addition to showing Dulles's belief in the necessary connection between diplomacy and moral principle, this passage shows his belief in an American mission to be the moral and spiritual leader of the noncommunist nations. This is yet another clear example of

Dulles's using the city-on-the-hill myth to shape his preferred conception of America's global role in the Cold War.

The three previous passages taken together also provide evidence in Dulles's worldview of certain elements of the Puritan representative character. He posited a diplomatic stance toward the Third World that consisted primarily of conversion and mobilization—the paradigmatic mode of social action of the Puritan representative character. He argued that the peoples of the developing world must be united around certain moral principles and political ideals and thus infused with a powerful sense of purpose and mobilized against the forces of international communism. This was a continuation of the Puritan character pattern in Dulles's basic approach to influencing world politics that we first noticed during his World War II involvement with the Federal Council of Churches.

Indeed, the transcripts of some of his speeches to the annual meetings of the Southeast Asia Treaty Organization (SEATO) and Central Treaty Organization (CENTO) paint a picture of the Puritan-as-diplomat-in-action. In the conclusion of his speech to the third meeting of the SEATO Council of Ministers at Canberra, Australia, Dulles took the tone of a worried pastor showing a wayward congregation how to avoid Satan's clutches.

> Let us put our own houses in order. Let us avoid communist traps baited with offers of trade and aid. Let us expose communist techniques of subversion. Let us make economic and social progress. Let us build up our educational systems. Let us give fair treatment to minority groups. Let us train capable trade union leaders. Thus we can do much to show other free nations how to seal off effectively the various traditional avenues of communist penetration.[136]

In a similar speech before an annual meeting of the Council of Ministers of the Baghdad Pact, Dulles made an appeal to unity based on his familiar mixture of moral principles and political ideals.

> The greatest danger is always the danger which comes from blindness to danger. Today we see the danger, and we are allied with forces that have repeatedly demonstrated their ability to prevail against the materialistic despotisms. There are, we know, God-given aspirations for freedom of mind and spirit and for opportunity. These are beyond the power of man to destroy. So long as we ally ourselves loyally and sacrificially with what is good, what is true, our cause surely will prevail.[137]

Dulles spent a great deal of his time as secretary of state flying around the world and organizing anticommunist coalitions. Once these coalitions (such as SEATO and CENTO) were organized, he continued to attend their ministerial meetings in an attempt to keep them mobilized against the forces of international communism. It is in these social contexts that we get the clearest picture of Dulles the Puritan-as-diplomat wielding his mixed arsenal of moral principles and Western political ideals in an attempt to create spiritual unity in the anticommunist world.

CONCLUSION

The foregoing analysis has produced significant evidence to indicate that certain elements of Dulles's worldview were influenced by the city-on-the-hill myth (and to a lesser extent in the 1920s and 1930s by the market myth). The analysis of several policymaking cases shows that his policy preferences and policymaking behavior were often consistent with those city-on-the-hill–influenced elements of his worldview. There was substantial city-on-the-hill mythical imagery in Dulles's communications beginning with his World War II involvement with the Federal Council of Churches and throughout his tenure as secretary of state.

On the philosophical level, Dulles believed strongly that there should be a close linkage between morality and diplomacy. Related to this pattern, but on a less philosophical level, Dulles believed strongly that the formulation and conduct of U.S. foreign policy should be guided by moral principles. In another related pattern, Dulles believed that the Cold War confrontation should and indeed must be viewed in moral terms.

Two other related questions yielded responses that are also consistent with a city-on-the-hill orientation: what forms of U.S. power were most effective in the Cold War, and what was the best strategy for dealing with the Soviets. With regard to the first question, analysis of Dulles's communications indicates that he believed military and economic power were necessary to counter the threat of communism, but these had to be supplemented by a moral/spiritual form of power. On the second, Dulles showed consistent pessimism about the prospects of direct negotiations with communist leaders—the clearest example of consistency between his worldview and policy preferences and behavior. Not only were his beliefs consistent with the city-on-the-hill myth, but quite often the statements relating these beliefs contained vivid city-on-the-hill imagery, and at times he used the myth itself to justify his arguments. At times (e.g., the 1955 Geneva Summit), his opposition to such negotiations was overruled by Eisenhower; at other times (such as the 1954 Geneva

conference on Korea and Indochina), Dulles was able to persuade
Eisenhower that the negotiations should not be supported by the
United States.

The evidence of the Puritan representative character influence on
Dulles's self- and role conceptions and behavior is less clear. There is
substantial evidence, however, of an overall orientation toward world
politics that is consistent with the moral and epistemological stance
and the paradigmatic mode of social action of the Puritan.

From the time of his involvement with the Federal Council of
Churches throughout his tenure as secretary of state, Dulles communicated his belief in the power of moral principles and political
ideals to convert and mobilize people around the world and thus to
alter the course of world politics. The fact that this fundamental approach to influencing world politics remained stable even as the
world and Dulles's roles changed is significant. It is precisely this
underlying stability in an individual's approach to a changing social
world and across roles that the representative character concept is
designed to capture. And this fundamental orientation does indicate some degree of identification on Dulles's part with the Puritan
character. This indication is strengthened by further evidence in
Dulles's self- and role conceptions.

Thorough examination of Dulles's speeches, writings, and let-
ters yielded only two instances where he actually reflected on his
role as a policymaker, but those two instances do provide interesting insights.[138]

The first comes from a draft of a 1955 speech entitled "Principles in Foreign Policy." Toward the conclusion of this speech Dulles
addressed the age-old question of whether statesmen could act
morally in their role of trustees of their nation's security:

> There are some who believe that moral considerations ought not
> to influence the foreign policy of a nation, that moral considera-
> tions are all right for the individual but not for the collective
> unity. Corporate bodies should be directed only by material con-
> siderations. . . . It is indeed the case that those who represent a
> government operate only for the immediate and direct self inter-
> est of the nation they represent. . . . The government of the
> United States has, I like to believe, a rather unique tradition in
> this respect. . . . Our institutions reflect the belief of our founders
> that all men were endowed by their creator with unalienable
> rights and had duties prescribed by moral law. They believed that
> human institutions ought primarily to help men develop their
> God-given possibilities and that our nation, by its conduct and ex-
> ample, could help men everywhere to find the way to a better and
> more abundant life.[139]

After describing how this unusual marriage of morality and diplomacy had brought great prosperity to the United States, Dulles went on:

> Thus there is a familiar pattern. Men who feel a sense of duty to some higher being strive here to do his will. Because of their faith, they have power and virtue and simple wisdom. They build not only for the day, but for the morrow; not merely for themselves, but for mankind. . . . No doubt we have made mistakes. But broadly speaking, our nation has played a role which I believe history will judge to have been honorable. It is a role which we could not have played unless those who exercised the power of government had believed that they were justified in putting moral considerations above material considerations.[140]

As these passages show, Dulles conceptualized his role as a statesman as being defined by a God-given duty to uphold the moral law. Perhaps even more significant is the fact that he justified this conceptualization using a city-on-the-hill interpretation of the nation's founding. Thus in this rare glimpse into Dulles's conception of his role as a statesman, we see certain elements of the Puritan representative character. We see the Puritan's strong sense of authority derived from God and adherence to divine law. This is consistent with the Puritan character's moral and epistemological stance—the good and the true are found in the word and the law of God. The only major element of the Puritan representative character missing from Dulles's conceptualization of his role as a statesman is the Puritan's paradigmatic mode of social action—using divine revelation to convert and mobilize people for God's purposes.

The other evidence of Dulles's role conceptions comes from a rare television interview in 1957. On the NBC show *Look Here!* Dulles responded to Martin Agronsky's questions about how he conceived of his role as secretary of state. At one point Agronsky asked Dulles to what extent he believed that he as an individual could make an impact on the course of human history.

> Well I don't say that man is totally independent of his environment or the conditions around him but I do believe whatever the conditions are you have an opportunity to mold them. There is a verse in the Bible I sometimes think about which says—starts out, "All things work together for good." But it doesn't stop there. It says: "All things work together for those who love God in accordance with His holy purpose." Now I think if you have the right kind of purpose, you can take advantage of conditions whatever they are, to make them somewhat different and somewhat better.[141]

Although Dulles's response was somewhat vague, he did seem to claim that because there was a congruence between his purposes and those of God, he was more able to make an impact on world politics. This is consistent with both the Puritan character's sense of authority derived from God and its adherence to God's law. This response with its hint of divine annointedness spurred Agronsky to delve further into the influence of religion on Dulles's conduct of diplomacy. He asked Dulles if it improved U.S. foreign policy to have a statesman who was constantly trying to apply Christian principles to its practice. Dulles responded:

> I believe that there are certain basic principles which undergird the world and are just as important and just as certain as the laws of physics. Now you wouldn't want to run foreign policy in violation of the laws of physics. I don't think any more can you run foreign policy without some of the great moral principles that have prevailed for all time. You can go back to the earliest days of history, you can go to all the great religions and you will find certain basic things, certain basic truths and I don't think you can defy those with impunity.[142]

This provides very clear evidence that Dulles conceived of himself as being guided in his conduct of foreign policy by moral principles. This statement is again quite consistent with the moral and epistemological stances of the Puritan representative character.

Can we therefore confidently classify John Foster Dulles as a Puritan American statesman? He was an extremely complex individual; it is apparent that myriad forces and experiences shaped Dulles's personality and worldview. Nonetheless, the case study does turn up evidence to indicate that Dulles was substantially shaped by both the city-on-the-hill myth and the Puritan representative character.

NOTES

1. Early interpretations presented Eisenhower as being somewhat disengaged in the foreign policy making process and as leaving many decisions up to Dulles. In the 1970s a revisionist interpretation began to appear, arguing that in fact Eisenhower was very much in charge but managed foreign policy from behind the scenes. For an excellent discussion of both the orthodox and revisionist schools on Eisenhower see Robert Kagan, "Why Like Ike?" *The National Interest* (Summer 1986): 88–94. For the most recent examples of the revisionist school see Fred Greenstein, *The Hidden Hand Presidency: Eisenhower as Leader* (New York: Basic Books, 1982), and Stephen Ambrose, *Eisenhower: The President and Elder Statesman* (New York: Simon and Schuster, 1984).

2. Eisenhower's trust and respect for Dulles is reflected throughout the president's memoirs, *Waging Peace* (New York: Doubleday, 1965).

3. For a good discussion of Dulles's religious upbringing, see Mark G. Toulouse, *The Transformation of John Foster Dulles: From Prophet of Realism to Priest of Nationalism* (Macon, GA: Mercer University Press, 1985), 3–15.

4. Ibid., 4–7.

5. Ibid., 5–6.

6. Quoted in Toulouse, 6.

7. Ronald W. Pruessen, *John Foster Dulles: The Road to Power* (New York: Free Press, 1982), 4–9.

8. Ibid., 5–7.

9. Ibid., 5.

10. Ibid., 8–9.

11. Ibid., 9.

12. Townsend Hoopes, *The Devil and John Foster Dulles* (Boston: Little, Brown, 1973), 20.

13. Pruessen, 9.

14. Quoted in Pruessen, 10.

15. Hoopes, 21.

16. Pruessen, 9, 24, 173.

17. Ibid., 31.

18. Ibid., 32–40.

19. Ibid., 44–45.

20. Ibid., 45–49.

21. Ibid., 73.

22. Ibid., 78–79.

23. John Foster Dulles, "The Allied War Debts," *Foreign Affairs* 1, 1 (September 15, 1922): 115–132.

24. Ibid., 129–132.

25. Ibid., 132.

26. Pruessen, 100.

27. Quoted in Pruessen, 141.

28. Ibid.

29. Ibid., 154–156.

30. John Foster Dulles, "The Road to Peace," *Atlantic Monthly* 156 (October 1935): 493.

31. Ibid., 496–497.

32. Pruessen, 155.

33. John Foster Dulles, *War, Peace, and Change* (New York: Harper, 1939).

34. Ibid., 9–16.

35. Ibid., 9.

36. Pruessen, 163.

37. Dulles, *War, Peace, and Change*, 121–122.

38. Ibid., 126–127.

39. Dulles's thoughts on the phenomenon of mirror imaging (i.e., deification of one's own state and demonization of other states) are most intriguing in light of his later tendency as secretary of state to engage in mirror imaging in his rhetoric regarding the Soviet Union. This paradox will be explored in more depth further on.

40. Dulles, *War, Peace, and Change*, 124–125.

41. Ibid., 126–127.

42. Ibid., 170.

43. Ibid., 113–117.

44. Ibid., 116.

45. Ibid., 117.

46. Ibid., 118.

47. One interesting issue that comes to mind is the extent to which these visions of world order are compatible or in conflict. Unfortunately, there is no evidence in his writings that he gave much thought to such questions.

48. Toulouse, 47–133.

49. Ibid., 58.

50. Dulles address at the First Presbyterian Church, Watertown, New York, Sunday, August 28, 1949. Reprinted in Henry P. Van Dusen, ed., *The Spiritual Legacy of John Foster Dulles: Selections from His Articles and Addresses* (Philadelphia: Westminster Press, 1960), 7.

51. Ibid., 11.

52. Toulouse, 58–63.

53. In his role as chairman of the commission, Dulles was a strong leader both administratively and intellectually, and many of his ideas about achieving vehicles for peaceful change, including the need for a liberalized international economic order, may be found in commission documents. See the commission report entitled "Moral and Spiritual Bases for a Just and Lasting Peace," in Van Dusen, 100–106.

54. Ibid., 101.

55. John Foster Dulles, "A Righteous Faith," in Van Dusen, 49.

56. John Foster Dulles, "A Nation's Foreign Policy," speech draft, January 26, 1944, Dulles Papers/Princeton, Box 23.

57. See, for example, *War, Peace, and Change*, 62–65.

58. Toulouse, 82–84, 142–143.

59. Ibid., 81.

60. Ibid., 92–93.

61. Ibid., 93–95.

62. Ibid., 97.

63. Ibid., 161.

64. Ibid., 153–157.

65. Ibid., 157–158.

66. Ibid., 158.

67. Pruessen, 261.

68. Toulouse, 160–180.

69. John Foster Dulles, "Appraisal of United States Foreign Policy," speech before the Economic Club of Detroit, February 5, 1945, 8–9, Dulles Papers/Princeton, Box 27.

70. Dulles manuscript of "Thoughts on Soviet Foreign Policy and What to Do About It" (which appeared in *Life* magazine, June 3 and 10, 1946), 1–2, Dulles Papers/Princeton, Box 30.

71. These developments included tensions resulting from Soviet failure to implement Yalta provisions regarding free elections in Eastern Europe, Soviet failure to remove troops from northern Iran, and Soviet pressure on Turkey. Other tension-producing developments during this period include Stalin's bellicose February 1946 speech and George Kennan's subsequent "Long cable" from Moscow.

72. John Foster Dulles, "The United Nations—Its Challenge to America," speech presented at Princeton University on February 22, 1946, 7, Dulles Papers/Princeton, Box 30.

73. Ibid., 7–9.

74. Ibid., 21.

75. John Foster Dulles, "Foreign Policy—Ideals, Not Deals," speech made before the Inland Daily Press Association in Chicago, Illinois, February 10, 1947, 1–2, Dulles Papers/Princeton, Box 31.

76. Ibid., 2–3.

77. Ibid., 3–4.

78. John Foster Dulles, "Appraisal of U.S. Foreign Policy," 9. For other examples of this theme see "Thoughts on Soviet Foreign Policy and What to Do About It" and "Foreign Policy—Ideals Not Deals."

79. John Foster Dulles, "Principle Versus Expediency in Foreign Policy," speech before the Missouri Bar Association in St. Louis, September 26, 1952, 1, Dulles Papers/Princeton, Box 64.

80. Ibid., 4.

81. Ibid., 1.

82. John Foster Dulles, "Morals and Power," speech at the National War College, Washington, D.C., June 16, 1953, 2, Dulles Papers/Princeton, Box 314.

83. John Foster Dulles, "Our International Responsibilities," commencement address at Vanderbilt University, June 4, 1950, 1–3, Dulles Papers/Princeton, Box 50. For more examples of this theme see "The Strategy of Soviet Communism," speech by Dulles at the Common Cause Dinner in New York, March 14, 1950, 6, Dulles Papers/Princeton, Box 50. See also "Our Foreign Policy: Is Containment Enough?" speech by Dulles before the Chicago Council on Foreign Relations, October 8, 1952, 5–9, Dulles Papers/Princeton, Box 59.

84. Dulles, "Our International Responsibilities," 3.

85. Ibid., 2.

86. John Foster Dulles, "A New Foreign Policy," manuscript for article in *Life* magazine, May 19, 1952, 1–3, Dulles Papers/Princeton, Box 57.

87. Ibid., 3.

88. Ibid., 10–11.

89. Ibid., 11.

90. Ibid., 12.

91. Ibid., 11–19.

92. Hoopes, 170.

93. Ibid., 170–171.

94. Minutes of the 136th meeting of the National Security Council, March 12, 1953, 8, *Minutes of Meetings of the National Security Council,* Microfilm Series, reel 1, University Publications of America.

95. Hoopes, 171.

96. Ibid., 171–173.

97. Emmett John Hughes, *The Ordeal of Power: A Political Memoir of the Eisenhower Years* (New York: Atheneum, 1963), 109.

98. Hoopes, 202.

99. Ibid., 202–205.

100. Minutes of the 161st meeting of the National Security Council, September 9, 1953, 2, *Minutes of Meetings of the National Security Council,* Microfilm Series, reel 2, University Publications of America.

101. Hoopes, 206.

102. Ibid.

103. John Foster Dulles, "Report on Berlin," transcript of television address to the nation, February 24, 1954, 8–9, Dulles Papers/Princeton, Box 324.

104. Hoopes, 206.

105. Minutes of the 186th meeting of the National Security Council, February 26, 1954, 6, *Minutes of Meetings of the National Security Council,* Microfilm Series, reel 3, University Publications of America.

106. George C. Herring, "A Good Stout Effort: John Foster Dulles and the Indochina Crisis, 1954–1955," in Richard H. Immerman, ed., *John Foster Dulles and the Diplomacy of the Cold War* (Princeton: Princeton University Press, 1990), 215.

107. Ibid., 217.

108. As Herring points out in "A Good Stout Effort," Dulles and Eisenhower were caught on the horns of a domestic political dilemma. On the one hand public and congressional opinion would not tolerate unilateral U.S. military intervention in Indochina so soon after Korea. On the other hand they could not afford to be perceived as merely standing by while communists made territorial gains in Indochina, whether those gains were made at the negotiating table or on the battlefield. See Herring, 218–219.

109. Ibid., 217.

110. Hoopes, 213–214.

111. Ibid., 222.

112. Herring, 225.

113. Hoopes, 239.

114. Quoted in Robert F. Randle, *Geneva, 1954: The Settlement of the Indochinese War* (Princeton: Princeton University Press, 1969), 322.

115. Press statement by Secretary Dulles, July 23, 1954, 1, Dulles Papers/Princeton, Box 81.

116. Eisenhower, *Waging Peace,* 505.

117. Ibid., 506.

118. Ibid., 504.

119. Hoopes, 290.

120. Ibid., 295.

121. Dulles memorandum to Eisenhower, June 18, 1955, 1, Dulles Papers/Princeton, Box 91.

122. Ibid., 2.

123. Ibid., 2–3.

124. Hoopes, 300–301.

125. As noted, his advising Eisenhower to be prepared to hold out East-West trade as a "carrot" to extract concessions from the Soviets in other areas was something of an anomaly. It does not seem to fit either his worldview or the larger pattern of his policy preferences or policymaking behavior.

126. Dulles statement on post-Geneva policy written for Eisenhower, September 13, 1955, Dulles Papers/Princeton, Box 91.

127. Ibid., 4.

128. Ibid., 8–10.

129. Hoopes, 417.

130. Dulles speech before the International Convention of Lions International, San Francisco, June 28, 1957, 8–9, Dulles Papers/Princeton, Box 356.

131. Hoopes, 415.

132. See Michael Guhin, *John Foster Dulles: A Statesman and His Times* (New York: Columbia University Press, 1972), 130–131.

133. John Foster Dulles, "Far Eastern Problems," speech before the French National Political Science Institute, Paris, France, May 5, 1952, 3, Dulles Papers/Princeton, Box 62.

134. John Foster Dulles, "Freedom and Its Purpose," speech before the National Council of Churches, Denver, Colorado, December 11, 1952, 12, Dulles Papers/Princeton, Box 62.

135. Dulles, "Principle Versus Expediency in Foreign Policy," 4–5.

136. Dulles speech to the opening session of the Third Meeting of the SEATO Council of Ministers at Canberra, March 11, 1957, 3–4, Dulles Papers/Princeton, Box 353.

137. Dulles speech before the Fourth Ministerial Council Session of the Baghdad Pact, Ankara, Turkey, January 27, 1958, 6, Dulles Papers/ Princeton, Box 360.

138. Unfortunately the analysis of Dulles's papers yielded no clear statements by Dulles on his self-conceptions as distinct from role-conceptions, so we are left with role-conception evidence only.

139. John Foster Dulles, "Principles in Foreign Policy," draft of speech, 7, Dulles Papers/Princeton, Box 335.

140. Ibid., 8.

141. Transcript of Martin Agronsky's interview of Dulles on NBC show *Look Here!* Sunday, September 15, 1957, 3–4, Dulles Papers/Princeton, Box 355.

142. Ibid., 6.

4

The Enterprising Diplomacy
of Averell Harriman

Averell Harriman was one of the more influential members of the postwar foreign policy establishment. Over a period of almost forty years he served five different Democratic presidents from Franklin Delano Roosevelt to Jimmy Carter in various important diplomatic posts. As Walter Isaacson and Evan Thomas point out in *The Wise Men: Six Friends and the World They Made,* he along with Dean Acheson, George Kennan, Charles Bohlen, Robert Lovett, and John Mc-Cloy formed an elite group of advisers who first reached the pinnacle of power by helping Truman shape postwar U.S. foreign policy and indeed the postwar world.[1] This same group came to be known as the Wise Men when at the height of the U.S. involvement in Vietnam they were called on to advise a desperate Lyndon Johnson.[2] Harriman's influence as a presidential adviser (particularly in the early stages of the Truman administration) is indisputable and is eclipsed only by the tremendous skill he showed as a high-level negotiator.[3]

Harriman did not even begin his diplomatic career until he was nearly fifty years old.[4] It is in his years as a famous and successful businessman (and in his childhood years, which served to prepare him for that career) that we must search for the experiences and cultural forces that shaped his later worldview and behavior as a diplomat.

BORN IN THE SHADOW OF THE "LITTLE GIANT"

W. Averell Harriman was the eldest (surviving) son of legendary railroad king E. H. Harriman and Mary Averell Harriman. He was born on November 15, 1891, in their Fifty-first Street mansion in New York City. Mary Williamson Averell came from a wealthy family; her father, William J. Averell, was a successful stockbroker and owned a small railroad near Lake Champlain in upstate New York.[5]

E. H. Harriman was the son of Orlando Harriman, an itinerant minister who filled in for parishes in the New York area for a number of years until he landed his own parish pulpit in West Hoboken, New Jersey, at a salary of $200 a year.[6] E. H. excelled in school, but at age fourteen he decided that he needed to quit school and help support the family.[7] In 1862, he obtained a job as an office boy for five dollars a week at a stock brokerage on Wall Street, and by 1869 he was the managing clerk at the brokerage. By 1870, at age 22, he had his own seat on the New York Stock Exchange. He quickly developed a reputation for shrewd investing and soon counted some of the richest and most powerful businessmen in New York among his clients.[8] He would later use these connections and the money he made to gain control of what would become a railroad and steamship empire of unprecedented size.[9] By outbargaining and outmaneuvering such business giants as J. P. Morgan and James J. Hill, Harriman was able to control and dramatically expand such huge railroad companies as the Illinois Central and the Union Pacific.[10]

Thus during the later part of the nineteenth century and the early part of the twentieth, E. H. Harriman accomplished the journey from poor boy to robber baron. He started out with little formal education and no capital and ended up with a personal estate worth $70 million.[11] His story is that of the self-made man, the central figure around which the market myth of America was built. It was under the shadow of this larger-than-life American entrepreneur that Averell Harriman would spend his childhood years, if not indeed his entire life. By the time Averell was old enough to realize it, E. H. was approaching the pinnacle of his spectacular business career. In his biography of the younger Harriman, Rudy Abramson describes the effect on Averell of his father's developing status as an American business legend.

> By the time he was ready for school, his father was fighting for control of the Union Pacific. He was not yet ten when his father took command of the Southern Pacific system and precipitated the Northern Pacific panic on Wall Street. By the time Averell reached his teens, E.H. was one of the most controversial figures in America, lampooned by cartoonists, investigated by Congress, and ridiculed by the President. . . . Always there was, from the man accused of ruthlessness and financial piracy, sermonizing on the responsibilities of wealth. . . . And there was pressure—constant pressure—to ride properly, to speak properly, to study, to achieve, to do better. . . . Life was a test, an obligation to please Pappa, to measure up to towering expectations of the man admirers called "the Little Giant," and sensational newspapers portrayed as an ogre.[12]

E. H. would sometimes take Averell along on business trips, which gave the younger Harriman the opportunity to watch his legendary father in action. He would later say that his own operational style was shaped partially by watching his father. In a 1978 interview with *Fortune* magazine, Harriman recalled watching his father conduct business on a trip to inspect his railroad: "My father used to ask the most precise questions. My impression was that he asked questions about every aspect of maintenance and operations. It impressed me, his interest in detail and his capacity to grasp detail. I inherited that and I've applied it throughout my whole life."[13]

In the same interview he discussed his father's infamous clash with fellow robber barons James J. Hill and J. P. Morgan over control of the Northern Pacific Railroad. Harriman spoke rather matter-of-factly about the all-out competition for controlling stock that actually triggered a huge panic on Wall Street. "My father had certain plans. He was very competitive himself and he didn't want to have them blocked. He was a great competitor of Hill's; he was a great competitor of Morgan's. I don't think he cared too much for Hill. There wasn't much love lost between them."[14] He went on to emphasize his father's sense of social responsibility, defending him against those who portrayed him as a greedy, soulless ogre: "He has been known as one of the Robber Barons, but he told me from an early age that the railroad had a three-way responsibility—to the stockholders, of course, to the employees, and then to the public that the railroad served."[15]

The driving competitiveness that Harriman attributed to his father is a key element of the entrepreneur representative character, fictionalized in portrayals of the entrepreneur from Silas Lapham to Frank Cowperwood (see Chapter 2). Not only does the younger Harriman explicitly refer to his father's competitive nature as important to understanding the man, he also explains that competitiveness by referring to his father's meager beginnings.

> My grandfather was an educated man—he'd been to Columbia. My father was born in Hempstead, Long Island, at the rectory there. He was brought up not poverty stricken, but not too comfortable. . . . His father had little money. But at the age of fourteen his father wanted him to get a higher education, and he said "no I'm going to go to work." He must have felt that his father had not made a financial success of his life, and he had a brilliant mind, of course, and I think he wanted to make money—to bring up a family in the way he would like to have been brought up. To make money—after all that's the job of Wall Street.[16]

It is significant that Harriman told his father's story using the classic American rags-to-riches allegory. The fact that he used this imagery to describe his father's rise suggests that he may have been influenced by the market myth and also indicates that he identified strongly with his father as an entrepreneur.

The extent of this identification is not surprising when one considers how hard the elder Harriman worked to shape his son in his own image. It is clear from accounts of Averell's childhood that his father worked hard to instill in him both competitiveness and the social responsibility of wealth.[17] Toward this end, E. H. sent Averell to the famous Groton prep school. The Groton School, run by a Cambridge-educated Episcopal rector named Endicott Peabody, was for E. H. perfect for instilling in Averell the proper values. As Isaacson and Thomas put it in *The Wise Men,* "Both Peabody and E.H. Harriman stressed the virtue of work, the burdens of privilege, and the obligation to repay society."[18] Indeed, many wealthy Protestant families sent their boys to Groton to prepare them for leadership roles.

While at Groton, Averell constantly struggled to meet his father's high standards, and his father, in close concert with Rector Peabody, kept a close watch on his academic progress. Peabody would send regular academic reports to E. H., who in turn constantly pushed Averell to do better even when his grades had recently improved.[19] E. H. also wanted Averell to be competitive in athletics. When Averell and his younger brother, Roland, became interested in the Groton rowing team, E. H. hired the coach of the Syracuse crew to train them on one of his lakes for an entire summer.[20] Much to his father's satisfaction, Averell went on to be a valuable member of the Groton crew and later became the student coach of the Yale team. Averell would later credit his father and his experience at Groton with giving him an ethic of obligation that would guide him throughout his long business and government careers.[21] In summers during the Groton years E. H. would take Averell along on business trips in the United States and abroad, an experience that allowed the younger Harriman to watch his father in action.[22]

Averell was only eighteen when his father passed away; it was 1909, and he was preparing to enter Yale. His father's passing placed a great deal of responsibility on the young college freshman. Averell's mother, Mary, did not want him to wait until he completed college to take on some of the official responsibilities that came with being the heir apparent to the Harriman empire.[23] Thus his college years would not be the carefree four-year interlude that was typical for someone of his pedigree. This pressure was exacerbated by the fact that the New York newspapers followed his every move, keeping their readers informed about how the future head of the

Harriman empire was handling college life. Also atypical was the level of responsibilities he took on at Yale. His work as coach of the freshman rowing crew and as technical adviser to the varsity helped to restore the program to its former glory days.[24] He was also inducted into the very prestigious Skull and Bones society.

INTO THE WORLD OF BUSINESS

Upon graduation from Yale in 1913, the young Harriman began his formal preparation to take over his father's railroad empire.[25] He spent the next two years as an intern at the Union Pacific, where he learned all of the various operational divisions of the railroad before being named a junior vice-president in charge of purchasing.[26] Shortly after, in September 1915, he married his first wife, Kitty. Newly married and with a brand new daughter, Averell enjoyed his position at the Union Pacific, and he succeeded in cutting a substantial amount of waste in the railroad's purchasing operations.[27] Nonetheless, he was eager to create a name for himself as an entrepreneur, as his father had done so magnificently.[28]

His opportunity to create his own business and identity came in fall 1916 as the U.S. government began to build up its merchant marine fleet for possible entry into World War I. With the advent of the war, Harriman had become aware of a worsening worldwide shortage of merchant vessels, and he began to explore the possibility of starting his own shipyards to take advantage of the seller's market.[29] In January 1917 as the United States was pushed toward entering the war by the German declaration of unrestricted submarine warfare, Harriman bought a large shipyard near Philadelphia. By the time Congress actually declared war on the Central Powers in early April 1917, Harriman was ready to bid for huge government contracts. He had quickly hired some of the best shipyard engineers in the country and in two months they had developed a revolutionary plan for the mass production of the desperately needed merchant freighters.[30] Harriman landed a government contract to produce sixty freighters and was able to get his shipyard up and running in just over four months.[31] The son of the "little giant" had seen this golden opportunity to launch his own business and had seized it adroitly.

In a 1921 interview in the *Marine Review,* Harriman intimated that in building up the American merchant marine, he was following through on a dream of his father's: "Father always had a desire to build up merchant shipping, but during his day the opportunity was not right."[32] This venture was only the beginning of his efforts to build his own business empire.

As the war ended in autumn 1918, Harriman anticipated that the government would stop placing orders for his ships, and he developed a plan to launch his own general steamship line. In April 1919 he purchased a one-fifth interest in the American-Hawaiian Steamship Company and was soon named its president.[33] With the backing of his mother and business partners on Wall Street, he created W. A. Harriman and Company to finance the rapid acquisition of further shipping interests.

He then sought to expand his shipping business into the vast European market via a cooperative arrangement with the German-based Hamburg-American shipping line. Another U.S. shipping firm, the American Ship and Commerce Corporation, was also trying to set up the same arrangement with Hamburg-American. In the face of this competition, Harriman put together sufficient capital with the help of his business partners and bought control of American Ship and Commerce, thus eliminating the competition.[34] With an operating style very much like that of his father, Harriman had consolidated a personal transatlantic shipping empire.[35] When asked what motivated him in this effort, Harriman echoed his father's sermons about the social obligations of wealth. "The rich man must not apply his money or his effort for purely selfish purposes. His duty is to consider how he can do the most to develop his nation's resources along sound lines and thus provide useful, remunerative employment to as many breadwinners as possible. . . . I am striving to do the thing which is the best and the most important thing I can do for the interests of America."[36]

Perhaps some of Harriman's sermonizing on the social obligations of wealth is a defensive reaction to the portrayal of his father as an unprincipled robber baron. Nonetheless, it is consistent with the ethic of obligation his father worked so hard to implant in him. Harriman clearly had a very positive conception of the role of the wealthy entrepreneur in building the U.S. economy. He also seemed anxious to avoid being seen as a wealthy aesthete who had everything handed to him. In the same interview he proclaimed, "It is the duty of everyone, rich or poor, to work. . . . I love work—I cannot see how anyone would prefer to be idle."[37]

In another interview with *Forbes* magazine during the same period, he described the nature of the satisfaction he derived from building a business empire. "Money, like most other things in this world must be regarded as a means to a larger end. . . . Money in itself can yield no joy. Joy comes from creating things, developing things, helping them to grow, and seeing them afford increasing numbers of human beings a comfortable livelihood."[38]

Taken together, these statements suggest that Harriman conceived of himself as an entrepreneur whose purpose was to build productive enterprises. Harriman's sense of social responsibility would not keep him from shifting capital investments when market conditions called for it. By 1926, a number of economic and political factors rendered the shipping business less profitable, and Harriman decided to reduce substantially his investments in it. W. A. Harriman and Company and the Harriman Brothers banks, both formed in partnership with his younger brother Roland, were heavily involved in international finance throughout this period, and Averell frequently traveled to Europe to drum up more banking business.[39] In 1925, against the advice of U.S. government officials and business associates, he negotiated a large Georgian manganese mining concession with the Soviet government.[40] Although this mining venture was unprofitable and short-lived, it is significant because it provided Harriman with the opportunity to negotiate at length with various Soviet officials, including Trotsky.[41] This would be the first of many face-to-face negotiations with Soviet leaders.

In the late 1920s Harriman began to eye the budding aviation industry as a promising business opportunity. In 1929 he and some business partners bought control of the Aviation Corporation of America (AVCO). Within a year AVCO would expand to include freight and passenger airlines, aircraft and engine manufacturing subsidiaries, airport operations, and even flying schools. Seeming to prefer dealmaking over corporate management, Harriman was responsible for negotiating many of the corporate acquisitions that went into making AVCO so large and diverse a company.[42] Mismanagement and the great stock market crash in 1929 weakened AVCO, and in 1932 a onetime competitor in the aviation business was able to gradually purchase a majority of the stock. Ironically, the competitor, E. L. Cord, used the same kinds of underhanded takeover tactics that E. H. and later Averell had used to get rid of competition. When Cord's bid to take control of AVCO appeared unstoppable, Averell quickly resigned his position as chairman of the board, a move that some observers said was an effort to avoid the humiliation of being publicly outmaneuvered.[43]

His quick exit from the aviation industry did not leave Harriman with nothing to do. He was still active in banking even though the Harriman Brothers banks had in 1931 merged with the Brown Brothers Bank to form Brown Brothers, Harriman. And in 1932 he was named chairman of the board at Union Pacific, a job that took the lion's share of his time and energy during the early 1930s.

In 1932 the Union Pacific was in dire straits, having been hit hard by the depression and by competition from other developing modes of transportation such as automobiles and airplanes.[44] Harriman launched a campaign to revolutionize rail travel by offering low-cost, comfortable accommodations to travelers. He also initiated the development of diesel-engine streamliner passenger trains, which traveled much faster than the conventional steam-powered trains.[45] When the first streamliner was ready for service, Harriman showed it off across the country. The futuristic machine drew huge crowds and made headlines everywhere it stopped. The publicity reached a fever pitch when the new streamliner carried Harriman and a group of dignitaries from Los Angeles to New York in fifty-six hours and fifty-five minutes, thus shattering the old transcontinental record (set by E. H. in 1906) by some fourteen hours.[46]

In an effort to boost passenger business in the Northwest, Harriman developed the Sun Valley ski resort in Idaho. Its opening in 1936 was attended by a crowd of Hollywood stars and other celebrities and a tremendous amount of nationwide publicity.[47] Harriman himself spent a great deal of time at the new resort, socializing with the many celebrities and seeming to enjoy the media spotlight.[48]

An examination of Harriman's business career to this point turns up some interesting patterns of behavior. Like his legendary father, he seemed to be constantly driven to make new business deals, to expand existing business enterprises, and to acquire new ones. In this sense he exhibited the restlessness that characterized his father's business career and seems to have typified the other entrepreneurs of the era. The previous interviews suggest that Averell identified strongly with his father's entrepreneurial identity and style and had also internalized his father's sermons about the social responsibilities of the wealthy entrepreneur.

Unlike his father, however, Averell developed a skill for shaping unavoidable publicity in favorable ways. Also unlike his father, he seems to have enjoyed and even encouraged media coverage of his business endeavors. This affinity for power and notoriety was probably what drew him to Washington and into politics during the early years of the Great Depression.

AN ODD SORT OF NEW DEALER

With the beginning of the New Deal era, Harriman and others in the business community began to sense that the real locus of power in U.S. society was now in Washington, not in Wall Street.[49] Harriman initially went to Washington because he was deeply concerned about New Deal securities reform legislation that was being hammered out during the first hundred days of the new administration.[50] Even though he had voted for Roosevelt, he had been angered and frightened by the new president's rhetorical attack on the financial community (which he referred to as "money changers" and "rulers of the exchange of mankind's goods") during his inaugural address.[51]

Harriman was concerned that the New Deal reformers knew very little about business and would draft securities reform legislation that would smother the financial community with government interference and kill any chance for economic recovery. This hostile perspective on New Deal reformism was commonly held by members of the U.S. business community at the time. Such a jealous defense of business from government interference is also a constitutive element of the market-mythical understanding of U.S. society.[52] The securities legislation, which was eventually passed as the Securities Reform Act, ended up being quite moderate. This was due in part to the lobbying of Harriman and other members of the financial community.[53] Nonetheless, Harriman's stay in Washington gave him a taste of the power that could be exercised there, and he decided to become involved in the creation and administration of other New Deal programs.

Through his older sister, Averell was given an entrée into the social milieu of the New Deal brain trust. Mary Harriman Rumsey was a close friend of the Roosevelts and of Frances Perkins, Roosevelt's secretary of labor. Through her powerful network of New Dealers, Averell got himself attached to the National Recovery Administration (NRA), which was run by General Hugh Johnson.[54] In July 1933, Johnson recruited Harriman to organize the NRA propaganda campaign in New York. Harriman did this so successfully that he was eventually given official positions in the NRA, first as administrator of its heavy-industry division and then as the senior assistant administrator of the entire agency.[55] This put him in the ironic position of administering a government agency whose function was to write codes to regulate all aspects of U.S. industry, albeit on a strictly voluntary basis. Harriman found himself strongly opposing business leaders who were pushing for the development of codes with built-in price-fixing provisions and other measures favorable to particular business interests.[56]

Harriman's rapid metamorphosis from financier concerned about government interference to moderate reformer administering the NRA is a bit difficult to explain. Biographer Rudy Abramson attributes the change to the influence of his older sister, Mary, who was a dedicated liberal reformer and who had always been a strong influence in Averell's life.[57] Whatever may have been the case, Harriman's stint at the NRA came to an abrupt end when the Supreme Court ruled it unconstitutional in spring 1935. This marked the end of his work with the New Deal; he then went back to New York to continue his work on revitalizing the Union Pacific. He did, however, remain abreast of political developments in Washington and kept in contact with Roosevelt, partially through his membership in the Business Advisory Council.[58]

ENVOY TO CHURCHILL

Harriman's long diplomatic career did not begin until February 1941, when President Roosevelt assigned him to the position of defense expediter to embattled Britain. Harriman was to be Roosevelt's personal envoy to Churchill and his ministers, handling all war-related matters from lend-lease to strategy. Roosevelt told him that his job was to "go over to London and recommend everything short of war that we can do to keep the British Isles afloat."[59] Thus his first diplomatic assignment was one of historic importance.

Harriman had gotten this vitally important position by gaining the trust and respect of Harry Hopkins, who was Roosevelt's closest adviser.[60] Helping Britain hold out against Hitler was not just a job; it was also a cause in which he believed fervently. Since the beginning of the war in Europe, Harriman had argued both privately and publicly that it was vital that the United States take strong measures to help the British stem the Nazi tide. He gave speeches in which he argued that the national security of the United States depended on providing effective support for the British even at the risk of war. He also argued strongly for granting emergency powers to Roosevelt so that he could make this aid to Britain effective.[61] In these speeches, which are some of the earliest statements of his views on U.S. foreign policy, his tone was decidedly realpolitik and pragmatic. The United States had to become involved in the war not out of duty or in defense of principle but because national security demanded it. Harriman reasoned that if Germany controlled all of Europe, it would not be long before it took control of Latin America, and the United States would be at its mercy politically and economically.[62] Thus Harriman believed very strongly in the historic task he was given by Roosevelt.

He discovered through conversations with various officials in Washington that many of them were skeptical of the value of sending war materials that were in short supply in the United States to Great Britain. As a result of these conversations he determined that his primary job would be to convey British needs and strategy back to Washington in a way that would provide effective justification for increasing lend-lease transfers.[63] Upon his arrival in London, he was immediately taken in almost as a member of the Churchill family, spending much of his time either at 10 Downing Street or, on weekends, at the prime minister's country retreat at Chequers. Churchill also saw to it that he was given access to all war-related information and that all ministers cooperated with him fully.[64] Having attained this high level of access and cooperation, Harriman set out to provide Roosevelt with the information he needed to justify increased flows of material assistance to the British.

In this first diplomatic assignment in London, Harriman developed a distinctive style of operation. From the start he sought to prevent himself from being encumbered in any way by the State Department bureaucracy. In addition to jealously guarding his independence, he guarded his access to Churchill as though others' access to the prime minister directly interfered with his own. Before Harriman's arrival, Ambassador John G. Winant had enjoyed unlimited access to Churchill, but Winant was, much to his own dismay, quickly nudged aside by Harriman.[65] Harriman also fought hard to maintain his access to information from Washington. In a cable to President Roosevelt he complained, "My usefulness will be in direct proportion to the extent to which I am kept informed of the developments in fact and thought in Washington."[66] Thus Harriman constantly competed for the two essential ingredients of power in the diplomatic world: access and information.

Having gained the full confidence of Churchill and full access to war-related information, Harriman carried out his job as defense expediter very effectively. Churchill even sent him on an extended inspection tour of Britain's forces in the Middle East, and he came back with a long list of recommendations for the prime minister, many of which were followed.[67] While Harriman was on his inspection trip in the Middle East, Hitler launched his attack against Russia, thus changing the entire strategic situation and creating Harriman's first opportunity to visit the Soviet Union in a diplomatic capacity.[68]

Churchill and Roosevelt picked Harriman to head a joint U.S.-British delegation that was to travel to Moscow and meet with the Soviet leadership to discuss Western assistance to the Soviet war effort against Germany. As the delegation was preparing to leave for Moscow, British foreign minister Lord William Beaverbrook made a bid to take control of the delegation, but Harriman successfully fought him off, using the argument that the United States would be providing the bulk of the assistance to the Soviets.[69] In the delegation's meetings with Stalin, Harriman studied the Soviet leader's negotiating style. In the first meeting Stalin was relatively open and easygoing, but in the second he was very rude and aggressive to the point of being insulting. After witnessing a relaxed Stalin at the third meeting, Harriman speculated in a report to Roosevelt that Stalin's aggressiveness during the second meeting must have been a calculated effort to bully him and Beaverbrook into offering more aid.[70] It was a negotiating tactic that he would see again in later meetings with the Soviet leader. Stalin's bad manners notwithstanding, Harriman left Moscow convinced that Stalin was committed to defeating Hitler and that the Western allies would be able to work with him.[71] He also was convinced that he alone had the negotiating skills and understood Stalin well enough to be successful with the Soviet leader. Apparently Roosevelt was convinced of this also, because after this trip, Harriman became the most important personal link between Roosevelt and Stalin.[72]

His next face-to-face meetings with Stalin came about as a result of developing friction between the Soviets and their Western allies over the issue of when and where to open up a western front. The Soviets desperately needed the Western allies to force the Germans to draw substantial forces away from the eastern front. Early in 1942, General Dwight Eisenhower had drawn up a plan for a small cross-channel invasion into France in late 1942 followed by a larger invasion in spring 1943.[73] Roosevelt and his military advisers were in favor of the plan, but Churchill and his advisers had doubts that an effective invasion could be organized and executed so soon. Unfortunately, open British opposition to an early invasion of France did not emerge until after Roosevelt had already made a commitment to Soviet foreign minister V. M. Molotov at a meeting at the White House in May 1942.[74] When it became clear that Churchill would not support an early cross-channel invasion, Roosevelt and Churchill decided that the latter must go to Moscow and explain to Stalin why the invasion of France must be delayed.[75] At the last minute, it was decided that Harriman should accompany Churchill to demonstrate that the Western allies were united on the decision to delay the opening of the second front.[76]

At their first meeting with Stalin, Churchill and Harriman found the Soviet leader visibly disappointed by their news of the delay, but he eventually warmed up to their presentation of a plan for an invasion of North Africa. They left the first meeting pleased with the way that Stalin had taken the bad news.[77] The second meeting with Stalin did not go nearly as well.

Upon their arrival, Stalin launched a verbal attack on the Western allies, questioning both their support of the Soviets and their courage in the face of the German challenge.[78] Harriman recognized Stalin's attack as a bullying tactic. However, he could see that Churchill was becoming infuriated by the outburst, and he quickly handed him a note that read, "Don't take this too seriously—this is the way he behaved last year."[79] When Stalin was finished, Churchill launched his own verbal counterattack, and Stalin, impressed by the prime minister's fiery spirit, became much less bellicose.[80] The rest of the meeting was much more relaxed, but Churchill left the Kremlin angry nonetheless. As they left together, Harriman reiterated to Churchill his belief that Stalin's aggressiveness had merely been a negotiating tactic, and he correctly predicted that the next meeting would be much more pleasant. The final meeting did go well with Stalin accepting Churchill's explanation of the delay of the second front and enthusiastically approving the plans to invade North Africa. Churchill and Harriman left Moscow, and the former cabled Roosevelt to inform him that "the bitter pill had gone down."[81]

Harriman had again gained valuable experience in dealing with Stalin face-to-face. At the same time, he was gaining the confidence of Roosevelt and Harry Hopkins as someone who really knew the Soviets and how to deal with them. Their increasing confidence in him would result in his being offered the position of U.S. ambassador in Moscow in June 1943.

AMBASSADOR TO MOSCOW

After Harriman accepted the Moscow position, his first order of business was to consolidate his control over the embassy. Previous U.S. ambassadors in Moscow had failed to gain control over all of the various agencies represented at the Moscow embassy, particularly the military mission.[82] Harriman made certain that he would not have this problem. He quickly replaced the key officers in the military mission and arranged to have the entire embassy reorganized so that all embassy personnel answered to him.[83]

As ambassador, he was not going to tolerate the kind of freelancing that he himself had engaged in under Ambassador Winant in London. Thus in consolidating his control in Moscow, he was quick to use the bureaucracy where it helped him, whereas in London his influence had depended on his ability to stay free of bureaucratic constraints. In Moscow he did, however, arrange to communicate with Roosevelt and Hopkins independent of the State Department network, a move that greatly enhanced his influence.[84]

This shrewd and rapid consolidation of influence and access, which Harriman first practiced during his tour in London, would manifest itself through the rest of his diplomatic career. It would also help him gain a reputation as one of the shrewdest and fiercest bureaucratic infighters in the foreign policy bureaucracy.

There is a strong similarity between Harriman's business style and his diplomatic operating style. As noted, Harriman the businessman worked very quickly and opportunistically to build his business empire. Harriman the diplomat was equally quick and opportunistic in building a bureaucratic power base. In building his business empire Harriman would not hesitate to neutralize a competitor by secretly acquiring enough stock to buy the competing firm. In his first diplomatic assignment in London, Harriman was quick to undermine Ambassador Winant as a rival for access to Churchill. Thus in both careers, Harriman manifested the fierce competitiveness his father had instilled in him during childhood.

His first tasks as ambassador in Moscow were to help coordinate the October 1943 foreign ministers' meeting there and to help set up the November 1943 Big Three conference in Tehran. The larger assignment given him by Roosevelt was to help secure Soviet cooperation in both the European and Pacific theaters and in the postwar era.[85] Toward these ends, Harriman set out to create more of an atmosphere of trust between the two allies.[86] In order to establish a better working relationship with the Soviets, he would try to maximize his personal contact with top Soviet officials such as Molotov and Stalin. This stress on face-to-face discussions was a carryover from both his business career and his days in London and would continue to be a trademark of the Harriman diplomatic style for the rest of his career.

In a cable to Roosevelt sent shortly after his arrival in Moscow, Harriman stressed the mistrust that the Soviets felt toward the United States, and he recommended that the president approve a Soviet request for captured Italian merchant and naval vessels as a trust-building measure. "Suspicions are present in the minds of many in official Soviet circles and Russian people as to the intentions of the United States toward Russia. There is no doubt of this. They have been reading during the past two years the comments and editorials of our press critical of Russia. The acceptance of this request, we believe, would go far toward allaying these suspicions."[87]

Also in connection with building an atmosphere of trust between these two allies, Harriman sent a cable to Secretary of State
Cordell Hull in which he recommended steps to alleviate the kinds
of misunderstandings that had plagued the U.S.-Soviet relationship
in the past. He recommended that direct communications between
Roosevelt and Stalin, some of which in the past had been miscon-
strued, should be sent only after great consideration of the wording
and implications. Of course, this step would also enhance his role
as a personal intermediary. He also warned that U.S. officials
needed to be more careful about promises that were made to the
Soviets: "We have an unfortunate record of offering more than we
have been able to carry out. These offers have been made in good
faith and with the usual qualifications. We have carried them out to
the best of our ability and at real sacrifice. On the other hand, a
better policy would be to make our offers more conservatively and
attempt to do a little more than had been indicated."[88] He went on
to complain about the slowness of U.S. responses to Soviet requests.
"Prompt responses to the requests of the Soviet Government,
whether important or trivial, will be an important factor in allaying
past suspicions and developing understanding."[89] This concern
with building a constructive diplomatic relationship with the Soviets on both important wartime matters and postwar issues would
color Harriman's policy preferences throughout his involvement
with the making of U.S. foreign policy during the Cold War.

Upon his arrival in Moscow, Harriman had immediately begun
to try to feel out the Soviet leadership on such important postwar
issues as the future of Eastern Europe and of a conquered Germany. Soon after arriving in Moscow he had a conversation with Soviet foreign minister Molotov regarding the future of Eastern Europe; he expressed sympathy (albeit qualified) for the Soviets'
position of wanting friendly countries on their western borders.[90]
In a subsequent cable to Roosevelt he informed the president that
he was concerned about Soviet insecurity regarding Eastern Europe
but that he thought Western interests in the region could be protected in any postwar settlement.[91] The Soviets, he informed Roosevelt, "indicated that although they would keep us informed, they
would take unilateral action in respect to these [Eastern European]
countries in the establishment of relations satisfactory to themselves. It is my feeling that this rigid attitude may well be tempered
in proportion to their increasing confidence in their relations with
the British and ourselves in the establishment of over-all world security."[92] Thus Harriman again showed his belief that by building
an atmosphere of trust, the Americans and the British would be

able to win the Soviets over to postwar agreements that were satisfactory to the West.

Harriman's confidence in the ability of the Americans and
British to negotiate favorable postwar agreements was tested constantly over the next year as he became a firsthand witness to Soviet
actions that indicated an unwillingness to cooperate even on small
issues. He was especially annoyed at the Soviets' refusal to allow
U.S. transport aircraft to come to Moscow to take diplomatic personnel such as himself on official trips.[93] The lack of Soviet cooperation was not limited to such seemingly unimportant issues, however. In March 1944, Harriman got word that a Soviet diplomat had
approached the Badoglio government in Italy about normalizing
diplomatic relations between the two countries. Harriman was quite
disturbed by this because the Soviets had not consulted their Western allies on this move. When Harriman approached Soviet deputy
foreign minister Andrei Vishinsky about it, Vishinsky was very eva-
sive and refused to give a straightforward answer. Harriman then
recommended that Washington make clear to the Soviets that this
type of behavior was harmful to the Grand Alliance.[94]

Faced with this and other evidence of Soviet bad faith, Harriman began to recommend that Washington consider using economic assistance as leverage over the Soviets. In an embassy cable to
the State Department in March, he wrote, "I am impressed with the
consideration that economic assistance is one of the most effective
weapons at our disposal to avoid the development of a Soviet
sphere of influence over Eastern Europe and the Balkans. . . . Such
assistance, as I have expressed in other telegrams, is one of our
principal practical levers, compatible with our principles, for influencing political action."[95] Thus, by 1944 Harriman was still somewhat optimistic about the ability of the United States to reach satisfactory agreements with the Soviets, but he was beginning to think
that it would require measured use of the carrot and the stick to
bring them around.

There were successes in obtaining cooperation from the Soviets
on military matters. In February 1944 after long, hard negotiations,
Harriman successfully obtained Stalin's permission for U.S.
bombers to use Ukrainian bases for shuttle-bombing missions. This
agreement gave Harriman great personal satisfaction and was politically and militarily quite significant because it opened the door
for similar negotiations regarding the future use of Far Eastern
bases for bombing Japan.[96] Harriman was also able to secure the release of downed U.S. airmen whom the Soviets had been holding
for some time in the Far East.[97] Overall, however, there were more

discouraging signs regarding the Soviet attitude on cooperation than encouraging ones.

By spring 1944, Harriman was becoming more and more concerned about the Soviet approach to the problem of Poland. The Soviets were showing no inclination to allow any governing role whatsoever for the Polish exile government in London, and they were pressing hard for an adoption of the Curzon line as the new border between Poland and the Soviet Union.[98] In conversations with Churchill during a May stopover in London, Harriman tried to make clear to the prime minister how rigid the Soviets were becoming on both the political and the territorial aspects of the Polish question.[99] However, while still in London, he expressed to Anthony Eden his belief that if the British and Americans would remain firm and continue to instill trust in the Soviets, they would be able to work out a satisfactory arrangement.[100]

The real problems in Poland did not come until late summer and the Warsaw uprising. As the Soviet army approached Warsaw in July 1944, Soviet radio broadcasts exhorted partisans in the city to rise up and fight the Germans in conjunction with the Red Army advance.[101] The Warsaw underground did respond with an uprising against the German occupiers, but unfortunately it was so poorly armed that the conflict quickly turned into a slaughter.[102] To the dismay of the British and American delegations in Moscow, Stalin refused to aid the badly outmatched Polish resistance by advancing into Warsaw with the Red Army, although initially he did agree to airdrop supplies to them.[103] Stalin then changed his mind and decided not to order the airdrops, apparently in response to Polish radio broadcasts that were (in hindsight, correctly) accusing the Soviets of deliberately setting the Warsaw resistance forces up for the slaughter that was occurring.[104]

Harriman and British ambassador Sir Archibald Clark-Kerr vigorously questioned Molotov about the Soviet refusal to help the desperate Poles. They were told by Molotov that the Warsaw uprising was "purely adventuristic" and that the "Soviet Government could not and would not be held responsible for this unhappy adventure."[105] They were read a cable from Stalin in which the Soviet leader stated, "The Soviet command has come to the conclusion that it should keep aloof from the Warsaw adventure since it cannot assume responsibility for the action there."[106] Harriman and Clark-Kerr pressed Molotov for permission for American planes to use the Ukrainian bases to drop supplies to the Warsaw resistance.[107] Molotov said the Soviets did not mind if the Americans used their planes to drop supplies over Warsaw, but they could not give permission for such missions to use Soviet bases.[108]

To add to Harriman's mounting frustration, in the same meeting Molotov announced that the U.S. shuttle-bombing missions would soon lose access to the Ukrainian bases that made such missions possible. Harriman responded that this action "would have a most desperate effect on American-Soviet collaboration."[109] A week after this meeting, Harriman cabled Roosevelt and informed him that the Soviets' failure to assist the Warsaw uprising had caused him to reevaluate Soviet intentions:

> I find no way to justify Stalin's position. The one solid faith that I have had was the validity of Stalin's word. He has now broken his promise [to assist the Warsaw resistance] . . . without any apparent cause except the ill-advised public statements of the Poles in London. . . . I can only draw the conclusion that this action is for ruthless political considerations in order that the underground may get no credit for the liberation of Warsaw, and that its leaders be killed by the Germans or give an excuse for their arrest when the Red Army enters Warsaw.[110]

He went on to warn that this behavior boded poorly for overall postwar cooperation with the Soviets. Yet he finished the cable by arguing that the United States could still bring the Russians around on important postwar issues if it negotiated more firmly and used sources of leverage such as economic assistance, which the Russians badly needed.[111] Thus even after being shocked and appalled by Stalin's ruthless handling of the Warsaw uprising, Harriman still believed that he could be brought around on important postwar issues.

As autumn 1944 wore on, however, Harriman began to become more concerned about Soviet intentions in postwar Eastern Europe. In a State Department cable in October he warned that the Soviets might try to create economic disruptions in Eastern European countries (with the use of harsh reparations demands) in order to substitute existing governments with communist ones.[112] On a trip to Washington in early November, he met with Roosevelt several times and warned him of the possibility of the Soviets attempting to dominate postwar Eastern Europe, but he worried that the president was not taking these warnings seriously.[113] He also came away from these meetings worried that Roosevelt was overestimating his own ability to personally iron out differences with Stalin. In a memorandum of his conversations with Roosevelt he wrote, "The President still feels that he can persuade Stalin to alter his view on many matters that I am satisfied Stalin will never agree to."[114]

Part of the reason Roosevelt did not yet wish to initiate a showdown over Poland or Eastern Europe was that he wanted the Soviets to commit to an early entry into the war against Japan. Harriman was charged with making sure that Stalin would enter the war as soon as possible after the Germans were finally defeated.[115] He was involved in frequent negotiations with the Soviet leader on this subject.

Nevertheless, when Harriman departed for the Big Three conference at Yalta in early February 1945, he was determined to meet with Roosevelt beforehand to persuade him to tackle the Poland and Eastern Europe issues head-on at the conference. Partly due to the president's failing health, however, he never got the chance.[116] Harriman then tried during the conference to persuade Roosevelt to get tough on the issue and to get guarantees that the new Polish government would at least contain some democratic elements, but the president refused. Harriman went back to Moscow disappointed that the matter had not been settled but determined to negotiate a suitable Polish arrangement with the Soviets.[117]

In early March Harriman, Soviet foreign minister Molotov, and British ambassador Archibald Clark-Kerr convened a conference in Moscow to settle the makeup of the new Polish government.[118] These meetings quickly produced a deadlock when Molotov insisted that the communist Poles should have the right of approval over which noncommunist Poles could participate in the deal.[119] This was completely unacceptable to Harriman and Clark-Kerr, but Molotov would not abandon his insistence on this procedural point.[120] In addition to the Soviet intransigence on the Polish issue, Harriman found extremely frustrating the Soviets' ongoing refusal to allow the repatriation of thousands of American war prisoners who had recently been freed in Poland.[121] Some of his cables to Washington during this period reflect this frustration. In a cable to Secretary of State Edward Stettinius in early April 1945 Harriman wrote, "I cannot in the compass of this message, list the almost daily affronts and total disregard which the Soviets evince in matters of interest to us. . . . I must with regret recommend that we begin in the near future with one or two cases where their actions are intolerable and make them realize that they cannot continue their present attitude except at great cost to themselves."[122]

CONFRONTING THE WORLD BULLY

The previous cable not only shows the degree of Harriman's frustration but also highlights the early formation of a Cold War worldview.

In this cable to Stettinius, Harriman also clearly laid out his belief that the Soviets would attempt to dominate Eastern Europe if the United States did not take a much firmer stand on the issue.

> For many months we have recognized that the Soviets have three lines of foreign policy. 1/Overall collaboration with us and the British in a world security organization; 2/the creation of a unilateral security ring through domination of their bordering states; and 3/the penetration of other countries through exploitation of democratic processes by communist controlled parties with strong Soviet backing to create a political atmosphere favorable to the policies of the Soviets. It has been our hope that, as we have, the Soviets would place No. 1 as their primary policy and would modify their plans for 2 if they were satisfied with the efficacy of plan 1. It now seems evident that they intend to go forward with unilateral action in the domination of their bordering states regardless of what they may expect from the World Security Organization.[123]

This is the first clear indication that Harriman believed a Soviet attempt to dominate Eastern Europe was imminent. He had speculated about the possibility before, but he had always assumed that preserving good relations with the United States and Britain was a higher priority for the Soviets.

After George Kennan (who had been sounding this warning for months), Harriman is thus one of the first policymakers to contemplate a rapid postwar deterioration of U.S.-Soviet relations.[124] Harriman's concern about an imminent U.S.-Soviet confrontation were still somewhat mitigated, however, by his belief that the United States could avoid this scenario if it adopted a tougher diplomatic stance toward the Soviets.[125]

Harriman went on to argue that the Soviets' heavy-handedness was a direct result of their perceiving the United States as weak:

> There is at hand evidence which satisfies me that the Soviets have interpreted our continued generous and considerate attitude towards them in spite of their disregard of our requests for cooperation in matters of interest to us as a sign of weakness on our part. Furthermore I am satisfied that the time has come when we must by our actions in each individual case make it plain to the Soviet Government that they cannot expect our continued cooperation on terms laid down by them. . . . I feel that our relations would be on a much sounder basis if on the one hand we were firm and completely frank with them as to our position and motives and on the other hand they are made to understand specifically how their interests will be adversely affected by a lack on their part of cooperation with our legitimate demands.[126]

Thus by early 1945, Harriman's view of the Soviets seems to have so-lidified. It would soon become very influential in Washington.

This early manifestation of Harriman's Cold War worldview pro-vides the first opportunity to subject his key beliefs to analysis. In the communications observed thus far, Harriman didn't address the abstract morality-diplomacy relationship at all: He did not di-rectly address to what degree U.S. foreign policy should be guided by moral principle or to what extent the Cold War should be viewed in moral terms. He consistently portrayed the Soviets as another great power with great-power interests (and one the United States could influence either positively or negatively).

With regard to more directly policy-relevant questions, such as how the United States should best use its power in the Cold War (and what forms it should take), Harriman's communications to this point provide a distinct, yet hybrid, answer. He consistently ar-gued that the United States could elicit favorable Soviet behavior if it took a more firm negotiating posture and used the Soviet need for economic assistance as leverage. Thus at this early stage of the Cold War, Harriman believed that the United States should focus mainly on diplomatic and economic means to deal with the Soviets. He would maintain this belief in the diplomatic approach with the Soviets throughout his career.

With regard to the question of what sources of Soviet power were most worrisome in the Cold War, Harriman's answer was again distinct but mixed. As early as 1944, his cables showed concern that the Soviets would attempt to disrupt the Eastern European economies with harsh reparation demands. These could be con-strued as a form of Soviet economic power, but they would have been impotent without the immediate threat of Soviet military power to back them up. Beginning in spring 1945, Harriman also showed concern over the Soviets' ability to penetrate Eastern Euro-pean governments through Communist Party participation in the electoral process.

Analysis of his communications up to this point yields little di-rect evidence of his Cold War worldview being influenced by any of our highlighted myths or representative characters. Throughout his wartime diplomatic career, Harriman showed a consistent belief in his ability to carry out face-to-face negotiations with Joseph Stalin. He showed belief in his ability to wrest postwar cooperation out of Stalin using U.S. economic assistance for bargaining leverage. In his cables to Washington he consistently portrayed Stalin as a leader who could be bargained with if only the United States negotiated firmly and showed a willingness to adversely affect Soviet interests in response to their uncooperativeness. This overall strategy is consistent with Harriman's business style as well as with the entrepreneur character's paradigmatic mode of social action.

George Kennan, who was Harriman's charge d'affairs at the Moscow embassy, commented on Harriman's "take me to your leader" style of diplomacy.

> He . . . regarded himself more as an operator than as an observer. He had no great interest in the general run of Foreign Service reporting. Accustomed to doing things in a big way and endowed with a keen appreciation for great personal power, always enjoying, in fact, the mere proximity of the very great, he dealt only with people at the very top. I have no doubt that he felt, and not without justification in a country where power was so highly personalized as in the Soviet Union of that day, that he could learn more that was important in one interview with Stalin than the rest of us could derive from months of pedestrian study of Soviet publications.[127]

This "operator" mode of diplomacy would be Harriman's trademark style for the rest of his career. Here again, one cannot escape the similarity between his style of diplomacy and his earlier style of conducting business. During the days when Harriman was trying to build his own business empire, he did not send teams of corporate lawyers to close important deals; he himself bargained with the other owners and hammered out the deal. One of his partners in AVCO during the late 1920s commented that Harriman had always preferred dealmaking to corporate management.[128]

With Roosevelt's death in early 1945, Harriman quickly got the chance to promote his "get tough" policy to a new president who was a neophyte in the area of foreign policy. Several days after Harry Truman inherited the Oval Office, he called Harriman back to Washington.[129] In his first meeting with Truman, Harriman told the new president that in his view, the Soviets were pursuing a two-track strategy of cooperating with their Western allies while simultaneously extending control over Eastern Europe. He further explained his view that the Soviets were mistaking U.S. generosity for weakness and his belief that if the United States would stand firm on vital issues, the Soviets would cooperate.[130] Harriman was pleased to find Truman very receptive to his arguments and in full agreement with his call for a much firmer negotiating stance.[131] This set the stage for Truman's famous meeting with Soviet foreign minister Molotov, in which the president browbeat the astonished

Soviet diplomat until Molotov protested, "I've never been talked to like that in my life." Truman responded, "Carry out your agreements and you won't get talked to like that."[132]

Far from pleased with Truman's toughness toward Molotov, Harriman was concerned that the new president had gone too far and that Molotov and Stalin would interpret it as a sign that Truman would no longer follow the policy of cooperation that Roosevelt had established. Indeed, as Rudy Abramson notes in *Spanning the Century,* Harriman would later look back on Truman's tongue-lashing of Molotov as the beginning of the Cold War.[133] Throughout the remainder of 1945, Harriman remained in Moscow as ambassador and dealt with Molotov and Stalin on postwar issues.

In January 1946 he resigned his Moscow post eager to get back to the United States.[134] When he first arrived in Washington, he gave speeches and presentations in which he told of the Soviets' uncooperative attitude and called for a tougher U.S. stance.[135] Truman then sent Harriman to London as ambassador to help settle the dispute that arose when the Soviets delayed their withdrawal from northern Iran, thus making the British (with huge oil interests there) very nervous. His stay in London was very short, however, as Truman called him back to Washington later that year to become secretary of commerce.

As commerce secretary, Harriman began to focus on the need to revitalize the world economy and rebuild war-torn Europe. In spring 1947, he was intimately involved in the early planning phases of what would become the Marshall Plan. Two weeks after Marshall's famous Harvard commencement speech outlining the plan, Truman named Harriman to chair a committee composed of business executives, labor leaders, and academics charged with assessing both the needs of Europe and the U.S. ability to meet those needs. In addition to chairing this important committee, Harriman traveled around promoting the Marshall Plan as a good way to both contain the Soviets and create strong overseas markets for U.S. goods.[136]

In addition to making him a principal salesman for the Marshall Plan, Harriman's position as secretary of commerce made him a key spokesman for U.S. economic policy both at home and abroad. He wrote newspaper and magazine articles in which he explained to Americans that it was important for them to buy more imports to stimulate the war-ravaged economies and close the dollar gap. As was the case with the Marshall Plan, he said, this type of farsighted economic behavior was not simply altruistic but was also in Americans' long-term self-interest because it helped to create strong foreign markets for U.S. goods.[137]

Harriman also used his articles and speeches to rally Americans to the world economic leadership role that the United States had inherited after World War II. In a draft article written for the *United Nations World,* Harriman wrote, "It is almost fair to say that the leadership of the United States among the free nations of the world has been thrust upon us. This leadership has come to us because of the strength of our nation and because of the ideals of freedom and justice on which it was founded. War has spent the vitality of many other nations, and free people the world over look to us for spiritual leadership and material assistance."[138] Although he stopped short of claiming that the United States had a divine destiny to lead the free world, the identity component of this passage is very similar to the identity component of the city-on-the-hill myth. In both instances much of the American identity derives from a leadership role and from strong adherence to certain ideals. This is the first city-on-the-hill rhetoric found in Harriman's writings and speeches.

In other articles written by Harriman during his tenure as secretary of commerce one finds rhetoric containing strong market myth themes. In one written for the *Financial Times of London,* Harriman argued that the United States derived much of its strength and uniqueness from its peculiarly competitive and individualistic brand of capitalism. Here he bragged, "It is generally agreed by people everywhere that, whatever else can be said for it, capitalism, based on enterprise, competition and initiative accomplished a task in the initial phases of American development which perhaps no other system could have done so fast or so well."[139] He went on to point out how successful the American brand of capitalism was in the mid-twentieth century:

> The United States produces close to two-thirds of the world's output of manufactured goods, owns two-thirds of the world's gold, and is practically its only source of international credit. These figures may arouse various reactions when viewed by non-Americans. But to an American they indicate above all one fact: Namely that the economic system under which he lives has worked well, by and large for him. He is still convinced that capitalism, individual initiative, competition and voluntary economic decisions by people in all aspects of our business life have been eminently successful in getting out the goods, and that generally speaking, all groups in the population have shared generously in this great production.[140]

In this passage Harriman touched on the identity component of the market myth. Americans understood that it was not simply capitalism that had made America so strong but *American* capitalism. And American capitalism was based on freedom and individualism, core components of the American collective identity. He went on to make the connection between faithfulness to these American ideals and economic success more explicit. "Any consideration of the American individual enterprise system cannot be complete without full recognition of the fact that our economic institutions are part of a national culture and political system rooted in a belief in democracy and the worth and dignity of the individual."[141] American economic prowess and fidelity to American political ideals thus went hand in hand for Harriman. In fact, his explanation of the relationship between these political ideals and U.S. economic success came close to taking the form of a theodicy.

In a 1947 article, Harriman again explored this relationship between faithfulness to the ideal of individual liberty and economic success. "We have afforded greater happiness and prosperity than men have ever known. Of first importance is the preservation of our liberties and second is the expansion of our productivity. The release of the energies and initiative of the individual has resulted in our unrivaled productivity. It is only by ever expanding our productivity that we can remain strong and free."[142] This linkage of the success of the U.S. economy to faithful adherence to foundational political values not only helped legitimize the system but also enhanced the power and the identity component of the market myth.

In another 1947 article, Harriman made an even more explicit connection between the U.S. free enterprise system and the collective identity of the American people. He also argued that Americans should be guided by that identity in their relations with the rest of the world.

> The American record of economic accomplishment since the end of the war is the greatest living testimony to the vigor and soundness of the free enterprise philosophy. In these days when other countries are experimenting with their social and economic institutions in an effort to find a way out of their material and spiritual difficulties, a practical demonstration of the potentialities of our free institutions is of the greatest importance. . . . Through the Office of Information and Cultural Affairs in the Department of State we are carrying on a vitally important program of telling the story about what kind of people we are and what we believe in. . . . I am sure that all persons who believe in our free institutions will support the efforts we are making on a wide front to attack the causes and not merely the symptoms of economic and political unrest. If we continue to live by our own principles and prove their effectiveness in terms of spiritual and material well being of all people, we will meet fully our responsibilities as the first nation in the world.[143]

In this passage Harriman provided a good insight into what he thought were the most important distinguishing characteristics of the United States as a society. By pointing to the American free enterprise system as an important indicator of "what kind of people we are and what we believe in," he not only clearly evoked a market myth identity for Americans but cast the American free market as a blueprint for the rest of the world to follow.

In another article later in 1947, Harriman came close to portraying the Cold War as a competition of economic models between the American free enterprise system and Soviet communism.

> Americans are increasingly aware of the vital role that their decisions play in world affairs. It is part of the American democratic faith that the people of all nations should have the right to develop their own patterns of political and economic progress. This means on the one hand, as President Truman has stated, that America will never seek to impose her pattern of economic development upon any country. It means also that America will not condone the imposition of any totalitarian power of its economic philosophy on others through the exploitation of chaos and the systematic stimulation of disorder. The United States recognizes that various patterns of economic development must necessarily co-exist and can cooperate. As far as we are concerned, the critical question is: are the governments of other countries controlled by their people or are the people without liberty and sovereign power and hence at the mercy of a totalitarian state.[144]

The implication here is that if people were allowed to make a choice, they would choose the free enterprise system.

Throughout 1947 and early 1948, Harriman worked hard at promoting the Marshall Plan both at home and abroad. Once the plan was approved by Congress, he was given the task of coordinating its implementation in Europe. In April 1948, he was named special representative of the Economic Cooperation Administration.[145] He was headquartered in Paris, but the task of coordinating the aid flows to the Europeans took him to all of the European capitals, where he was able to stay involved in European security issues even as he was coordinating the Marshall Plan programs.[146] By spring 1950 the European recovery was way ahead of schedule, and Harriman, feeling he had completed his assignment, wrote to Truman asking to be reassigned to Washington.

Truman responded by naming Harriman special assistant to the president for national security affairs. Harriman arrived in Washington just after the Korean War broke out. Among the first tasks Truman gave Harriman was to dampen the feud that had developed between Secretary of State Acheson and Secretary of Defense Louis Johnson.[147] Harriman was able to mediate the ongoing conflict for a time, but it eventually ended in Johnson's resignation. Another big assignment came when Truman sent him to meet with Douglas MacArthur in an effort to rein in the outspoken general with regard to his tendency to deliver off-the-cuff foreign policy proclamations.[148] Harriman had what seemed like productive talks with MacArthur, although as later events showed, he was unable to stop MacArthur's independent attempts at policymaking.

In September 1951, Harriman was named chairman of the North Atlantic Commission on Defense.[149] His job was to steer this committee, made up of representatives of the twelve NATO members, in its task of synchronizing the NATO defense contributions of member states with their economic capacities. Harriman pushed the committee relentlessly until it produced a report that called for a substantial buildup of NATO forces. Later that fall, he was named director of the Mutual Security Administration, a position that put him in charge of U.S. foreign aid programs. He remained in this capacity until Truman left office.

During his tenure at the Mutual Security Administration, Harriman continued to use articles and appearances to warn the public about the threat posed by Soviet communism. These warnings had become much more strident than those in the immediate postwar years. In a November 1951 draft article for the *New York Times,* he warned,

> The leaders of the Soviet Union have combined police state methods with ancient imperialism and a will to believe ideological dogma that amounts to religious fanaticism. Having seized control of Russia after World War I and weathered a frightful series of internal strains and emerged more powerful than ever from World War II although at frightful cost, these men are determined to dominate the world. They believe it is their destiny to develop a world revolution and they are utterly convinced they will succeed.[150]

This view that the Soviets were on an ideological crusade to dominate the world contrasts with his earlier view that Soviet expansionist behavior was attributable to traditional Russian insecurity. However, even though he described the Soviets as ruthless and power hungry, he stopped short of characterizing the Soviet program as evil. This is important because it indicates that he still viewed the Cold War as a global political power struggle, not as a battle between the forces of good and evil. There is still no indication that Harriman felt either that U.S. foreign policy should be guided by moral principles or that the Cold War should be viewed in moral terms.

In this *New York Times* article, Harriman still portrayed the most worrisome forms of Soviet power as being derived from military, economic, and subversive methods. His defensive strategy of military preparedness and political vigilance was very consistent with the containment doctrine adopted during the Truman years, although he now placed more emphasis on military forms of U.S. power.[151] He also pushed for more active efforts to expand the global free market to the Third World in order to inoculate it against the influence of communism.

> We have a much more attractive form of civilization to sell than do the communist propagandists, but we must make certain, by expanding the world's economy, developing the underdeveloped areas, and lifting the standard of living of a large part of the world's population, that we practice what we preach and that we eliminate so far as possible those cesspools of poverty which Stalin saw as the breeding ground of future communist adherents.[152]

This statement is consistent with the articles he wrote while commerce secretary in which he argued that the primary U.S. responsibility was to spread the word about the effectiveness of the free market. But in this passage, Harriman wove strands of the market myth into his Cold War policy prescriptions. This is the first direct evidence of market myth influence on Harriman's Cold War worldview.

After laying out a political, military, and economic game plan for containing the Soviets, he concluded that the United States had to "work toward the day when we have created sufficient strength in the free world that once again we may hope to settle our problems with the Russians by negotiation, and expect the Soviet leaders will live up to their promises."[153] Thus even though Harriman was skeptical about the possibility of fruitful negotiations with the Soviets in the short term, he retained his belief, unchanged since his earliest communications from Moscow during World War II, in the efficacy of negotiation as a long-term strategy. This consistent belief makes him virtually unique among important U.S. cold warriors during this period.

GOVERNOR AND CRITIC OF THE NEW LOOK

In the years 1952–1958, Harriman made several attempts to gain elected office nationally and in the state of New York. In 1952 he ran for the Democratic nomination for president and lost by a wide margin. In 1954 he was elected governor of New York. During his term as governor he made another unsuccessful attempt, in 1956, to gain the Democratic presidential nomination, and he kept close watch on Washington and was one of the harshest critics of the Eisenhower administration's foreign policy.

In a 1954 article in *Foreign Affairs,* Harriman criticized the Eisenhower-Dulles approach to Cold War diplomacy. He was particularly critical of the Eisenhower administration's "new look" defense posture with its heavy reliance upon nuclear weapons: "Our overemphasis on atomic and thermonuclear weapons has alarmed even those who are confident that we will never in fact begin a war, since they see that it has decreased the strength of our conventional defense and the effectiveness of our diplomacy."[154] Harriman argued that the reduction in conventional forces had weakened U.S. diplomatic leverage with communists in areas such as Southeast Asia (where at the time the French had just given up their fight against the Vietminh). Here again is the increasing emphasis on military power in Harriman's Cold War worldview, although he did view military power as an important complement to diplomatic efforts to contain communism in Southeast Asia.

In the same article he was also extremely critical of Dulles's handling of negotiations with the Allies over the situation in Southeast Asia. He argued that Dulles's heavy-handed diplomatic approach to the Allies had been an obstacle to securing British and French cooperation in the effort to contain the southward spread of communism in the area.[155]

Later in this article he returned to the subject of the art of diplomacy and pointed out the flaws in Dulles's approach to foreign leaders. He outlined the proper way to negotiate with leaders in the developing world:

> These discussions must always be conducted as between equals, with full understanding and respect for the problems and compulsions of the other, and on the basis that getting a job well done is of mutual benefit. Above all, every effort must be made to avoid putting foreign leaders in the position of bowing publicly to American will. The art of diplomacy lies in inducing the leaders of other countries to come forward publicly with desirable ideas and proposals, rather than obligating them to support and defend policies publicly demanded by a more powerful country in return for favors granted.[156]

This passage highlights nicely the vast difference in diplomatic style between Harriman and Dulles. Whereas Dulles bluntly attempted to browbeat and "convert" foreign leaders to the Western cause, Harriman would first learn the concerns and motivations of the other leaders and then work with them to find a solution that both addressed their concerns and served U.S. interests.[157] For Harriman, such was the essence of the lost art of diplomacy.

This discourse also highlights Harriman's consistent belief in the effectiveness of properly conducted diplomatic negotiations for furthering U.S. interests in the Cold War context. The article also provides an indirect glimpse into Harriman's role conceptions.

Throughout the rest of Harriman's term as governor of New York, he continued to publicly critique Eisenhower and Dulles's handling of the Cold War. In a 1956 article in the *Atlantic Monthly*, he argued that the Soviets had begun to follow a new strategy for global conquest and that the Eisenhower administration had failed to pick up on it.[158] According to Harriman, by 1953

> the Kremlin's drive after World War II—by means of aggression, pressures, threats, and subversion—to extend its control and influence in Europe and the Middle East beyond where its armies were found at the war's end had clearly failed. The West had become so strong and united that further advance by these crude methods was stopped in that area. . . . It was in these circumstances that Stalin shifted the offensive to economic, political and psychological grounds and transferred the center of attention to Asia and other underdeveloped areas.[159]

He went on to argue that the Soviets were masking this new, less overtly aggressive approach behind their self-proclaimed policy of "peaceful co-existence." Specifically, they were taking steps (such as signing the 1955 Austrian treaty) to create a period of reduced superpower tensions during which they could catch up with the West economically while simultaneously using peaceful rhetoric and economic aid packages to lure newly independent states into the communist camp. He criticized the Republican administration for ignoring the importance of development aid as a counter to communist influence in the Third World, and he argued that the belligerent rhetoric of Secretary Dulles played right into the Soviets' attempts to paint themselves as the peacemakers. He concluded that it was not too late to counter the new Soviet strategy, but that would require a complete rethinking of U.S. policy in those areas.[160]

Thus we see Harriman's Cold War worldview changing in response to a noticeable shift in Soviet behavior. Now he placed much more emphasis on diplomatic efforts to hold the moral high ground in the eyes of the world. He also placed more emphasis on developmental and economic aid programs to the developing world as a means of "inoculating" developing countries against communism.

Clearly, part of Harriman's attack on Eisenhower's foreign policy was politically motivated; by spring 1956 he had decided to seek once again the Democratic nomination for president.[161] Even though he had a better organization this time and was able to win the endorsement of Harry Truman, he was unable to defeat Adlai Stevenson for the nomination. Back in Albany, he set his sights on reelection as governor in 1958, but his bid was unsuccessful. Thus in 1959 he found himself unemployed, and he decided to work his way back into the world of diplomacy. In order to increase his stock in the eyes of what he hoped would be a new Democratic administration in 1960, he set out on an extensive schedule of world travel that included long trips to both India and the Soviet Union.[162]

His extended trip through the Soviet Union included a long meeting with Soviet premier Nikita Khrushchev, and this meeting gained him the attention in Washington he was seeking. During the course of the meeting Harriman and Khrushchev discussed both Soviet domestic policy and U.S.-Soviet relations.[163] In an article in *Life* magazine, Harriman described his discussions with Khrushchev in some detail, recounting Khrushchev's threats of war over Berlin and use of military force in support of China's claim to Formosa.[164] But in spite of Khrushchev's bellicosity during the meeting, Harriman concluded the article by reaffirming his belief that the Soviets could be dealt with through the proper use of diplomacy.[165]

INTO THE NEW FRONTIER

As noted, Harriman's meeting with Khrushchev received a great deal of publicity in the United States, particularly in Washington, where he was hoping to impress John F. Kennedy. Kennedy had won the Democratic nomination for president while Harriman was in the Soviet Union. Harriman now sought to earn himself a high-level diplomatic post in the Kennedy administration by advising the candidate on foreign policy issues and by supporting the campaign financially.[166] He hoped that he would be asked to be secretary of state, but that offer never came, and he had to settle for an appointment as ambassador-at-large.

His first big assignment as a member of the Kennedy foreign policy team was to negotiate a settlement of the Laotian crisis, which had been inherited from the outgoing Republican administration.

Under the guidance of John Foster Dulles, the Eisenhower administration had attempted to convert Laos into an anticommunist stronghold on the border of North Vietnam and China. Eisenhower and Dulles were not satisfied with the neutralist Souvanna Phouma regime, which had been in place since the mid-1950s, so they began to provide military aid to anticommunist general Phoumi Nosavan.[167]

In 1959 Nosavan overthrew the neutralist Phouma regime and installed anticommunist Boun Oum as prime minister; this government was in turn overthrown several months later by military supporters of Phouma, who reinstalled him as the head of government. The United States continued to provide aid to the anticommunist Phoumi, who not only fought the communist Pathet Lao but also once again overthrew the neutralist government of Souvanna Phouma.[168] At this point the neutralist forces led by Kong Le teamed up with the communist Pathet Lao, and with substantial military aid from the Soviet Union, they routed Phoumi's anticommunist forces and threatened to take over the entire country. This led the UN Security Council to call for a cease-fire and a convention to settle the Laotian civil war. This was the situation the Kennedy administration inherited in spring 1961.

Having encouraged Kennedy to back a neutralist solution to the Laotian problem, Harriman was sent to negotiate such a solution at the Geneva conference on Laos in May 1961.[169] Harriman's desire to work toward a neutralist solution was in stark contrast to the position taken by Dulles and the Eisenhower administration. It will be recalled that Dulles's attitude toward neutralist regimes was very clear: He believed them to be immoral for refusing to take part in the struggle against world communism. Harriman believed that a neutralist solution was the best that could be obtained by the United States unless it was willing to intervene militarily (which would risk intervention by the North Vietnamese and Chinese).[170]

However, Harriman was not sure that the United States would be able to obtain a viable neutralist settlement given its lack of diplomatic leverage in the regional military context. He therefore prepared a fallback position consisting of a de facto three-way partitioning of the country with the anticommunists controlling the South, the neutralists controlling the central and western regions, and the Pathet Lao controlling the eastern regions. This de facto partitioned Laos would be cosmetically unified by a central coalition government led by the neutralist Phouma but with representatives from all three factions. Harriman was aware that without the dismantling of the Pathet Lao, this solution would only stall their eventual takeover of the entire country.[171] After more than two months of meetings in Geneva, it turned out that Harriman's fallback partition plan was the best settlement he could obtain at the table.[172]

Once he realized that this arrangement was the best he could obtain, he set out to make it work. The first problem he faced was constraining both the communist Pathet Lao and the anticommunist forces of Phoumi Nosavan. He realized that the Soviets were the only party with leverage over the Pathet Lao. He also assumed (perhaps with hindsight incorrectly) that the Soviets wanted the neutralist solution to work. Thus he spent a great deal of time during the Geneva conference trying to persuade the Soviets to rein in the Pathet Lao.[173] He did not limit these efforts to his own personal meetings with Soviet ministers but also he asked President Kennedy to personally pressure Khrushchev.[174] At the same time he realized that the United States would have to assert control over the anticommunist forces, and he used the threat of cutting off U.S. military aid toward this end.[175] He also proposed the use of similar economic leverage to keep the coalition government of Souvanna Phouma on a genuinely neutralist course.[176]

Harriman worked the Laotian crisis in the consummate dealmaker fashion. First he determined what would be the best arrangement he could get at the table given his relatively weak bargaining position. Then, having achieved this agreement, he set out to make all the parties honor the agreement, using whatever forms of leverage he had at his disposal. Thus the Harriman approach was to make lowest-common-denominator deals and make them work without Dulles's concern for overarching moral principles.

By spring 1962 it was obvious that the North Vietnamese had violated the Geneva agreement by staying in eastern Laos, and widespread fighting had broken out between Phoumi Nosavan's anticommunist forces and the Pathet Lao.[177] Even though Harriman's Laos settlement proved to be very fragile, his stock as a member of the Kennedy foreign policy team continued to rise and he was given a new assignment as assistant secretary for Far Eastern affairs.

In spring 1963 he was appointed undersecretary of state for political affairs. Shortly after his appointment he was assigned to lead the team sent to Moscow to negotiate a limited nuclear test ban treaty. Kennedy's instructions to Harriman were that he should initially strive for a comprehensive ban on testing, but if that was not feasible, he should work for a limited ban.[178]

Once again Harriman settled into the role of dealmaker, feeling the Soviets out on the possibility of a comprehensive test ban. He quickly found that they would not agree to any on-site inspections, which effectively killed the prospects for a comprehensive ban.[179] He then set his sights on a limited ban that covered only atmospheric, underwater, and space testing of nuclear weapons. His first obstacle was a Soviet suggestion that a NATO–Warsaw Pact nonaggression agreement be linked to the completion of a test ban agreement. Under instructions to avoid such a linkage, Harriman agreed to mention future nonaggression pact talks in the final test ban treaty communiqué, and this satisfied the Soviets.[180] In only ten days of negotiating, from July 15 to July 25, 1963, the parties reached an agreement on the text of a limited test ban treaty, and Harriman returned to something of a hero's welcome back in Washington.[181]

In the course of negotiating with Khrushchev and other Soviet leaders, Harriman developed his own theory about the Soviets' eagerness to conclude some form of test ban treaty. He realized the Soviets were competing with the communist Chinese for the leadership of the international communist movement. He also realized that if the Chinese refused to sign the treaty (which was a likely outcome), they would be discredited in the eyes of the developing nations. He felt that this competitive impulse was the driving force behind the Soviets' push for the treaty.[182]

This early recognition of the emerging Sino-Soviet split was a significant change in Harriman's worldview and one that would have significant impact on his future policy preferences and negotiating strategies. His early recognition of this split also made him rare, if not unique, among high-level policymakers in the Kennedy administration. Aside from this recognition, however, many of the core beliefs in his worldview remained relatively unchanged. He still believed that the essence of the Cold War competition was a contest between the superpowers to provide the model of development for the Third World.

In an article for the *New York Times Sunday Magazine,* he described this competition.

> It is quite clear that we and the Soviets want—and are working for—quite different worlds. We want a world in which men and nations are free, in which independent states are able to work in their own way toward goals of their own choosing without the intervention of ambitious and aggressive neighbors. . . . The communists are determined to create quite a different world. They are trying to shape the world in their own image. Their emphasis is on atheism, discipline, conformity and rigid central control over every aspect of political, economic and social life. . . . But in spite of this irreconcilability of long-range goals, there are areas of common interest or of possible agreement between us and the Soviets.[183]

Harriman seemed confident that in spite of the grand modeling competition between the superpowers, there were still areas in which they could negotiate their differences. He also seemed confident that the United States and the West could win this competition to shape the developing world because of the self-evident superiority of the market model.

In another article he wrote at length about the triumph of market forces in the rebuilding of war-torn Europe and Japan while simultaneously pointing out the abject failure of centrally controlled industry and agriculture in the Soviet Union and China.[184] He argued that the United States had to convince the peoples of Asia that the market model was superior in all respects to the communist model and that the United States should serve to show how market forces bring dynamism to a society. "One of the matters of basic importance is bringing home to ourselves and to the rest of the world that ours is the true revolution and that we are still involved in a dynamic, changing and revolutionary society. . . . Today revolutions are taking place almost every year changing our dynamic society to fit our growing needs and our responsibilities."[185]

As the previous examples illustrate, Harriman's writings during this period manifested a strong market myth influence. For Harriman it was the success of its special brand of free market system that made the United States a worthy model for the rest of the world. At the philosophical level he viewed the Cold War as a competition between the market model and the communist model for predominance in shaping developing societies.

On the surface, this image of U.S. society as the ideal market model for the rest of the world seems similar to the city-on-the-hill myth, but there are vast differences of meaning between the two. The city-on-the-hill myth holds America's uniqueness as derived from its special relationship with the divine creator and the special moral status that therefore attends America's actions in the world. In the market myth, America's exceptionalism derives not from any divinely transmitted moral quality but rather from the tremendous success of its special brand of market society. According to the market myth, Americans have a right to shape the world not because they are morally superior but because their brand of capitalism has proven itself to work better than any other system.

For Harriman, then, giving the market model a chance to prove itself in the developing world involved actively countering communist tactics such as infiltration, propaganda, and "wars of liberation." Indeed, an analysis of Harriman's personal politico-diplomatic strategy for Southeast Asia reflects just this kind of thinking.

His proposals reflect an emphasis on expanding trade and developmental assistance as instruments of Cold War diplomacy. However, though he focused on the economic and development aspects of the Cold War, he did not ignore the regional military competition that formed the context within which these market societies would have to sprout. Indeed, he viewed economic development strategy and military strategy as being complementary elements in an overall plan to bring market forces to Southeast Asia.

In a May 1962 article for the *New York Times Magazine,* Harriman laid out his preferred politico-diplomatic strategy for Southeast Asia.[186] He pointed to a January 1961 speech by Nikita Khrushchev as evidence that the Soviets had adopted a strategy of using propaganda, economic aid, and other diplomatic instruments to persuade the developing world that communism was the best development model available. He also noted that the Soviets were not relying solely on the merits of the communist model but instead were supporting local military proxies such as the Pathet Lao and North Vietnamese in Laos and the North Vietnamese and Vietcong in South Vietnam.[187]

Harriman argued that the United States had to accept the Soviets' challenge to show which model worked best but that first the United States had to take steps to counter the local communist military proxies so that the economic, psychological, and social competition could take place on a level playing field.

> Our willingness to accept this challenge is based not only on our desire to see the evolutionary struggle in Southeast Asia resolved peacefully, but also on our confidence that communism is not "the wave of the future" and that free peoples can devise more attractive solutions to the problems of Southeast Asia than can communists. The fact is, however, that in Southeast Asia the North Vietnamese are not pursuing "peaceful co-existence" but instead are engaging in armed aggression. Therefore, before we can respond to Khrushchev's challenge on political, social, and economic grounds, it is necessary that the North Vietnamese stop their armed aggression.[188]

Both in Vietnam and in Laos, Harriman drew up similar tactics for creating a level playing field. In both cases he advocated holding international conferences to achieve agreements between the superpowers and between their local proxies that would outlaw the military presence of any outside power in those countries (as well as any superpower military aid to factions there) so that development could take place unhindered.[189] As was discussed earlier, the Laotian conference actually took place, and Harriman pursued an agreement that would achieve these goals. Unfortunately, the International Control Commission set up to enforce the agreement was weak, and the Soviets proved unable or unwilling to rein in the North Vietnamese and the Pathet Lao.

In South Vietnam, however, Harriman was trying to bring about an international agreement that he hoped would extend and strengthen the provisions agreed to at the 1954 Geneva conference on Vietnam, provisions that he had hoped would secure South Vietnam from outside interference so that it could develop into a prototype of a new Southeast Asian market society. In a memorandum to Kennedy, written while he was in Geneva trying to wrap up the Laotian conference, Harriman recommended that he be allowed to make "a direct approach to the U.S.S.R. through our present relationship at the Geneva conference on Laos."[190] The purpose of this approach would be to convince the Soviets to restart talks on Vietnam within the framework of the ongoing Geneva conference on Laos. Harriman argued that the Soviets should be given the message that

> the progress made toward the settlement of the Laos question is meaningless if hostilities continue in neighboring Viet-Nam. The United States believes that an effort should be made to resolve that situation peacefully and end the aggression against SVN. The violation of the 1954 Accords by NVN has caused the United States to support SVN. A peaceful settlement should be built on the foundation of the 1954 Accords. The U.S.S.R. and the United Kingdom . . . should bring together a small group of the powers directly concerned to review the Accords to see how compliance can be secured and how they can be strengthened to meet today's needs.[191]

Harriman based his argument for such an approach on his personal observation that "there are some indications that the Soviet Union would be interested in the establishment of a peaceful and stable situation in Southeast Asia."[192] This was consistent with his strengthening conviction that the Soviets wanted Southeast Asia to serve as a buffer zone against southward expansion by the communist Chinese. According to Harriman, once the Vietnam talks were reopened, the United States would push for an enforceable agreement that stipulated the "cessation of hostilities, and acceptance . . . of the division of Viet-Nam with non-interference of any kind by one side in the other's affairs." There would also have to be "agreement that eventual reunification [of Vietnam] be sought only by peaceful means."[193] Finally, he called for an agreement that would create "mutually advantageous trade and economic relations between North and South Vietnam" and a "strengthened and modernized ICC [International Control Commission]" for enforcement of the agreement.[194]

Harriman concluded the memorandum with an interesting assessment of political conditions inside South Vietnam: "The best any international settlement can do is to buy time. If the government of South Vietnam continues a repressive, dictatorial and unpopular regime, the country will not long retain its independence. Nor can the United States afford to stake its prestige there. We must make it clear to DIEM that we mean business about internal reform."[195] Over the next two years, Harriman would become the symbolic head of a growing faction within the State Department's Far Eastern Bureau that viewed the corrupt Diem government as untenable unless drastic reforms were made.[196] Harriman would continue to push this argument until summer 1963, when he and others would decide that Diem could not be salvaged as an effective leader.

The previous memorandum to Kennedy shows that Harriman believed strongly in a political as opposed to a military approach to the Vietnam problem. Most significant, he believed he could negotiate a diplomatic settlement with the Soviets whereby they would restrain the North Vietnamese from further interference in South Vietnam in return for reduced American involvement there. In hindsight, it appears that Harriman's early settlement proposals might have provided the United States an early way out of the Vietnam quagmire it was slowly wading into. Others in the State Department, such as George Ball, would make similar arguments before the United States became fully committed militarily;[197] however, Harriman's proposal is remarkable in that it appeared as early as 1961.

This proposal fits with a consistent pattern in Harriman's overall Cold War modus operandi. From the end of World War II, when Cold War tensions first began to flare, Harriman's preferred approach was firm negotiation. This is consistent with the entrepreneur representative character's paradigmatic mode of social action and with Harriman's preferred mode of operation during his business career. Of course, we can never know how successful Harriman's attempt at a diplomatic settlement would have been, but it is hard to imagine how the United States or the South Vietnamese could have fared any worse than they eventually did.

As noted, Harriman's belief in the efficacy of negotiating with the Soviets is in marked contrast to the Cold War modus operandi of John Foster Dulles, who viewed sitting down with communists as a compromise of American principles. This contrast is especially stark when one thinks of Dulles's attitude toward the 1954 Geneva conference on Vietnam. He wanted nothing to do with the conference, which he felt would lend legitimacy to communist aggression. Seven years later, Harriman wanted not only to revive the 1954 Geneva framework but to use the Soviets as close diplomatic partners in the enterprise.

Harriman's proposed diplomatic solution to the Vietnam problem was also consistent with his overall philosophical approach to the developing world as evidenced in his writings. He believed that if the United States could find a way to remove communist subversion and military interference in developing societies, the market model of development could compete with the communist model on a level playing field, where it would inevitably win out.[198] This is more evidence of substantial market myth influence on Harriman's Cold War worldview. There was also consistency between Harriman's worldview and his policy preferences and policymaking behavior. In this case his policy preference was to sit down with the Soviets and negotiate a neutral South Vietnam that would be protected from outside interference with its (inevitable free market) development. His policymaking behavior (sending a cable to Kennedy in which he tried to sell this approach) was also consistent with his Cold War worldview as evidenced in his writings on the communist challenge in Southeast Asia.

Harriman's proposal for a "Geneva solution" to the Vietnam problem was ignored by Kennedy, McNamara, Rusk, and others, who by fall 1961 were already focusing on a course of forced nation-building and reinforcing South Vietnam militarily.[199] Harriman would continue to believe that something like his Geneva solution was possible right up to the end of the Johnson administration, and he would pursue it until the bitter end. He was never able to persuade Kennedy of the merits of such a diplomatic approach, who in the remaining two years of his administration followed the advice of McNamara, Rusk, and others who felt that militarily strengthening the South Vietnamese government was the proper course.

As mentioned, by the time he became undersecretary of state for political affairs in spring 1963, Harriman was convinced that the Diem regime could not last unless Diem got rid of his brother, Ngo Dinh Nhu, and reformed his corrupt government.[200] The last straw for Harriman had been Diem's brutal handling of the Buddhist uprising in spring 1963, which led to a string of highly publicized self-immolations by Buddhist monks. By summer 1963, Harriman and other State Department officials including undersecretary of state

George Ball, assistant secretary of state for Far Eastern affairs Roger Hilsman, and Vietnam expert Paul Kattenburg began to argue that the United States should withdraw its support of the corrupt Diem regime unless Diem immediately removed Nhu from the government and began reforms.[201] By late August, Harriman and Hilsman began to argue that the United States should encourage a coup against Diem by anti-Diem generals.[202]

On the weekend of August 24, while President Kennedy and Diem supporters such as McNamara, Rusk, and CIA director John McCone were out of town, Harriman and Hilsman sent a controversial cable to the new U.S. ambassador to Saigon, Henry Cabot Lodge.[203] The cable never explicitly asked Lodge to set the wheels in motion for a coup against Diem, but the cable's essence was that the United States could no longer tolerate Diem's incompetent rule. As McNamara recalls in his memoirs, Lodge nonetheless interpreted the cable as authorization to approach South Vietnamese generals about the possibility of a coup, and he did so.[204]

Many of the Diem supporters in the administration were infuriated by Harriman and Hilsman's sending the cable while they were out of town, considering it an underhanded bureaucratic end run.[205] Such behavior on the part of Harriman was not out of character, however; by this time he had developed a strong reputation as a bureaucratic infighter. Roger Hilsman, Harriman's coconspirator in the Lodge cable episode, confirmed this reputation, saying that Harriman "had more experience in the guerilla warfare of interagency policy battles than anyone else."[206] At any rate, this episode illustrates that Harriman had not lost his jungle-fighting instincts over the years.

In early November 1963 the coup took place, and three weeks later JFK was killed in Dallas. Kennedy's death and the succession of Lyndon Johnson to the presidency brought about a drastic decrease in Harriman's power and influence within the foreign policy making circle.

STRUGGLING FOR INFLUENCE WITH LBJ

Johnson did not hold Harriman in the same confidence and esteem as had previous presidents Roosevelt, Truman, and Kennedy.[207] Another problem was that Harriman's forceful anti-Diem arguments and participation in the Lodge cable during summer 1963 had severely alienated Secretary of State Dean Rusk.[208] When Johnson took over, Rusk became much more powerful due to his strong relationship with the new president, and as a result Harriman became increasingly isolated and was virtually cut out of the policy-making inner circle.[209] Harriman remained isolated and was given marginal diplomatic assignments until finally he was again named ambassador-at-large in February 1965.[210]

Harriman's isolation and loss of policymaking influence hurt him deeply. Longtime friend and colleague Milton Katz describes this period as a low point in Harriman's life.

> Separated from his role in important affairs, he had a horrible feeling that he had no personal significance as a human being. There wasn't an independent, defining sense of who he was. When you got down to the inner core, you found it wasn't filled. There was a vacuum, and he sensed it himself. He was at his best when he had a big job, as he had in World War II, the Marshall Plan, and NATO days, and in a sense he was at his worst when he didn't have a big job, because he was fleeing the vacuum inside him.[211]

Thus Harriman had come to genuinely need to be an important diplomatic player, not just for his ego but for his very identity.

Harriman would struggle for the remainder of Johnson's administration to gain his confidence and to get him to pursue seriously a negotiated settlement in Vietnam. Working from his position as ambassador-at-large, Harriman continued to explore the possibility of a negotiated settlement brokered in cooperation with the Soviet Union. In March 1965, he conveyed to Johnson his belief that the intensifying competition between the Soviets and the Chinese could be exploited by the United States. It could convince the Soviets to help broker a settlement to head off the deepening U.S. military involvement in Vietnam.[212] In private conversations during this time Harriman expressed frustration at Johnson's failure to allow him to explore the potential of a joint U.S.-Soviet brokered settlement. In such a conversation with Arthur Schlesinger Jr., he said, "I wish we had a little more willingness to experiment here. . . . We have got to have a settlement. Why don't we try to do something? Why don't we have some imagination about trying to develop some relationship? [Walter] Lippmann for the first time wrote sensibly about the 'carrot and the stick' in Viet-Nam. We are applying the stick without the carrot."[213]

Of course, while Harriman was trying to develop support for a negotiated settlement, the rest of the administration was rapidly committing the United States to a military course in Vietnam with the start of the bombing campaign known as Operation Rolling

Thunder and with rapid increases in the number of U.S. combat troops being sent to Vietnam.[214] Harriman would not give up, however.

On April 1, 1965, he sent a memorandum to National Security Adviser McGeorge Bundy, who had much more influence with Johnson than Harriman. In this memorandum, Harriman laid out his whole theory about the intensifying Sino-Soviet competition and the potential for the United States to exploit it. He also explained how a settlement could be made attractive to all the communist entities whose interests would be involved, including the Soviets, the North Vietnamese, and the Chinese. He argued that the president should make a "statement to capture world opinion as well as to give the enemy a political and economic carrot."

> The statement should imply that NVN could have a political and economic future free from fear of Chinese domination. It would also imply that NVN would be recognized as a state and would share in the development of the area. . . . The statement should propose a non-aligned area for Indochina with its security guaranteed by the U.S., USSR, Red China etc. This would assure the Soviets against Chicom advance to the south. . . . By the non-aligned set-up, Peiping could have the security of a comfortable buffer area. They might be ready to accept such a buffer, as long as they were sure that there would be no attempt to make it a western bastion. . . . To achieve these purposes, the statement should propose a close economic relationship among the four Indochinese countries. This economic relationship should include free exchange of products, and common development planning. . . . The U.S. should indicate a willingness to be generous, but show no desire to control.[215]

This proposal for a negotiated settlement was vintage Harriman. It was very consistent with his Cold War worldview as expressed in his writings on Southeast Asia since the early 1960s. In fact it was remarkably similar to the settlement proposal he recommended to President Kennedy in November 1961.[216] He premised both proposals on the emerging Sino-Soviet split and the motivation that might give the Soviets to work for a neutral buffer zone in Southeast Asia to block southward expansion by the Chinese. Both proposals also offered an economic "carrot" to the North Vietnamese by suggesting that they could participate in a regional cooperative development plan. Aside from being a carrot to the North Vietnamese, the regional economic development plan also represented continuity in Harriman's belief in the importance of expediting the spread of market forces to Southeast Asia as a way to prevent further communist expansion there. This was consistent with Harriman's Cold War writings from as early as the mid-1950s. This latest proposal was incredibly ambitious, and the negotiations to bring it about would be very complex. The fact that Harriman thought it could be done was also consistent with his strong belief in the effectiveness of diplomatic negotiations for solving difficult problems when handled by the right people (i.e., himself). It was also further indication of Harriman's consistent entrepreneurial style as a statesman.

Although there is no direct evidence that Johnson was persuaded by Harriman's proposal, there is evidence that after Bundy received Harriman's memo, he and McNamara urged Johnson to announce publicly a U.S. willingness to start negotiations on Vietnam.[217] Shortly thereafter, Johnson gave his highly publicized Johns Hopkins speech, where he indicated U.S. willingness to begin negotiations and proposed a huge Mekong valley cooperative development project that would include the North Vietnamese.[218] Thus Johnson's proposal certainly resembled Harriman's in important ways. Later in May, Johnson agreed to a brief bombing pause to see if the North Vietnamese would negotiate, but nothing came of it.[219]

For the next three years, as the Johnson administration became more and more committed to a doomed military effort, Harriman continued to push for a negotiated settlement. Finally, on March 31, 1968, after realizing that the Vietnam War had ruined his presidency, Johnson gave his bombshell speech announcing his decision not to run for the Democratic nomination in the upcoming campaign and to deescalate the war. In that same speech, he designated Harriman as the head of the U.S. negotiating team in peace talks that he hoped could now begin.[220] Thus Harriman finally had the diplomatic assignment he had wanted for years. But it was to be a very frustrating six months for him. When his team left for the peace talks in Paris, Johnson and Rusk gave it very rigid negotiating instructions.[221] And when the White House received a tip in June from Soviet premier Aleksey Kosygin that a bombing halt might stimulate more cooperation from the North Vietnamese, Johnson ignored Harriman's pleas to try it.[222] Defense Secretary Clark Clifford informed Harriman that Johnson could not stand the idea of South Vietnamese cities being shelled while Hanoi went untouched.[223] Harriman came to view this as a lost opportunity of monumental proportions, a chance to commit the Soviets to the point where they might pressure the North Vietnamese to be more cooperative at the bargaining table.[224]

With that June opportunity lost, the Paris peace talks droned on through the summer, and Harriman struggled to find a diplomatic solution within the tight negotiating parameters given him. He finally returned to Washington in January 1969 as the incoming Nixon administration was taking over the negotiating process.

At age seventy-eight, Harriman went into semiretirement. His further involvement in official diplomatic affairs would be limited to participation in several official U.S. delegations to foreign head-of-state funerals and UN conferences. He died in 1986.[225]

CONCLUSION

The foregoing exploration turns up some interesting patterns of continuity in both Harriman's worldview and behavior. The analysis of his childhood and business years produces evidence that Harriman was substantially influenced by his father's career as one of the high-profile American entrepreneurs of the Gilded Age. There is evidence in some of Harriman's communications during this period that he identified rather strongly with his father and wanted to build his own business empire. During the years when he was doing so, he developed a style of business operation characterized by a preference for negotiations and dealmaking over day-to-day administration.

His competitive and aggressive style of dealing with rival business owners carried over into his diplomatic career; he developed quite a formidable reputation among his colleagues as a bureaucratic infighter. With the exception of his years in the Johnson administration, Harriman showed great skill in quickly building a bureaucratic power base with each new assignment.

Unfortunately, examination of Harriman's communications during his diplomatic career yields no solid evidence of his self-conceptions. The evidence of a representative character influence, based as it is on patterns of operational style, is merely suggestive.

The evidence for market myth influence on Harriman and on his Cold War worldview is somewhat stronger. Starting in the late 1940s, Harriman's communications began to show substantial evidence of market myth influence. His speeches and articles during this period contained not only clear market myth imagery but also appealed to the market myth for a collective identity for the American people. In the mid-1950s, Harriman began to weave strands of the market myth into his Cold War worldview and policy prescriptions. He began to argue that the best way to inoculate the developing world against the spread of communism was to show Third World leaders the dynamism and developmental potential of the free enterprise system while expediting the spread of free market forces to those regions.

When Harriman officially reentered the foreign policy bureaucracy at the beginning of the Kennedy administration, his policy preferences and policymaking behavior regarding the situation in Southeast Asia were clearly consistent with his market myth–influenced Cold War worldview as it had evolved since the late 1940s. He proposed diplomatic settlements (to be pursued with the Soviets as cosponsors) that would neutralize Laos and South Vietnam in order to rid them of communist interference and thus allow them to (inevitably?) develop into market societies. Although his efforts regarding Laos failed fairly quickly, he continued to push for this kind of solution for South Vietnam until the end of the Johnson administration.

Another important pattern of continuity in Harriman's worldview was his consistent belief—from his wartime term as ambassador to Moscow to his assignment as head of the U.S. delegation to the Paris peace talks in 1968—in the efficacy of negotiations with the Soviets as a way of influencing their behavior. This belief not only was a constant part of his worldview from the end of World War II until 1968 but also was reflected in his policy preferences and policymaking behavior during this period. This consistency across time and, more important, across many different official assignments is very significant and is also extremely rare (if not unique) among senior policymakers during the high Cold War. Taken together with his operational style of preferring dealmaking and negotiation to administration that spanned his business and diplomatic careers, we have a pattern of continuity that supports the notion of his being influenced by and identifying with the entrepreneur representative character in U.S. culture.

NOTES

1. Walter Isaacson and Evan Thomas, *The Wise Men: Six Friends and the World They Made* (New York: Simon and Schuster, 1986), 19.
2. Ibid., 20.
3. Rudy Abramson, *Spanning the Century: The Life of W. Averell Harriman, 1891–1986* (New York: William Morrow, 1992), 17.
4. Ibid., 16.
5. W. Averell Harriman and Elie Abel, *Special Envoy to Churchill and Stalin: 1941–1946* (New York: Random House, 1975), 37.
6. Abramson, 29.
7. Lloyd Mercer, *E. H. Harriman: Master Railroader* (Boston: Twayne, 1985), 8–9.
8. Ibid., 10.
9. Ibid., 10–25.
10. See Abramson, ch. 2.

11. Abramson, 91.
12. Abramson, 65.
13. Rush Loving Jr., "W. Averell Harriman Remembers Life with Father," *Fortune* (May 8, 1978): 206.
14. Ibid.
15. Ibid., 216.
16. Loving, 198.
17. Isaacson and Thomas, 42–43.
18. Ibid., 49.
19. Abramson, 72–74.
20. Ibid., 79.
21. Isaacson and Thomas, 49.
22. Ibid., 74.
23. Ibid., 92.
24. Abramson, 102–103.
25. Ibid., 107.
26. Loving, 216.
27. Abramson, 108.
28. Ibid., 119.
29. Ibid.
30. V. G. Iden, "W. A. Harriman Seeks and Wins Front Rank in Marine Field," *Marine Review* (March 1921), 124.
31. Ibid., 119–120.
32. Ibid., 121.
33. Abramson, 123–124.
34. Ibid., 124–127.
35. Ibid., 130–131.
36. Iden, 122.
37. Ibid., 122.
38. B. C. Forbes, "New Business Star: Harriman II," *Forbes* (October 30, 1920): 65.
39. Harriman and Abel, 47.
40. Abramson, 142–143.
41. Ibid., 152–153.
42. Ibid., 190–192.
43. Ibid., 202–206.
44. Ibid., 209.
45. E. J. Kahn, "Profiles Plenipotentiary: W. A. Harriman," *New Yorker* (May 10, 1952): 51.
46. Abramson, 219.
47. Kahn, 52.
48. Abramson, 228–231.
49. Ibid., 243.
50. Ibid., 238.
51. Ibid., 239–240.
52. Indeed, the market myth attributes America's remarkable economic development to an almost total lack of government interference with business activity.
53. Abramson, 243.
54. Ibid., 245–249.
55. Ibid., 255–256.

56. Ibid., 259.

57. Ibid.

58. Ibid., 260.

59. Harriman and Abel, 3.

60. Ibid., 270–276.

61. See Harriman speech before the Yale Alumni Association, New York, February 4, 1941, Harriman Papers/Library of Congress (HPLC hereafter), chronological file, January-February 1941, Container 158. See also Harriman speech before the Traffic Club of Washington, February 13, 1941, HPLC, chronological file, January-February 1941, Container 158.

62. Abramson, 266.

63. Harriman memorandum of conversations before leaving Washington for London, March 11, 1941, HPLC, chronological file, March 1–17, 1941, Container 158.

64. Harriman and Abel, 23.

65. Ibid.

66. Harriman cable to President Roosevelt, April 10, 1941, HPLC, chronological file, April 1941, Container 158.

67. Abramson, 283–287.

68. Harriman and Abel, 66.

69. Abramson, 290.

70. Harriman and Abel, 87–93.

71. Abramson, 295.

72. Ibid., 293–294.

73. Abramson, 325.

74. Ibid., 328.

75. Ibid., 331.

76. Harriman and Abel, 146–147.

77. Ibid., 154–155.

78. Ibid., 156–158.

79. Abramson, 340.

80. Harriman and Abel, 156–157.

81. Quoted in Abramson, 341.

82. Harriman and Abel, 228.

83. Abramson, 350–351.

84. Ibid., 350–351.

85. Harriman and Abel, 226–227.

86. Harriman cable to Roosevelt, November 5, 1943, HPLC, chronological file, November 1–7, 1943, Container 170.

87. Harriman telegram to Roosevelt, October 25, 1943, HPLC, chronological file, October 21–25, 1943, Container 170.

88. Harriman memorandum to Hull, November 1, 1943, HPLC, chronological file, November 1–7, 1943, Container 170.

89. Ibid.

90. Harriman memorandum of conversation with Molotov, October 23, 1943, HPLC, chronological file, October 21–25, 1943, Container 170.

91. Harriman cable to Roosevelt, November 5, 1943, HPLC, chronological file, November 1–7, 1943, Container 170.

92. Ibid., 6.

93. Harriman letter to Foreign Minister Molotov, March 10, 1944, HPLC, chronological file, March 9–15, 1944, Container 171.

94. Harriman cable to Hull, March 12, 1944, HPLC, chronological file, March 9–15, Container 171.

95. Harriman telegram to the Department of State, March 13, 1944, HPLC, chronological file, March 9–15, 1944, Container 171.

96. Abramson, 364.

97. Ibid., 378.

98. Harriman cable to Hull, March 10, 1944, HPLC, chronological file, March 9–15, 1944, Container 171.

99. Harriman memorandum of conversations in London, May 2, 1944, HPLC, chronological file, May 1–15, 1944, Container 172.

100. Harriman memorandum of conversation in London, May 4, 1944, HPLC, chronological file, May 1–15, 1944, Container 172.

101. Harriman and Abel, 335–336.

102. Ibid., 336–339.

103. Harriman memorandum of conversation with Molotov, August 11, 1944, HPLC, chronological file, August 8–12, 1944, Container 173.

104. Harriman memorandum of conversation with Clark-Kerr and Molotov, August 17, 1944, 3, HPLC, chronological file, August 17, 1944, Container 173.

105. Ibid., 2.

106. Ibid., 3.

107. Ibid., 7.

108. Ibid., 1.

109. Harriman memorandum of conversation with Clark-Kerr and Molotov, August 17, 1944, "Operation Frantic Bases," 1, HPLC, chronological file, August 16–18, 1944, Container 173.

110. Harriman cable to the president and secretary of state, August 25, 1944, HPLC, chronological file, August 19–25, 1944, Container 173.

111. Ibid.

112. Harriman State Department telegram, October 16, 1944, HPLC, chronological file, October 15–16, 1944, Container 174.

113. Harriman memorandum of conversations with Roosevelt during trip to Washington, D.C., October 21–November 19, 1944, 8, HPLC, chronological file, Container 174.

114. Ibid., 8.

115. Harriman memorandum of conversation with Stalin and Anthony Eden, October 15, 1944, HPLC, chronological file, October 15, 1944, Container 174.

116. Abramson, 389.

117. Ibid., 390–391.

118. Ibid., 391.

119. Minutes of the Polish Commission, Moscow, March 5, 1945, 1–5, HPLC, chronological file, March 3–6, Container 177.

120. Ibid., 3.

121. Harriman and Abel, 419–420.

122. Harriman cable to Stettinius, April 6, 1945, 3, HPLC, chronological file, April 5–9, 1945, Container 177.

123. Ibid., 1.

124. George Kennan, *Memoirs: 1925–1950* (Boston: Little, Brown, 1967), 222–226.

125. See Daniel Yergin, *Shattered Peace: The Origins of the Cold War and the National Security State* (Boston: Houghton Mifflin, 1977), 75–85. Yergin

calls Harriman's early mitigated Cold War worldview the "world bully" perspective because it portrays the Soviets as a bully who might be made to behave if someone would only stand up to them.

126. Harriman cable to Stettinius, April 6, 1945, 3.

127. Kennan, 233.

128. Abramson, 191.

129. Ibid., 395.

130. David McCullough, *Truman* (New York: Simon and Schuster, 1992), 371.

131. Abramson, 395.

132. Yergin, 83.

133. Abramson, 396–397.

134. Ibid., 404.

135. Ibid., 407.

136. Ibid., 414–417.

137. W. Averell Harriman, "Buy American Is a Dead Slogan," *Washington Post* (April 13, 1947): 6.

138. W. Averell Harriman, "The State of the World Economy," draft article written for *United Nations World,* June 17, 1947, 1, HPLC, article file, Container 853.

139. W. Averell Harriman, "America's Faith in Free Enterprise and Individual Initiative," draft article written for the *Financial Times of London,* November 1947, 3, HPLC, article file, Container 853.

140. Ibid., 7.

141. Ibid., 9.

142. Averell Harriman, "U.S. Task in Promoting World Peace," *Commercial and Financial Chronicle* 166, 4624 (August 28, 1947): 9.

143. Averell Harriman, "Our Primary Task—A Healthy Economy," *Commercial and Financial Chronicle* (May 8, 1947): 8.

144. Harriman, "America's Faith in Free Enterprise and Individual Initiative," 11.

145. Abramson, 426.

146. Ibid., 439.

147. Ibid., 444.

148. Ibid., 449–453.

149. Ibid., 463.

150. W. Averell Harriman, draft of "The Road to Peace," *New York Times,* November 1, 1951, 1, HPLC, article file, Container 853.

151. Ibid., 9.

152. Ibid.

153. Ibid., 12.

154. W. Averell Harriman, "Leadership in World Affairs," *Foreign Affairs* 32, 4 (July 1954): 528.

155. Ibid., 528–529.

156. Ibid., 536.

157. For a description of the Dulles diplomatic style with leaders of the developing world, see Chapter 3.

158. W. Averell Harriman, "Danger Unrecognized: The Soviet Challenge and American Policy," *Atlantic Monthly* (April 1956): 42–47.

159. Ibid., 42–43.

160. Ibid., 43–47.

161. Ibid., 533–536.

162. Ibid., 573.
163. Harriman draft of eighth article on Russian trip, HPLC, article file, Container 854.
164. Ibid., 33–34.
165. Ibid., 35.
166. Abramson, 577–581.
167. Ibid., 582–583.
168. Ibid., 583.
169. Harriman memorandum to Kennedy, May 8, 1961, HPLC, chronological mission files, Container 527.
170. Ibid., 2–3.
171. Ibid., 4–5.
172. Abramson, 587.
173. Harriman memorandum of conversation with Soviet minister Pushkin, June 7, 1961, HPLC, chronological file, June 1–16, 1961, Container 527.
174. Harriman memorandum to the president on Laos, September 5, 1961, 1, HPLC, chronological file, September 1961, Container 538.
175. Abramson, 589.
176. Harriman memorandum of White House conversation on Southeast Asia, August 29, 1961, Papers of John F. Kennedy, JFK Library, Boston (hereafter JFK Papers), national security files, Box 217 A, 2.
177. Abramson, 590–591.
178. Ibid., 596.
179. Ibid., 597.
180. Harriman telegram to Rusk, July 13, 1963, 1, HPLC, chronological file, Container 540.
181. Abramson, 599.
182. Harriman telegram to Rusk, July 18, 1963, 1–2, HPLC, chronological file, Container 540.
183. W. Averell Harriman, "An Appraisal of Khrushchev by Harriman," draft of article for *New York Times Sunday Magazine*, August 25, 1963, 1–2, HPLC, article file, Container 854.
184. W. Averell Harriman, "The United States and the Far East," *Annals of the American Academy of Political and Social Science* 342 (July 1962): 90–95.
185. Ibid., 97.
186. W. Averell Harriman, "What We Are Doing in Southeast Asia," *New York Times Magazine*, May 27, 1962, article draft found in HPLC, article file, Container 854.
187. Ibid., 2.
188. Ibid.
189. For a good overview of Harriman's diplomatic strategy for the 1961 Geneva conference on Laos, see Harriman memorandum to Kennedy, May 15, 1961, HPLC, chronological file, May 9–31, 1961, Container 527. For his recommendations for a similar conference on Vietnam see Harriman memorandum to Kennedy, November 11, 1961, JFK Papers, national security files, meetings and memoranda, Box 194.
190. Harriman memorandum to Kennedy, November 11, 1961, 1.
191. Ibid., 2.
192. Ibid., 1.

193. Ibid., 3.
194. Ibid., 4.
195. Ibid., 5.
196. Abramson, 609.
197. For an excellent discussion of Ball's efforts to get LBJ to pursue a diplomatic solution in fall 1964 and early 1965, see Robert S. McNamara, *In Retrospect: The Tragedy and Lessons of Vietnam* (New York: Times Books, 1995), 156–159.
198. Harriman, "What We Are Doing in Southeast Asia," 2.
199. This two-track approach was largely the result of the findings of the Taylor-Rostow mission to Saigon in October 1961. For an excellent discussion of this mission, its findings, and its impact on U.S. policy in Vietnam see David Halberstam, *The Best and the Brightest* (New York: Penguin Books, 1972), ch. 9.
200. Abramson, 616.
201. Ibid., 619–623.
202. Harriman memorandum of conference with the president on Vietnam, August 28, 1963, JFK Papers, national security files, meetings and memoranda, Box 316.
203. McNamara, 52–55.
204. Ibid., 55–56.
205. Ibid., 55.
206. Roger Hilsman, *To Move a Nation: The Politics of Foreign Policy in the Administration of John F. Kennedy* (New York: Dell Books, 1968), 139.
207. Abramson, 627–632.
208. Ibid., 621–623.
209. Ibid., 632.
210. Ibid., 635.
211. Quoted in Abramson, 631.
212. Harriman memorandum to President Johnson, March 15, 1965, 3, HPLC, chronological file, March 1965, Container 567.
213. Harriman memorandum of conversation with Arthur Schlesinger Jr., March 20, 1965, 1, HPLC, chronological file, March 1965, Container 567.
214. For an excellent discussion of this see McNamara, ch. 7.
215. Harriman memorandum to Bundy, April 1, 1965, 2–3, HPLC, chronological file, April 1965, Container 567.
216. Harriman memorandum to Kennedy, November 11, 1961.
217. McNamara, 180–181.
218. Seyom Brown, *The Faces of Power: United States Foreign Policy from Truman to Clinton* (New York: Columbia University Press, 1994), 192–193.
219. Ibid., 193–194.
220. Abramson, 657.
221. Ibid., 658–660.
222. Harriman memorandum of review, December 14, 1968, HPLC, trips/missions file, Paris peace talks, Container 562.
223. Ibid., 3.
224. Ibid., 1.
225. Abramson, 675–696.

5

Robert McNamara: Cold War Manager

Robert S. McNamara was clearly one of the most influential foreign policy advisers in both the Kennedy and Johnson administrations. There is also little doubt that he was one of the most influential secretaries of defense ever to hold that position. In his eight years at the head of the Department of Defense, he revolutionized the way business was conducted at the Pentagon, rationalizing its worldwide operations with the same kinds of statistical control methods used in the management of huge corporations. In addition to forever changing the way the Pentagon was run, he overhauled U.S. nuclear weapons doctrine and strategy.

Given these impressive achievements, it is somewhat sad that many people remember McNamara simply as one of the principal architects of America's tragic military involvement in Vietnam. There is no doubt that McNamara was one of the key participants in the many decisions that led the United States into that quagmire.[1] But ironically, it was McNamara's growing doubts about the ongoing war that put him at odds with Lyndon Johnson and brought about his not-so-subtle reassignment to the World Bank in late 1967.

Both Kennedy and later Johnson were greatly impressed by McNamara's overpowering intellectual and managerial style. Before going to Washington, McNamara's upbringing, education, and tremendous drive had channeled his extraordinary intellectual talents toward a career at the top of Ford Motors. But almost as soon as he reached the presidency at Ford he was summoned to Washington by a young senator from Massachusetts one year his junior who had himself just scaled the pinnacle of American politics.

In *The Best and the Brightest*, David Halberstam describes how McNamara's pragmatic operating style fit so perfectly with the leitmotif of the Kennedy administration and made him an indispensable member of the Kennedy team.

He was very much a man of the Kennedy administration. He symbolized the idea that it could manage and control events in an intelligent, rational way. Taking on a guerilla war was like buying a
sick foreign company; you brought your systems to it. He was so
impressive and loyal that it was hard to believe . . . that anything
he took command of could go wrong. He was a reassuring figure
not just to both presidents he served but to the liberal good community of Washington as well; if McNamara was in charge of something he would run it correctly; if it was a war, it would be a good
war.[2]

THE SHAPING OF A MANAGER

Robert Strange McNamara was born June 9, 1916, in San Francisco,
California.[3] His father, Robert James McNamara, was a sales manager of a wholesale shoe distributor and the son of Irish Catholic
immigrants. His mother, Claranel Strange, was from a middle-class
Methodist family with Scottish and English ancestry. When McNamara was seven, his family moved into a middle-class neighborhood
in Oakland, partially because the location offered good public
schools for young Robert and his younger sister, Margaret.[4]

Young Bobby, as he was called as a child, was noticed very early
on for his intelligence by his parents and teachers. In the classic
American middle-class pattern, his parents (particularly his
mother) raised him to be relatively free of emotion and drove him
relentlessly to achieve in school.[5] In his memoirs, McNamara described the impact of this early parental pressure on the course of
his life. "My drive for scholastic excellence reflected the fact that
neither my mother nor my father had gone to college (my father
had never gone beyond eighth grade), and they were fiercely determined that I would. Their resolve shaped my life."[6] McNamara
responded to this pressure by excelling in school and by competing
aggressively in childhood athletic activities.

After four years of overachieving in high school, McNamara en-
rolled at the University of California at Berkeley, starting in fall
1933. McNamara biographer Deborah Shapley argues that his studies and experiences during those years at Berkeley were crucial for
the formation of his identity.[7] The Berkeley intellectual milieu was
dominated by the growing belief in rationalism and scientific methods that was taking the country by storm in the 1930s.[8] Building on
his strong high school math background, McNamara quickly
learned how to use statistical techniques and formal logic to build
persuasive arguments.[9] The value of these techniques was much
more than merely instrumental to the young McNamara, however.

McNamara told Shapley that during those college years, attacking problems with quantitative analysis gave him a sense of personal style and identity.[10] Majoring in economics, McNamara was named to Phi Beta Kappa after his sophomore year and went on to become a member of the leading secret societies at Berkeley, all of which made him a leading member of the student body.[11] Nonetheless, Berkeley's biggest contribution to McNamara's intellectual development seems to have been his discovery of quantitative analysis. Shapley sums up the importance of this discovery. "He had discovered an internal identity, bolstered by his talent for numbers and logic. To a young man growing up in a working-class household, this was not just any talent. His facility matched the forward direction of the age, possibly yielding him the special insights in the new gospel of rationalism that some Cal faculty preached."[12]

In his memoirs, McNamara reflected on the importance of his Berkeley experience as a shaping influence.[13] He emphasized the impact of his introduction to logic and quantitative analytical techniques.

> The defining moments in my education . . . came in my philosophy and mathematics curricula. The ethics courses forced me to begin to shape my values; studying logic exposed me to rigor and precision in thinking. And my mathematics professors taught me to see math as a process of thought—a language in which to express much, but certainly not all, of human activity. It was a revelation. To this day I see quantification as a language to add precision to reasoning about the world. Of course it cannot deal with issues of morality, beauty, and love, but it is a powerful tool too often neglected when we seek to overcome poverty, fiscal deficits, or the failure of our national health programs.[14]

We can see that McNamara's undergraduate years at Berkeley had a profound effect on his epistemological orientation toward the world. There he developed a high degree of confidence both in his own reasoning ability and in the power of quantitative analytical methods for helping policymakers understand a complex social reality and solve complex problems. This quotation supports Shapley's conclusion that while at Berkeley, McNamara began to build an identity around his newfound analytical powers. We also see in this passage the first evidence of an epistemological hubris similar to that which Alasdair MacIntyre argues is used to justify managerial authority within the modern corporation (although without the appeal to covering laws).[15]

On graduating from Berkeley, McNamara was accepted into the graduate program at the prestigious Harvard Business School in fall

1937. At Harvard, McNamara was introduced to the new approach to corporate management known as financial or statistical control. This was a revolutionary new method of corporate accounting that allowed for all aspects of the production and distribution process (i.e., production labor, materials, transportation, etc.) to be assigned specific cost values and to be inventoried statistically using these cost values.[16] This information could then be compared with statistical information about income from sales to give managers a precise measurement of profits and rates of return. This in turn gave corporate managers the ability to measure precisely the performance of corporate divisions and to make future cost and income projections.[17] Needless to say, McNamara found himself perfectly suited to learning this new statistical control approach to managing huge corporations, and this facility was reflected by his excellent grades at Harvard. In her interviews with McNamara's Harvard classmates Shapley learned that they were in awe of McNamara's analytical abilities.[18] It seems that McNamara picked up at Harvard where he had left off at Berkeley. He mastered statistical control techniques with lightning speed and used them with an amazing ability to find optimal solutions to hypothetical management problems.[19]

McNamara finished Harvard with a distinguished record and went home to work for Price Waterhouse in San Francisco as an accountant. But he was unhappy with this simple job and after a year accepted an instructor position at Harvard.[20] Before returning to Cambridge, he married his longtime girlfriend, Margy Craig. He taught at Harvard for a year and a half, until the United States entered World War II, when he became restless to join the war effort.[21] His chance came when General Hap Arnold approached the Harvard Business School about having some of its instructors install a statistical control system for the Army Air Forces, which he commanded. With the U.S. entry into the war, the AAF was forced to expand instantly, and the generals had no way to keep track of and allocate the thousands of new flight crews and new airplanes and operate the huge maintenance infrastructure. With this new statistical control system they could manage the vast resources of the AAF the same way corporate chiefs managed mammoth manufacturing firms.[22] McNamara had his first opportunity to apply the methods of statistical control to a real-world management problem, and he went into the project with energy and confidence.[23]

Although developing a statistical control system for an ongoing and ever-expanding air war was a huge challenge, McNamara and colleagues from Harvard were up to the task of teaching hundreds of AAF officers the system while simultaneously getting the reporting system up and running.[24] First McNamara spent time developing the system in England, where the air war against Germany was just getting under way; then, after a stint in Kansas monitoring the manufacture of B-29s, he was assigned to the Twentieth Bomber Command in the India-Burma-China theater of operations. There he monitored the dangerous transport of bombers, crews, and supplies from India over the Himalayas into China (a route known as the Hump), where they would be readied for bombing operations against Japan.[25] From India he went to the Pacific in 1944 to monitor the mounting bombing campaign against Japan; he was then transferred briefly to the Pentagon and then to Wright Field in Ohio, which had become the headquarters of the worldwide statistical control operation.[26]

At the end of the war, the statistical control operation was deemed a huge success by the army, and McNamara and his colleagues were decorated for a job well done. McNamara and his fellow statistical control officers came away from their war experience in awe of the seemingly unlimited power and control that this new system could put into the hands of leaders of large bureaucratic organizations.[27]

With the war over, McNamara had intended to return to his teaching career at Harvard, but his wife, Margy, was suddenly stricken with polio and paralyzed. They faced the prospect of huge medical bills that would devour his meager teaching salary. He was approached by Charles Thornton, who had been one of the leaders of the statistical control team in the army. Thornton's idea was to market the brightest members of the statistical control team en masse to various corporations that were in financial trouble and therefore in need of a statistical control system.[28] After exploring several smaller corporations, Thornton focused on the financially troubled Ford Motor Company, which was in dire need of a new management system. He made a deal with Ford to hire his group of ten. McNamara, who was considered one of the brightest of the "whiz kids," as they would come to be called, was offered a salary of $12,000 a year, more than four times his teaching salary at Harvard.[29]

THE FORD YEARS

McNamara's wife gradually recovered completely, and he and the other whiz kids settled in to bring the struggling Ford empire back to financial health. The task was monumental. The automaking giant was lurching through the transition from war- to peacetime production with an organizational scheme riddled with duplication and poorly defined lines of responsibility.[30]

Thornton and the others set out to create a statistical control system that would provide the top-level managers with detailed cost and income inventories. The precise cost and profit projections made possible by this information could then guide their all-important production and marketing plans.[31] McNamara was first assigned to head the company's planning and financial analysis office; in 1949 he was promoted to controller of the firm.[32] In these positions he was given access to all of the cost and sales statistics that filtered up from the bottom of the organization. He became a master at interpreting those reams of statistics (without the aid of computers) and used his interpretations to give sage planning and financial advice to the top managers of the company.[33] It was in these meetings with Ford's upper-level management that he developed his highly impressive yet intimidating intellectual style of rattling off endless streams of seemingly unimpeachable statistics (without notes) to bolster his arguments.[34] John Byrne describes how McNamara used this aggressive debating style at Ford.

> He would fire away, one question after another until people were overwhelmed, if not terrified. McNamara's personal style was to rush through everything at high speed, cowing subordinates and peers with how much he knew and how much they didn't. . . . He was so dominating at meetings that people were afraid to contradict him and tended not to say what they really thought. If you took issue with Bob, you had to be as ready as he was to do battle with a flurry of facts and numbers. Bob did not tolerate fools gladly.[35]

This style would become his trademark in the Kennedy-Johnson years and would create many enemies in those administrations. It flowed naturally from his belief that there was virtually no problem he could not solve as long as he was armed with the relevant, quantitatively coded "facts" of the situation. Once he had access to those "facts," proper rational and objective analysis would lead to the optimal solution. Byrne provides an excellent description of his problem-solving approach at Ford.

> He brought to the job a tremendous discipline. It had to do with the way Bob thought through a problem, lusting for every detail, then assembling all the facts and coming up with as logical and rational a decision as possible, a decision based solely on the numbers. . . . It required dispassionate analysis devoid of intuition or

> emotion or of that gut feel so many of the auto men often relied on to base their decisions. . . . Those who "felt," those whose "gut" led them to a conclusion were scorned and scolded, compelled to base their decisions on imperative fact.[36]

He had begun to believe in his analytical powers and the power of statistics in his undergraduate and graduate years. His wartime experience in setting up the AAF statistical control system strongly reinforced those beliefs. Now his experience at Ford was showing him just how much bureaucratic power and influence this statistically based knowledge could give him. But statistics did not always suit his purpose, and during his time at Ford, it seems he developed a disturbing habit of altering them either to support his argument or to remain in agreement with superiors he wanted to please, such as Henry Ford II.[37] Perhaps this tendency of the professional McNamara to stifle personal doubts or convictions in order to remain in good graces with superiors—and thus to remain in power—could be characterized (in a superficial sense) as loyalty. Whatever the case, it would stay with him throughout his tenure as secretary of defense.

From his position as controller in 1949 McNamara used his statistics and his loyalty to Ford to gain power in the company and rise through the upper-management ranks until he was named president of Ford Motors on November 9, 1960. Ironically, this was one day after Kennedy was elected president. A month after he had been made president, he was contacted by Kennedy's transition team and asked to meet with the president-elect about the possibility of his serving as secretary of defense. After a couple of meetings with Kennedy, McNamara accepted the nomination for the position on December 13, 1960.[38]

An examination of McNamara's biography up to this point yields some very definite patterns. His experiences at Berkeley and Harvard and later in the AAF and at Ford gave him tremendous confidence in both his own reasoning abilities and ability to use quantitative analytical techniques for solving complex problems. His manipulation of a complex bureaucratic organization using these techniques is the paradigmatic mode of social action of the manager representative character.

MacIntyre argues that the manager's claim to effectiveness is based on the "stock of knowledge by means of which organizations and social structures can be molded."[39] In fact, McNamara's confidence in the "facts" and his debating style are almost a textbook example of this orientation. As noted earlier, he learned how to dominate policy debates by forcefully showing his mastery of "the numbers."[40] He also exhibited the "factual" and "quantitative" attitudes that, according to Sumner, characterize the "managerial mind."[41] Before he even joined the executive corps at Ford, McNamara was clearly exhibiting many of the key attributes of the manager representative character. And his climb up the corporate ladder at Ford only reinforced these attributes.

MANAGING THE PENTAGON

Upon taking office as secretary of defense in January 1961, McNamara set out to implement Kennedy's campaign promises to enlarge and revitalize the nation's defenses. His first task was to close the "missile gap" that the Kennedy campaign alleged had widened during the later Eisenhower years. Soon after taking office, however, he received intelligence reports indicating that no such gap existed and that in fact the United States was substantially ahead in numbers of nuclear missiles.[42] Nonetheless, McNamara began to expand U.S. nuclear forces to counter the growing (albeit still numerically inferior) Soviet nuclear forces. Almost immediately he ordered a substantial expansion of the navy's Polaris SLBM (submarine launched ballistic missile) program, an expansion of the air force's Minuteman ICBM (intercontinental ballistic missile) program, and an increase in the percentage of manned bombers to be on constant fifteen-minute alert.[43]

Whereas the force expansions themselves were significant, the way that McNamara decided on these changes is even more interesting. Upon arriving at the Pentagon, McNamara was dismayed to find that rational planning of defense programs had been rendered nearly impossible by interservice rivalry and pork barrel political pressures in Congress.[44] Coming fresh from Ford, where he had been instrumental in utilizing the methods of financial control to rationalize planning and operations, McNamara decided that a similar system was needed at the Department of Defense. He set out to develop a comprehensive system for force planning and budgeting of defense programs.

His comptroller at the Pentagon, Charles Hitch, had previously worked at the RAND Corporation and had been working on developing just such a system.[45] When Hitch presented his system (the Planning-Program Budgeting System, or PPBS), McNamara ordered that it be set up at the Pentagon as quickly as possible. Using the proven methods of statistical or financial control, McNamara would be able to assess accurately the cost effectiveness of individual weapons programs. This would allow him to recommend to the president and Congress the optimal mix of weapons systems to provide the necessary combat or deterrent capability for the least amount of defense dollars.[46]

Decisions on which weapons systems to fund would no longer be based on irrational political wrangling between the military services or between members of Congress looking out for their districts. McNamara later described his new system to a congressional subcommittee: "The basic objective of the management system we are introducing and trying to operate, is to establish a rational foundation as opposed to an emotional foundation for the decisions as to what size force and what type of force this country will maintain."[47] In a later description of PPBS he argued that he was "convinced that this approach not only leads to far sounder and more objective decisions over the long run but yields as well the maximum amount of effective defense we can buy with each defense dollar expended."[48] Thus McNamara picked up at the Pentagon where he had left off at Ford in his quest to harness the quantitative techniques of financial control to rationally guide the behavior of huge bureaucratic enterprises.

In his memoirs McNamara indicated that he viewed the task of guiding the Defense Department as being basically no different from managing Ford.

> I had no patience with the myth that the Defense Department could not be managed. It was an extraordinarily large organization, but the notion that it was some sort of ungovernable force was absurd. I had spent fifteen years as a manager identifying problems and forcing organizations—often against their will—to think deeply and realistically about alternative courses of action and their consequences. My team and I were determined to guide the department in such a way as to achieve the objective the president had set: security for the nation at the lowest possible cost.[49]

He went on to say that his approach to managing the Pentagon flowed from a basic philosophy of management he had developed since Harvard.

> This all reflected an approach to organizing human activities that I had developed at Harvard and applied in the army during the war and later at Ford. . . . Put very simply it was to define a clear objective for whatever organization I was associated with, develop a plan to achieve that objective, and systematically monitor progress against the plan. Then, if progress was deficient, one could either adjust the plan, or introduce corrective action to accelerate progress.[50]

McNamara conceived of his role at the top of the Pentagon as that of a manager. His description of his management philosophy reads like the summary of the rational actor model of decision-making in an undergraduate international relations textbook. It also indicates an extreme degree of confidence in his ability to monitor and control the behavior of the largest bureaucracy in the world. Here again we see the paradigmatic mode of social action of the manager character: manipulation of resources of the bureaucratic organization until the optimal resource mix is found. He also exhibited the manager character's myopic moral stance: Whatever works is good.

During his first year in office, McNamara used his new system to show that future increases in strategic nuclear forces should be in ICBMs rather than in manned bombers (which were the sacred cow of the air force) because the ICBMs provided more mission capability for less money.[51] This meant that the air force's new pet bomber project, the B-70, would need to be discontinued (although not, as it turned out, without a fight from supporters in the air force and in Congress).[52]

EMERGING FOREIGN POLICY ADVISER

McNamara was quick to take charge of the Pentagon and defense policy; his emergence as a foreign policy adviser to the president came a bit more slowly. His performance as an adviser to Kennedy during the run-up to the Bay of Pigs fiasco was less than exemplary. He is on record as having doubts that the invasion could succeed without substantial U.S. military involvement, but he voted to go ahead with the operation when Kennedy asked for a final show of hands from his advisers.[53]

It wasn't until the Berlin crisis of summer 1961 that McNamara really surfaced as an influential voice.among Kennedy's foreign policy advisers. After Khrushchev had presented Kennedy with an ultimatum on Berlin at the June 1961 Vienna summit, Kennedy put his foreign policy team to the task of coming up with the best way for deterring the Soviets from violating U.S. and Western interests in Berlin.[54] Working with former secretary of state Dean Acheson and others on a Berlin task force that he chaired, McNamara carefully analyzed the relevant military balance in Berlin.

The task force quickly discovered that existing Western plans to combat a Soviet move on Berlin relied heavily on an early use of tactical nuclear weapons, and they set out to remedy this immediately. In addressing this overreliance on nuclear weapons, the group began to develop the outlines of what would come to be known as the doctrine of "flexible response."[55] Although McNamara and Acheson agreed that the best way to deter the Soviets in Berlin was to vastly increase U.S. and Western conventional capabilities as a show of resolve, they disagreed on what form the show of resolve should take.

Acheson argued for an immediate declaration of national emergency and early call-up of the reserves, and McNamara argued that the president should put off asking Congress for a declaration of national emergency and should initiate the call-up of reserves in phases rather than immediately. McNamara believed that the delayed mobilization of reserves would preserve flexibility of action (coupled with the conventional forces buildup) while still sending a message of resolve to the Soviets.[56] His concern was that the U.S. signal to the Soviets be sufficiently firm yet not overly provocative, and eventually his argument persuaded Kennedy that delayed reserve mobilization was the best course.[57]

Eventually, in August 1961, the Soviets solved their German emigration problem by building the Berlin Wall, but Khrushchev never carried through on his threat to sign a treaty with the East Germans, which would effectively have negated Western rights in West Berlin. Looking back on the summer 1961 Berlin crisis, McNamara became convinced that supplementing the U.S. nuclear deterrent with improved conventional capabilities had sent an effective signal to the Soviets and had led to Khrushchev's backing down from his earlier ultimatum.[58] This belief in the efficacy of manipulating the military context of a superpower confrontation in order to influence the Soviets' behavior would continue to guide McNamara's policy prescriptions in the years to come.

It is not really until 1962 that we begin to see McNamara making statements about the world political situation that are broad enough to allow a glimpse of his Cold War worldview. In most of his statements during this period, McNamara laid out what he considered to be the Soviets' strategy for extending their influence in the world, and then he put forth his preferred counterstrategy. In a February 1962 speech to the Fellows of the American Bar Foundation, McNamara began by warning of Khrushchev's intention to support and foster "wars of national liberation" throughout the developing world. "What Chairman Khrushchev describes as wars of liberation and popular uprisings, I prefer to describe as subversion and overt aggression. We have learned to recognize the pattern of this attack. It feeds on conditions of poverty and unequal opportunity, and it distorts the legitimate aspirations of peoples just beginning to realize the reach of human potential."[59]

He argued that the Soviets had adopted this low-level conflict strategy because they realized that high-level conflict between the superpowers would probably end in general nuclear war. And although they wanted to avoid nuclear war, they wished "to keep alive the threat of nuclear war as a means of intimidation, a form of blackmail intended to discourage the free world from resisting Communist encroachment at other levels."[60] Thus we begin to see McNamara's conceptualization of the ladder of escalation that forms the basis of the flexible-response strategy.

Having laid out the Soviet military threats that confronted the United States across the spectrum of conflict intensity, McNamara argued directly for flexible response as the proper strategy for dealing with those threats.

> But it is equally clear that we require a wider range of practical alternatives to meet the kind of military challenges that Khrushchev has announced he has in store for us. Unless the Free World has sufficient forces organized and equipped to deal with these challenges at what appears to be the highest appropriate levels of conflict, we could be put into difficult situations by the communists. In such situations we could lose by default; or we could lose by limiting our response to what appears to be the highest appropriate level—but a level at which we may be inferior; or we could resort to thermonuclear war—the level at which we are superior—but at costs which could be out of proportion to the issues and dangers involved.[61]

Here we see McNamara conceptualizing the superpower confrontation as though it were a strategic game-theory scenario, reflecting the influence the game theorists from the RAND corporation had on his thinking during this period.[62] For him, the proper U.S. response to this strategic escalation and bargaining game was to ensure the ability to respond to Soviet uses of force at the appropriate level of conflict intensity (or on the appropriate rung on the ladder of escalation). For if the United States relied only on nuclear deterrence, it would become vulnerable to "salami slice" tactics, repeated acts of aggression so low on the scale of intensity that a nuclear deterrent against those acts was simply not credible.

> There is no need however, for the Free World to be vulnerable to this dangerous Soviet [salami slice] tactic. An adequate level of non-nuclear military strength will provide us with the means to meet a limited challenge with limited forces. We will then be in a

position of being able to choose, coolly and deliberately, the level
and kind of response we feel most appropriate in our own best interests; and both our enemies and friends will know it.[63]

Implicit in this argument is the notion that if the United States responded at the proper level of conflict intensity, the Soviets would
behave "rationally" and deescalate the conflict.

One thing that stands out immediately in these statements is
McNamara's tendency to focus on the military aspects of the Cold
War. This is no doubt partly a function of role constraints.[64] As Pentagon chief, his primary responsibility was defense policy. This
focus also makes sense because the military dimensions of the Cold
War were one aspect of U.S foreign policy over which he could
exert some degree of personal control. There is little evidence that
McNamara put much faith in the use of diplomatic negotiations to
resolve superpower conflicts. He did seem to think the Soviets
could be bargained with, albeit at gunpoint.

McNamara did not directly address the question of whether
U.S. foreign policy should be guided by a set of overarching moral
or geostrategic principles. But his emphasis on maintaining as wide
a range of response options as possible suggests that his policy recommendations were not based on such principles. Further, he
viewed moral principles as constraining U.S. behavior in the Cold
War while not similarly constraining the Soviets or the rest of the
communist bloc:

> To the extent that we deter the Communists from initiating larger
> wars, we may anticipate even greater efforts on their part in so-
> called "wars of national liberation." . . . We must face up to the
> fact that the Communists have a distinct advantage over the
> democracies in this type of conflict. They are not inhibited by our
> ethical and moral standards—political assassination, robbery,
> arson, subversion, bribery are all acceptable means to further
> their ends. We still have a long way to go in devising and imple-
> menting effective countermeasures against these techniques.[65]

Thus although McNamara considered moral principle to be a factor
influencing U.S. foreign policy, it was a negative constraint (putting
the United States at a disadvantage in the Cold War) rather than a
positive guide for the formulation of that policy (as conceptualized
by John Foster Dulles).

Up to this point there is no direct evidence (i.e., mythical imagery contained in statements) that his Cold War worldview was influenced by any of the three societal-level myths. However, two elements of McNamara's worldview are consistent with the pragmatic

myth. His discussion of the merits of flexible-response doctrine with its emphasis on adaptability in the face of Soviet aggression is very much in the spirit of this myth. And the implication that the United States would be more effective in its prosecution of the Cold War if it were unhindered by moral principle does not have to be expanded very far before one arrives at the vulgarized pragmatic dictum that "whatever works is good."

MANAGING THE CUBAN MISSILE CRISIS

The next major confrontation with the Soviets after the 1961 Berlin crisis was the Cuban missile crisis. The Soviet attempt to secretly put offensive nuclear missiles in Cuba was discovered by U-2 reconnaissance overflights on October 14, 1962. McNamara first found out about the Cuban missiles the evening of October 15, and working with his Pentagon subordinates, he immediately began making the necessary preparations for U.S. military operations against the missiles.[66] The first meeting with Kennedy to discuss the missiles was held on Tuesday, October 16.[67]

Initially McNamara argued that the United States should launch a quick airstrike against the missile sites (before the missiles could be made operational), as well as the Cuban airfields, some of which contained Cuban air defense forces and some of which contained Soviet bombers that were capable of carrying nuclear bombs to targets in the southeastern United States. He argued further that the United States should be prepared to follow the comprehensive airstrikes with an invasion of Cuba.[68]

Following the Tuesday morning meeting, McNamara spent the afternoon conferring with his subordinates at the Pentagon, including the Joint Chiefs of Staff, and he began to think through the possible consequences of the military actions he had recommended that morning. At lunch he and his deputy, Roswell Gilpatric, played an informal wargame, going through the likely Soviet responses to possible U.S. military actions against the missiles in Cuba. This exercise convinced McNamara that some form of blockade would be the best initial option because it would not sharply provoke the Soviets and would preserve all other U.S. military options.[69] It also reveals McNamara's continued belief in his ability to manage the most emotionally intense Cold War confrontation by conducting rational and objective analyses of possible escalatory scenarios.

At a Tuesday evening meeting, McNamara presented three separate courses of action to the group: a public diplomatic protest of the Soviet moves in Cuba (suggested by Rusk in the morning meeting), a comprehensive airstrike followed by an invasion, and a middle course consisting of open, continuous surveillance of the island together with a blockade to prevent further offensive systems from reaching Cuba.[70] He quickly discounted Rusk's diplomatic option because, in his words, it "seemed likely to lead to no satisfactory result, and it almost stops subsequent military action."[71] He disapproved of the diplomatic option because if taken it would (by alerting the Cubans and Soviets to U.S. knowledge of the missiles and giving them a chance to hide or speed up activation of the missiles) preclude taking other more forceful actions later.

Having argued against Rusk's diplomatic option, he then warned of the possible consequences of the military attack options (airstrike and invasion):

> It seems to me almost certain that any one of these forms of direct military action will lead to a Soviet military response of some type some place in the world. It may well be worth the price. Perhaps we should pay that. But I think we should recognize that possibility, and moreover, we must recognize it in a variety of ways. We must recognize it by trying to deter it, which means we probably should alert SAC, probably put on an airborne alert, perhaps take other alert measures.[72]

McNamara's argument for increasing the alert status of U.S. nuclear forces is another subtle example of his preference for manipulating the military context of a confrontation in order to influence Soviet behavior.

After discussing the escalatory dangers associated with direct military action against the Cuban missiles, McNamara advocated the middle course of intensive aerial surveillance combined with a blockade (to stop additional offensive systems from reaching the island) and an ultimatum to the Soviets stating that any attack on the United States by offensive weapons in Cuba would be treated as an attack by the Soviets and would bring a retaliatory attack on the Soviet Union.[73] McNamara had become a strong advocate for the "quarantine" strategy because it preserved maneuvering room for both the Soviets and the United States.[74]

The following Monday night, October 22, President Kennedy announced to the American people the discovery of the missiles in Cuba. He also announced the decision to follow McNamara's strategy, and he passed on the ultimatum to Khrushchev that McNamara had suggested. During the next several days McNamara maintained a very close supervision of the U.S. navy's implementation of the quarantine strategy because he was afraid that the navy commanders did not understand the delicate political nature of the operation.[75] McNamara shared Kennedy's concern that the blockade be implemented in as unprovocative a fashion as possible.[76] He wanted to create as many opportunities as possible for the Soviets to act "rationally" and back down without seeming to be humiliated. Much to his dismay, the navy commanders wanted to run the blockade according to long-standing naval regulations, which called for—among other things—drawing the quarantine line hundreds of miles off the Cuban coast (giving the Soviets less decision time) and forcing Soviet submarines to surface.[77]

McNamara's micromanagement of the quarantine operations greatly disturbed Chief of Naval Operations George Anderson. After a confrontation with Anderson over the quarantine, McNamara resolved to see that Anderson would not be reappointed as chief of the navy, a resolution he carried through on the following year.[78] The following Sunday, the crisis was resolved as a result of Khrushchev's promise to remove the offending missiles in return for Kennedy's agreement not to invade Cuba (supplemented by a secret agreement for the United States to remove Jupiter missiles in Turkey).

McNamara's later statements indicate that he was favorably impressed by the effectiveness of the quarantine strategy with its preservation of escalation options and its nonprovocative approach to the Soviets.[79] His later statements also indicate that the Cuban crisis had a profound effect on his thinking about nuclear weapons and nuclear war.[80]

MAKING NUCLEAR STRATEGY

McNamara had initiated a major reevaluation of U.S. nuclear strategy almost immediately on taking office in January 1961. In early February 1961 he had toured the headquarters of the Strategic Air Command near Omaha, Nebraska. There he and a group of his subordinates had been fully briefed on the nation's nuclear war fighting plan, known as the Single Integrated Operational Plan (SIOP). McNamara was greatly dismayed by the plan as the generals presented it to him.[81]

Plan 1-A of SIOP called for immediately releasing all of the U.S. nuclear weapons against the Soviet Union, China, and Eastern Europe in response to an actual (or even merely threatened) Soviet invasion of Western Europe.[82] McNamara was concerned by the inflexibility of the plan, which gave the president (and himself as number two in the nuclear chain of command) no choice except to launch a full nuclear strike, killing hundreds of millions of people and ensuring a full retaliatory strike on the United States.[83] This lack of options did not fit with McNamara's belief in the potential for managing and controlling superpower conflict, and he quickly set out to develop a nuclear strategy that had more flexibility.

A week later, on February 10, 1961, McNamara was given a briefing by William Kaufmann of the RAND Corporation. Kaufmann presented a new strategic concept he had developed that he called "counterforce/no cities."[84] According to this plan, the United States would limit its initial nuclear strike to military and strategic nuclear targets and withhold a large reserve force that would remain targeted on Soviet population centers. The United States would, in effect, hold the Soviet population hostage and would use the reserve force as leverage with the Soviets to end the hostilities under conditions favorable to the United States.[85] The Kaufmann counterforce concept was based on game-theory research being done by economists and mathematicians at the RAND Corporation.[86]

Although McNamara did see some problems with the counterforce strategy, he found that its advantages outweighed its disadvantages. He was impressed with the counterforce approach's flexibility and its allowance for the preservation of options even once a nuclear exchange had begun, thus giving the president more control over any escalating superpower conflict.[87] Immediately after the Kaufmann briefing, he set out to make the counterforce concept the foundation of U.S. nuclear doctrine.[88]

In addition to being attracted to the inherent flexibility of the counterforce concept, McNamara thought this approach might limit the destructiveness of a nuclear exchange and even provide a way to bring a nuclear conflict to an end.[89] In a January 1962 speech in Chicago, he highlighted the flexibility as well as the damage-limiting and bargaining-leverage aspects of the concept.

> Our forces can be used in several different ways. We may have to retaliate with a single massive attack. Or we may be able to use our retaliatory forces to limit damage done to ourselves, and our allies, by knocking out the enemy's bases before he has had time to launch his second salvos. We may seek to terminate a war on favorable terms by using our forces as a bargaining weapon—by threatening further attack. In any case our large reserve of protected firepower would give an enemy an incentive to avoid our cities and to stop a war. Our new policy gives us the flexibility to

choose among several operational plans but does not require that we make any advance commitment with respect to doctrine or targets. We shall be committed only to a system that gives us the ability to use our forces in a controlled and deliberate way, so as best to pursue the interest of the United States, our Allies and the rest of the free world.[90]

Here again we see a tendency to avoid commitment "with respect to doctrine" that is very consistent with the pragmatic myth. Perhaps more important, the bargaining aspect of the counterforce strategy, called intrawar deterrence by the inventors of escalation and bargaining theory at RAND, was consistent with McNamara's policy preferences in previous situations of superpower confrontation— both the 1961 Berlin crisis and the 1962 Cuban missile crisis.[91] In both these situations McNamara sought to manipulate the military context of the confrontation in an effort to make the Soviets "act rationally" and deescalate the conflict. McNamara seems to have thought that U.S. leaders would be able to exert intrawar deterrence to make the Soviets back down in the middle of a nuclear conflict. This assumption of rational behavior on the part of government leaders (Soviet or American) in the midst of a nuclear exchange is indeed a dubious one, but the ability to inject such rationality into conflict situations was something that McNamara seemed to constantly strive for and was consistent with his style of management and his belief in his ability to manage conflict.

McNamara continued to promote the counterforce strategy through most of 1962. After the Cuban missile crisis, however, he began to have serious doubts about it. In an interview with Shapley, he indicated that the dramatic events of the Cuban missile crisis made him question his belief that a nuclear exchange could be rationally managed in the way that the counterforce strategy assumed.[92] And as Shapley points out, U.S. public opinion had been reawakened during the crisis to the potential horrors of nuclear war, and therefore it became less politically acceptable for leaders to talk about rationally managing and bargaining within a nuclear exchange.[93]

There were other factors that began to sour McNamara on the counterforce strategy. One was that despite his best efforts to promote it to the Soviets as a nonprovocative damage-limitation strategy, they sent signals that they considered it a U.S. effort to achieve first-strike capability.[94] Another development was a July 1962 intelligence review of Soviet nuclear forces that determined the Soviets would have a survivable second-strike capability within two or three years.[95]

This 1962 intelligence finding started McNamara thinking about basing U.S. nuclear doctrine on the principle of mutual and stable deterrence instead of war fighting and damage limitation.[96] Throughout 1963, he began to back away from the counterforce strategy in favor of one that would come to be known as mutually assured destruction (MAD). He commissioned some of the "whiz kids" from the RAND corporation to produce a computer-based quantitative study to determine the force size and structure that would provide a survivable second-strike capability for the United States.[97]

The study, complete with graphs and computer printouts, showed that a nuclear force of roughly 400 megatons would destroy 50 percent of Soviet industrial capacity and 30 percent of the population. The study's charts showed further that increasing the survivable yield over 400 megatons would not produce appreciable gains in the percentage of Soviet industry and population destroyed.[98] This was the kind of quantitative analysis that McNamara had used to solve problems since his statistical control days with the Army Air Forces, and its logic appealed to him immediately. He went on to use the 400-megaton figure as his basic measure of nuclear sufficiency, and he used the findings of the study as the foundation of his new strategy of mutually assured destruction.[99] McNamara believed that MAD would not only produce a better deterrent posture vis-à-vis the Soviets but also would allow him to hold down requests from the service chiefs for new weapons systems.[100] Thus he was impressed by its economic logic.

In spring 1964, McNamara's assistants from RAND produced another quantitative study the economic logic of which would finally destroy damage limitation–counterforce as a viable strategy in McNamara's mind.[101] This new study showed that a damage limitation–counterforce strategy (which would include large-scale antiballistic missile deployment) would simply not be cost-effective in the face of Soviet quantitative and qualitative improvements in offensive forces. The study's graphs illustrated the point that costly U.S. investments in antiballistic missile systems and improvements in counterforce capabilities could be effectively offset by much less costly Soviet offensive improvements. The economic logic of this study was irresistible to McNamara, and he used it to publicly kill counterforce as official U.S. nuclear strategy.[102]

Thus the game-theory propositions of one set of whiz kids from RAND had sold McNamara on the counterforce strategy, and the quantitative studies of another set of whiz kids had now given McNamara "objective evidence" that the counterforce strategy was not viable. The graphs of the latest counterforce study showed clearly that a counterforce strategy was simply not cost-effective. This is yet another example of McNamara's reliance on the quantitative control methods he had learned at Harvard Business School. It shows that his faith in this quantitative "spotlight on the truth" was as strong as ever.

Interestingly, though, even with his conversion to MAD as official U.S. nuclear doctrine, he continued his established pattern of attempting to influence the Soviets by manipulating the military context of the confrontation. Having seized on the concept (which was not his invention) of maintaining a stable deterrent balance, McNamara set out to send signals to the Soviets that the United States welcomed the establishment of such a balance. In December 1962 (the aftermath of the Cuban missile crisis) McNamara had told journalist Stewart Alsop that he would welcome the Soviet development of a survivable second-strike capability "the sooner the better."[103] Although this remark brought down a firestorm of criticism from the right wing in the United States, it may also be seen as a tension-reducing signal to the Soviets.[104] When McNamara elaborated on the logic of mutually assured destruction, he noted with great interest and pleasure the number of copies of the statements that the Soviet embassy in Washington purchased.[105]

MANAGING THE VIETNAM CONFLICT

This pattern of policy preferences and behavior may also be found in McNamara's involvement in the decisionmaking that led to the U.S. military involvement in Vietnam. His major involvement in Vietnam decisionmaking did not begin until fall 1961, when Kennedy sent General Maxwell Taylor and Walt Rostow to Vietnam on a major fact-finding mission. Taylor and Rostow returned to Washington in early November 1961 and reported that the situation on the ground in Vietnam was deteriorating due to increasing Vietcong strength.[106]

They recommended an enlargement of the U.S. advisory role in South Vietnam as well as an increase in U.S. logistical support and the start of U.S. development programs to "win the hearts and minds" of the South Vietnamese peasants.[107] Perhaps most significant, they recommended that 8,000 combat troops be sent to South Vietnam (disguised as flood control workers).[108] In response to the Taylor-Rostow report, McNamara drafted a memorandum to Kennedy more or less in support of it:

> The fall of South Vietnam to communism would lead to the fairly rapid extension of Communist control, or the complete accommodation to communism, in the rest of mainland Southeast Asia

and in Indonesia. The strategic implications worldwide, particularly in the Orient would be extremely serious. . . . The chances are against, probably sharply against, preventing that fall by any measures short of the introduction of U.S. forces on a substantial scale.[109]

He went on to argue that

the introduction of a U.S. force of the magnitude of an initial 8,000 men in a flood control context will be of great help to Diem. However it will not convince the other side (whether the shots are called from Moscow, Peiping, or Hanoi) that we mean business. Moreover, it will probably not tip the scales decisively. We would be almost certain to get bogged down in an inconclusive struggle. . . . The other side can be convinced we mean business only if we accompany the initial force introduction by a clear commitment to the full objective stated above, accompanied by a warning through some channel to Hanoi that continued support of the Viet Cong will lead to punitive retaliation against North Vietnam.[110]

McNamara also wrote that the total U.S. forces needed to accomplish the mission outlined would probably not exceed 205,000.[111] He finished the memo by stating, "We do not believe major units of U.S. forces should be introduced unless we are willing to make an affirmative decision on the issue stated at the start of this memorandum. We are inclined to recommend that we do commit the U.S. to the clear objective of preventing the fall of South Vietnam to Communism and that we support this commitment by the necessary military actions.[112]

In this memorandum to Kennedy, written on behalf of the Joint Chiefs of Staff, his deputy, Roswell Gilpatric, and himself, McNamara clearly showed a preference for using military force to influence the behavior of the North Vietnamese (as well as the communist Chinese and the Soviets).[113] He eschewed the policy of sending only 8,000 U.S. troops because that would fail to "convince the other side that we mean business."

This approach clearly fits the previously noted pattern of McNamara's policy preferences and behavior in confrontations with the Soviets. He again attempted to modulate the use of U.S. military force in order to persuade the communist adversaries to change their behavior.

Kennedy rejected the recommendations of the McNamara memorandum and in fact even rejected sending the 8,000 combat troops that Taylor and Rostow had recommended. He did, however, agree to the increased advisory, logistical support, and development roles that had been recommended by the Taylor-Rostow report.

Thus although Kennedy did not follow the McNamara-JCS-Gilpatric recommendations to commit large numbers of combat troops in 1961, he certainly did not take steps to lessen the U.S. involvement in Vietnam, and in fact he expanded it. McNamara set out immediately to implement the steps that Kennedy had authorized.[114]

For most of the remainder of Kennedy's term as president, the administration's policy remained one of propping up Diem as the South Vietnamese president while providing him with massive advisory, logistical, and development support and avoiding the introduction of U.S. combat troops. By 1963 there were signs that the repressive and corrupt Diem regime was unable both to maintain civil order and to successfully prosecute the war against the Vietcong. A faction within the State Department led by Averell Harriman began to argue that the United States must force Diem to broaden and reform his government.[115] Others in the administration including McNamara and Secretary of State Dean Rusk argued that the United States must continue to support Diem militarily, that the war was being won under him, and that there was no alternative to him.[116]

McNamara was by far the strongest advocate of staying with Diem. A big reason was that the statistics bubbling up to him through his Vietnam reporting system were telling him that the war was being won.[117] Unfortunately, officers at every level of the reporting system felt pressure to give their superiors what they wanted to hear—news that the war was going well—so that by the time the statistical information made it to McNamara, it had been significantly skewed in an optimistic direction.[118]

So while journalists' reports indicated that the South Vietnamese army was corrupt and ineffective in the field and that Vietcong control over the South Vietnamese countryside was expanding, McNamara's statistical indicators (body counts, kill ratios, infiltration rates, etc.) were telling just the opposite story. When members of Harriman's anti-Diem faction argued that Diem was losing the loyalty of the population in the South, McNamara would ask them for percentages (which they were unable to provide).[119] McNamara, meanwhile, could rattle off reams of impressive-sounding statistics to bolster his argument that the war was being won.

This is an excellent example of McNamara's epistemological hubris. He argued in meetings as though his statistical control methodology gave him a window on the true conditions in Vietnam. Anyone who did not use statistical information to build policy positions was seen as "epistemologically underprivileged."[120] Feelings of loyalty or disaffection among the peasants could not be operationalized into a clean statistical indicator, yet this was the basis of the argument being made by Harriman's anti-Diem faction at the State Department. Its more interpretive arguments were dismissed by McNamara as "poetry."[121]

McNamara's epistemological hubris is, again, very consistent with the manager representative character's knowledge-based claims to authority, as discussed in Chapter 2 and by Alasdair MacIntyre.[122] McNamara had learned very early in his career at Ford that he could use quantitative analysis to give himself an epistemologically privileged position that would greatly enhance his power within the bureaucracy. This behavior in the context of Vietnam decisionmaking is merely a continuation of a consistent and significant behavior pattern that is nicely illumined by the representative character concept.

In his memoirs, McNamara wrote about his continuing faith in quantitative measurements of war progress even though the reports on Vietnam had been flawed.

> I always pressed our commanders very hard for estimates of progress—or lack of it. The monitoring of progress—which I still consider a bedrock principle of good management—was very poorly handled in Vietnam. . . . Uncertain how to evaluate progress in a war without battle lines, the military tried to gauge its progress with quantitative measurements such as enemy casualties (which became infamous as body counts), weapons seized, prisoners taken, sorties flown, and so on. We later learned that many of these measures were misleading or erroneous.[123]

This passage provides important evidence indicating that McNamara conceptualized his role in running the U.S. military effort in Vietnam as that of a modern rational manager: He developed a bureaucratic action plan, quantitatively measured the progress of its execution, and then made adjustments if progress was unsatisfactory.

In summer 1963 a major Buddhist uprising and an accompanying brutal crackdown by the Diem regime further convinced the Harriman faction that the war against the Vietcong could not be won under Diem's leadership.[124] It began to argue that Washington should begin to think about alternative leadership for South Vietnam. McNamara and others such as Dean Rusk continued to argue that support for Diem (combined with pressures on him to reform) was the proper policy to follow.[125] McNamara argued that there was no viable leadership alternative to Diem in South Vietnam, and therefore U.S. support of a coup against Diem was ill-advised.[126] Eventually the anti-Diem faction in Washington won out, and in

November 1963 a group of South Vietnamese army officers staged a coup.[127]

After the Kennedy assassination and in the aftermath of the Diem overthrow, extremely pessimistic reports began to flow out of Vietnam.[128] In December 1963, President Johnson dispatched McNamara to Vietnam to investigate.[129] In his report to Johnson on his return, McNamara warned that "Viet Cong progress has been great during the period since the coup." He recommended that the United States redouble its efforts to strengthen the South Vietnamese government and military, but he stopped short of recommending a major increase in the U.S. military presence there.[130]

In winter and spring 1964, McNamara and Johnson's other foreign policy advisers were faced with increasing evidence that the Vietcong were gaining strength in the South. In addition to finding ways to strengthen the South Vietnamese government and military against this threat, McNamara and others began to focus on ways to coerce the North Vietnamese government into withdrawing their support of the Vietcong. In late February 1964, McNamara ordered the Joint Chiefs of Staff to explore actions against North Vietnam. In his memoirs McNamara wrote that these actions were "designed to induce that government to terminate its support and encouragement of the insurrection in South Vietnam."[131] This is another example of McNamara's confidence in his ability to influence the behavior of a communist adversary by carefully modulating the application of U.S. military force.

One of the ideas implemented was Operation Plan 34-A, which consisted of low-level covert actions against various North Vietnamese facilities.[132] The explicit rationale behind the 34-A operations was to increase the cost to the North Vietnamese of their support for the Vietcong in the hopes that they would discontinue this support.[133] In addition to the covert actions of Plan 34-A, McNamara and others began to plan for the use of bombing strikes as a coercive measure against the North Vietnamese.[134]

Returning from a March 1964 fact-finding trip to Vietnam, McNamara wrote a report to Johnson in which he recommended that the Pentagon begin to plan for such coercive airstrikes against the North Vietnamese. In the report, McNamara called for planning to begin on "retaliatory bombing strikes and commando raids on a tit-for-tat basis by the GVN [South Vietnamese government] against NVN [North Vietnamese government] targets." He also recommended that the Pentagon begin planning "graduated overt military pressure by GVN and U.S. forces. This would include air attacks against military and possibly industrial targets."[135] The purpose of these attacks, according to McNamara, would be to erode the morale of the Vietcong as well as to persuade the North Vietnamese to stop supporting them. It is important that McNamara was merely recommending that the bombing strikes be planned for and was not yet advising that they be carried out.[136] Nonetheless, these recommendations are significant because Johnson did accept them, and this set in motion the planning of what would become the extensive U.S. air war against North Vietnam.

In response to McNamara's recommendation to begin planning a coercive air campaign against North Vietnam, the Joint Chiefs of Staff drew up a list of ninety-four North Vietnamese targets of military or industrial importance. McNamara, however, viewed the chiefs' bombing plans as too extensive and dangerous because they might provoke a large-scale North Vietnamese invasion of South Vietnam or the intervention of Chinese forces.[137]

By summer 1964 McNamara was beginning to prefer a carefully controlled and limited air campaign against the North Vietnamese, one that would not risk provoking a larger war. His thinking on this approach was being influenced by Assistant Secretary of Defense John McNaughton.[138] McNaughton had been a protégé of Thomas Schelling, a professor of political economy at Harvard who had developed theories of bargaining using the game-theory approach familiar to McNamara's whiz kids from RAND.[139] Schelling had written about using bargaining strategies in war that were similar to the coercive strategy that was the foundation of Kaufmann's counterforce/no cities nuclear doctrine.[140]

McNaughton adapted Schelling's theories to the problem of limited conventional war in Southeast Asia. He argued that carefully controlled and limited bombing strikes could be used to convince the North Vietnamese to stop supporting the Vietcong. The idea was not to destroy North Vietnam with the bombing but rather to gradually increase the level of pain inflicted by the bombing until the North Vietnamese gave in.[141] McNaughton's game theory–inspired bombing plan appealed to McNamara because it seemed to avoid the risk of provoking a larger war with China and because it would seemingly be subject to his control.[142]

McNamara and McNaughton both believed that in order to make U.S. strikes less provocative vis-à-vis the Chinese, they would have to be timed so that they would appear to be reprisals for Vietcong or North Vietnamese actions.[143] In early August 1964, U.S. officials declared that North Vietnamese torpedo boats had attacked the U.S. destroyer *Maddox* in international waters off the coast of North Vietnam, assuming it to be part of a Plan 34-A harassment operation that had attacked coastal facilities in the area two days earlier.[144] President Johnson ordered the *Maddox* and another destroyer to return to the same waters two days later, and he ordered U.S. carrier-based aircraft to stand by to bomb North Vietnamese targets if the destroyers should be attacked again. Johnson also prepared a request to ask Congress for what would become the infamous Tonkin Gulf Resolution. On the night of August 4, 1964, the two U.S. destroyers came under what they thought was an attack by North Vietnamese patrol boats.[145] Despite the ambiguous evidence on the attack, Johnson seized the opportunity to ram through the Tonkin Gulf Resolution and to launch limited reprisal attacks against North Vietnamese targets.[146] The air war against North Vietnam had begun.

In the months following the Tonkin Gulf reprisal raids, McNamara and McNaughton continued to plan for the limited air war, although publicly the subject of Vietnam fell into the background with the November presidential elections coming up. In October, Undersecretary of State George Ball produced a long paper questioning all of the secret plans to involve the U.S. military more deeply in Vietnam.[147] More significant from McNamara's point of view, Ball argued forcefully that once the United States became militarily involved in the war, it would not be able to control its escalation.[148] Ball questioned the effectiveness of the limited air war. He argued that the bombing would not improve the morale of the South Vietnamese forces and that, more important, bombing would not significantly lessen the North Vietnamese war-making capability in the South. To bolster his argument he cited the results of the Pentagon's Sigma II war games showing that the North Vietnamese could fight on even after all of the ninety-four proposed bombing targets were effectively hit. He argued further that since the bombings would have no military effect, they would also fail to give the United States the type of bargaining leverage that McNaughton and McNamara had planned for.[149]

McNamara was disturbed by Ball's memorandum, partly because Ball did not share his belief in the ability of the United States to coerce the North Vietnamese while controlling the escalation of the war and partly because he did not share McNamara's assumption that the United States had no choice but to defend the South Vietnamese against the communists. McNamara dismissed Ball's arguments, as did Secretary of State Dean Rusk, National Security Adviser McGeorge Bundy, and, most important, President Johnson.[150] Throughout November and December, Johnson was presented with different bombing plans with McNamara arguing for his coercive escalation bombing plan and the Joint Chiefs arguing for more massive bombing attacks.[151] During this period, Johnson refused to commit to any sustained-bombing plan.

An analysis of McNamara's communications in winter and spring 1965 indicates that he believed the communists had given up on general war as a means of achieving their objectives and the most dangerous communist challenge stemmed from their support of wars of national liberation. He laid out his view of the state of the Cold War in a February 1965 appearance before the House Armed Services Committee.

> Like their predecessors, the new leaders of the Soviet Union fully appreciate the perils of general nuclear war and the dangers of local wars escalating into nuclear war. I also believe that the leaders of Communist·China, too, are reluctant to challenge the full weight of our military power. But both the Soviet Union and Communist China continue to support "wars of national liberation" or "popular revolts" which we know as covert armed aggression, insurrection and subversion.[152]

In this same testimony he elaborated on the threat posed by these wars of national liberation, but he put this threat in the context of an emerging Sino-Soviet split. He argued that the Chinese were trying to establish themselves as the symbolic leaders of the communist world by proving the effectiveness of their model of revolution.

> A Communist Chinese success in South Vietnam would be claimed as proof positive that the Chinese communist position (vis à vis the Soviets) was correct and they will have made a giant step forward in the struggle for control of the world communist movement. Such a success would also greatly enhance the prestige of Communist China among the non-aligned nations and strengthen the position of their following everywhere. Thus the stakes in South Vietnam are far greater than the loss of one small country to communism. . . . Thus the choice is not simply whether to continue our efforts to keep South Vietnam free and independent but, rather, whether to continue our struggle to halt communist expansion in Asia. If the choice is the latter, as I believe it should be, we will be far better off facing the issue in South Vietnam.[153]

With the exception of his acknowledgment of the Sino-Soviet split, McNamara's Cold War worldview was much the same as in his earlier communications. He still viewed the Cold War as mostly a military struggle, and he still viewed wars of national liberation as the most dangerous communist challenge.[154]

In late January 1965, McNamara teamed up with National Security Adviser McGeorge Bundy to persuade Johnson that the deteriorating situation in South Vietnam called for decisive U.S. military action.[155] On January 27, Bundy presented Johnson with a memo in which he and McNamara argued that the time had come to use U.S. military power to force a change in the behavior of the North Vietnamese.[156]

> Both of us are now pretty well convinced that our current policy can only lead to disastrous defeat. . . . We are pinned to a policy of first aid to squabbling politicos and passive reaction to events we do not even try to control. Or so it seems. Bob and I believe that the worst course of action is to continue in this essentially passive role. . . . We see two alternatives. The first is to use our military power in the Far East and to force a change in Communist policy. The second is to deploy all our resources along a track of negotiation. . . . Bob and I tend to favor the first course, but we believe that both should be carefully studied and that alternative programs should be argued out before you.[157]

In a meeting to discuss the memo with Bundy and McNamara, Johnson told them that he was persuaded and was ready to "move strongly."[158] Just over a week later, Vietcong forces attacked an American barracks at Pleiku in the Central Highlands, killing eight Americans and wounding sixty more. That same day the National Security Council met and the members unanimously advised Johnson that a reprisal strike should be launched immediately.[159] The strike that was promptly carried out was code-named Flaming Dart. A subsequent Vietcong attack on a U.S. base at Qui Nhon was answered by another reprisal bombing operation code-named Flaming Dart II.[160] The tit-for-tat series of bombing signals to the North Vietnamese that McNamara had envisioned had begun in earnest. Only now, pressure was being generated elsewhere in the national security bureaucracy to widen the airstrikes into more than simply reprisals for specific Vietcong attacks.

On returning from a trip to Saigon in early February, McGeorge Bundy wrote a memorandum (partially drafted by John McNaughton) to President Johnson in which he recommended a bombing policy he called "sustained reprisal."[161] In essence this policy linked reprisal attacks not to specific communist attacks but to the aggregate of communist activity in South Vietnam.[162] The Bundy memo explained,

> We are convinced that the political values of reprisal require a continuous operation. Episodic responses geared on a one-for-one basis to spectacular outrages would lack the persuasive force of sustained pressure. More important still, they would leave it open

to the communists to avoid reprisals entirely by giving up only a small element of their own program. . . . It is the great merit of the proposed scheme that to stop it the communists would have to stop enough of their activity in the South to permit the probable success of a determined pacification effort.[163]

Although Bundy and McNaughton proposed a significant escalation over the controlled-bombing tactic, they were operating on the same premises about the utility of coercive, signal-sending bombing campaigns that McNamara and McNaughton had adopted in summer 1964. Implicit in the proposed new "sustained reprisal" policy was the assumption that the United States could influence Hanoi to reduce its efforts in South Vietnam by threatening an increase of bomb-induced "pain." In the memo, Bundy noted that the bombing was still a "means of effecting the will of Hanoi."[164]

Bundy's policy of "sustained reprisal," along with a variation developed by Maxwell Taylor called "graduated reprisal," became the basis for the sustained bombing campaign against North Vietnam known as Rolling Thunder, which President Johnson formally approved on February 13, 1965. The operation did not begin until March 2, 1965. After the first round of Rolling Thunder attacks, McNamara indicated that although he was satisfied that the bombing attacks had communicated "our political resolve," he was concerned about their cost effectiveness.[165]

In a memorandum to Johnson recording an April 20 meeting in Hawaii with the Joint Chiefs and the country team from Vietnam, McNamara reflected the consensus among that group that Rolling Thunder and sustained reprisal were correct policy. He wrote that the group agreed that "the present tempo [of bombing attacks] is about right [and] that sufficient increasing pressure is provided by repetition and continuation." He also noted that there was a "shared view" among the group "that it was important not to 'kill the hostage' by destroying the NVNese assets inside the Hanoi donut."[166]

This shows McNamara was still firmly convinced of U.S. ability to manipulate Hanoi with a carefully modulated bombing campaign into reducing its efforts in the South. Years later he reiterated his belief at the time that bombing could persuade Hanoi to settle the war on terms favorable to the United States. "I never did believe bombing could win wars. And I didn't believe bombing could stop infiltration or destroy the war-making capacity of North Vietnam. I did not believe it was likely we could win a military victory. I did believe that the military action should be used as a prod towards moving towards a political track: to increase the chance of initiating or achieving or movement on the political track."[167]

Although McNamara may have believed in the efficacy of coercive bombing in April 1965, by summer of that year he was receiving substantial evidence that the North Vietnamese were not responding to the bombing the way that McNaughton's game theorizing said they should. Reports from Vietnam showed that infiltration rates from the North were increasing fast, and intelligence indicated that the communists were preparing a massive offensive to cut South Vietnam in two.[168] In June McNamara was persuaded by Commander William Westmoreland of Military Assistance Command Vietnam (MACV) that only a large-scale commitment of U.S. troops could save South Vietnam from the communists. Westmoreland also convinced him that a sufficiently large American force using an attrition strategy could be effective against the communists.[169] In a July 20 memorandum to President Johnson, McNamara recommended that the United States should deploy 175,000 combat troops into South Vietnam to defend against the communist forces and to persuade them that they could not win in the South.[170] In his memoirs, McNamara emphasized the signal-sending aspects of the recommended troop deployments. "My memo centered on the idea that U.S. and South Vietnamese military strength should be increased 'enough to prove to the VC that they cannot win and thus to turn the tide of the war.'"[171] Here is yet another example of McNamara attempting to influence the behavior of the North Vietnamese and Vietcong by manipulating the military context (in this case increasing the number of U.S. troops on the ground). The purpose of the troop deployment was not to militarily defeat the communists but rather to "send a signal" of U.S. resolve in the hopes of persuading them through coercion to alter their aggressive behavior. This is consistent with the manager character's quasi-experimental, manipulative mode of social action.

President Johnson accepted McNamara's recommendation and soon announced that the United States would be sending the requested numbers of combat troops.[172] In addition to the combat troops, McNamara recommended that extensive bombing raids (which included B-52s) be used to support military actions against the communists in the South, and Johnson accepted this recommendation also.[173] McNamara had hoped that these actions would indicate U.S. resolve to the communists and persuade them to deescalate their efforts in South Vietnam, but by fall 1965 he had substantial evidence that the opposite was in fact occurring. Intelligence showed that the North Vietnamese infiltration was increasing to match the U.S. buildup.[174] In a November 30 memorandum to President Johnson he noted the dramatic increase in communist force levels in the South and advised that another 200,000 U.S. troops be deployed in order to counter that increase.[175]

In spite of the fact that the North Vietnamese were not deescalating in response to his bombing campaign and troop deployments, McNamara did not give up on his efforts to manipulate the military context of the confrontation to persuade the North to "behave rationally." In the November 30 memo to Johnson he recommended that a bombing halt of several weeks be attempted to see if the North Vietnamese would respond by slowing down their infiltration of the South:

> It is my belief that there should be a three or four week pause in the program of bombing of the North before we either greatly increase our troop deployments to VN or intensify our strikes against the North. . . . The reasons for this belief are, first that we must lay a foundation in the mind of the American public and in world opinion for such an enlarged phase of the war, and second we should give NVN a face saving chance to stop the aggression. I am seriously concerned about embarking on a markedly higher level of war in VN without having tried, through a pause, to end the war or at least having made it clear to our people that we did our best to end it. . . . The best chance of achieving our stated objectives lies in a pause followed, if it fails, by the deployments mentioned above.[176]

In an earlier November memo to Johnson, McNamara had argued that the United States should be prepared to conduct a finely orchestrated combination of military moves, not to defeat the communists militarily, but to persuade the communists that they could not win and that they should negotiate a settlement. He described this memo in his memoirs.

> After analyzing alternative courses open to us, I recommended: (1) increasing U.S. troop commitments to 350,000 by the end of 1966, compared with the 275,000 Westy [Westmoreland] had estimated in July; (2) implementing a month-long bombing pause . . . and (3) making an all out effort to start negotiations. I recognized that negotiations at that time seemed unlikely to succeed, but I argued a bombing pause "would set the stage for another pause, perhaps in late 1966, which might produce a settlement." If a pause proved fruitless, I recommended intensifying Rolling Thunder strikes against North Vietnam—not to win the war (which I considered impossible short of genocidal destruction) but as one prong of a two prong strategy to prove to the Vietcong and North Vietnamese that they could not win in the South while penalizing Hanoi's continued support of the war.[177]

One cannot help but notice the experimental quality of his thinking here. It is as though he was convinced that the perfect combination of military moves existed that would motivate the North
Vietnamese and Vietcong to act as the United States wanted them
to act; all he had to do was find that perfect combination.

In late December 1965, President Johnson halted the bombing
of the North for thirty-seven days. The North Vietnamese responded by dramatically increasing their infiltration of the South
during those days, which infuriated Johnson and led him to resume
the bombing at prepause levels.[178] After the Christmas bombing
pause failed to bring the North Vietnamese around, McNamara
began to reassess his strategy of calibrating and modulating the application of military force to alter their behavior. He anticipated
that they would greatly increase their infiltration and large-unit actions and again recommended that Johnson authorize an additional 200,000 American troops to counter the communist
buildup.[179] However, now McNamara was worried that the spiral of
escalation was beginning to work in favor of the North Vietnamese.
In a memo to Johnson he shared this fear:

> Even though the communists would continue to suffer heavily
> from our ground and air action, we expect them, upon learning
> of any U.S. intentions to augment its forces, to boost their own
> commitment and to test U.S. capabilities and will to persevere at
> a higher level of conflict and casualties (U.S. killed-in-action with
> the recommended deployments can be expected to reach 1000 a
> month). . . . It follows, therefore that the odds are about even
> that, even with the recommended deployments, we will be faced,
> in early 1967 with a military standoff at a much higher level.[180]

Yet even though he was beginning to worry that the North Vietnamese might be getting into a position where they could use military force to "test U.S. capabilities and will to persevere," he still
clung to the idea that the United States could pressure the communists into negotiations. He concluded his discussion as follows:
"This prospect intensified my conviction that the United States
needed negotiations leading to a diplomatic resolution of the conflict. I hoped our increased effort would 'condition' [Hanoi] toward [such] negotiations and an acceptable end to the war."
(brackets and quotation marks in original).[181]

Throughout spring 1966 McNamara was under a great deal of
pressure by the Joint Chiefs to expand the bombing campaign in
the North to include heavy industrial targets and petroleum-storage
facilities. In June McNamara finally came to agree with the Chiefs,
and he recommended a major escalation in the bombing campaign.[182]

This more than doubled the number of bombing missions against the North, but the communists merely responded by increasing their activity in the South.

McNamara finally began to realize that the bombing could have no effect on the behavior of the North Vietnamese.[183] He was also beginning to realize that the war could not be won, but he would not begin to air these doubts to Johnson until later in 1966.

LEAVING THE PENTAGON

When McNamara finally did begin to share his growing doubts about the war with Johnson, the effect was to alienate the president, who did not want to hear bad news about the war effort. By 1966 McNamara had commissioned his chief whiz kid, Alain Enthoven, to run a thorough statistical control analysis on the effectiveness of existing and hypothetical troop deployments to Vietnam. This analysis provided "hard" proof for McNamara that dramatic increases in new troop deployments along the lines of those being requested by Westmoreland would be futile.[184] McNamara began to see these requested increases in troop deployments (as well as arguments for intensifying the bombing campaign) as not only militarily ineffective but as representing a new phase in the war wherein the U.S. involvement and commitment in Vietnam was beginning to spin out of the control of the policymakers.[185]

In May 1967, McNamara presented Johnson with a long memo in which he laid out his arguments against intensifying the bombing campaign and against the deployment of the 200,000 additional troops requested by Westmoreland and the Chiefs. This memo, in which McNamara relayed his concerns that the war was escalating out of control, argued for carefully limiting the bombing of the North, and argued for keeping additional troop deployments under 30,000, had an explosive impact within the top policymaking circles in the Johnson administration. McNamara described this event in his memoirs. "My May 19, 1967 memorandum to the president unleashed a storm of controversy. It intensified already sharp debate within the administration. It led to tense and acrimonious Senate hearings that pitted me against the Joint Chiefs of Staff and generated rumors they intended to resign en masse. It accelerated the process that ultimately drove President Johnson and me apart. And it hastened my departure from the Pentagon."[186]

For the remainder of 1967 until McNamara was reassigned to the World Bank, he was virtually alone among Johnson's principal advisers in arguing for deescalation of the war. After that May memorandum, he became increasingly alienated from the president. It is deeply ironic that McNamara's estrangement from the inner circle of power should be brought about as a result of his growing fears that the conflict in Vietnam was in danger of escalating beyond his control. His hubristic sense in 1964 and 1965 that the situation in Vietnam could be controlled had helped him to persuade Johnson to Americanize the war. It is not surprising that when, in May 1967, he pointedly argued that the United States should now reverse course, Johnson would begin to question his value as an adviser.

CONCLUSION

Analysis of McNamara's Cold War worldview as it evolved during his tenure at the Pentagon turned up no direct evidence (i.e., mythical imagery in statements) that he was influenced by any of the three myths highlighted in this study. However, certain elements of his worldview were remarkably consistent with the pragmatic myth. His early emphasis on adaptability (i.e., flexible response) in Cold War confrontations and his complaints about adherence to moral principle putting the United States at a tactical disadvantage in the Cold War both have a distinct pragmatic myth ring to them.

This case study also provides strong role evidence to suggest that McNamara was greatly influenced by the manager representative character. It is clear from examination of his early biography that he was exposed to an educational milieu that shaped him in some very definite ways. At Berkeley in the 1930s, he was heavily affected by the predominant rationalistic and scientistic intellectual currents. According to his own recollections, it was at Berkeley that he first discovered his talent for quantitative analysis and developed tremendous confidence in his reasoning abilities, in effect finding a new identity. At Harvard he was initiated into the field of scientific management and given the tools of statistical control that he would later use to revolutionize both Ford and the Pentagon. By the time he arrived at Ford, he was already showing many of the attributes of the manager representative character.

Throughout his career at Ford and at the Pentagon, he manifested an epistemological hubris, an extreme overconfidence in his ability to discern the "facts" of a complex bureaucratic operation and to use these "facts" to manipulate the behavior of the bureaucracy to achieve optimal performance. This manipulation of human and material resources fits the paradigmatic mode of social action of the manager representative character perfectly. This mode of social action may also be seen in McNamara's role conceptions.[187] Further, his hubristic attitude fits MacIntyre's description of the manager representative character's knowledge- and effectiveness-based claims to authority.[188] McNamara used his mastery of statistical facts and his reputation for managerial "effectiveness" to intimidate people into supporting his positions in policy debates. He was making a claim to authority based on his knowledge and his "effectiveness" in much the way that MacIntyre describes.

McNamara came to Washington convinced that the same statistical control techniques he and others had used to centralize and control Ford Motor Company could be used to rationalize the Pentagon and to evaluate the success or failure of U.S. political and military operations abroad. Using these modern business accounting methods, he would simply quantify and measure the resources that the U.S. government was using to achieve its goals (which could also be quantified) and then determine whether these goals were being met in the most efficient manner. If the current approach to the problem wasn't working efficiently, he would simply look for an approach that would work.

At the foundation of this technocratic approach to foreign policy making lies an important (although unchallenged at the time) epistemological assumption—that a complex sociopolitical phenomenon (i.e., the guerrilla war in Vietnam) can be intellectually grasped by breaking it down into component material facts or discrete statistical indicators (i.e., rate of infiltration from the North or number of Vietcong killed annually) that can then be quantitatively analyzed like industrial factors of production to yield the proper operational solution (number, types, tactics, and locations of U.S. forces) to achieve the stated goals (e.g., forcing the communists to cease their attacks in South Vietnam). That McNamara consistently operated under this assumption is borne out in his statements over and over again. This leads to another unexamined assumption—that the behavior of the adversary in a confrontation (whether the Soviets, the Chinese, the North Vietnamese, or the Vietcong) can be manipulated by simple modulation of the amount of force being used against it. McNamara's policy preferences and policymaking behavior (from the 1961 Berlin crisis to the escalation of U.S. military involvement in Vietnam in 1965–1966) consistently reflected this belief. Thus this case study provides strong evidence that McNamara's role conceptions, policy preferences, and policymaking behavior were influenced by the manager representative character.

NOTES

1. For the single best history of the political and decisionmaking process that led to the U.S. involvement in Vietnam, including McNamara's role, see David Halberstam, *The Best and the Brightest* (New York: Penguin Books, 1972).

2. Ibid., 264.

3. Henry Trewhitt, *McNamara* (New York: Harper and Row, 1971), 26.

4. Deborah Shapley, *Promise and Power: The Life and Times of Robert McNamara* (Boston: Little, Brown, 1993), 8.

5. Ibid., 8–10. For an excellent discussion of this pattern of twentieth-century child rearing and motivation, see Robert N. Bellah, *The Broken Covenant: American Civil Religion in Time of Trial* (Chicago: University of Chicago Press, 1992), 78–80.

6. Robert S. McNamara, *In Retrospect: The Tragedy and Lessons of Vietnam* (New York: Times Books, 1995), 4.

7. Shapley, 12–15.

8. Ibid., 12–13.

9. Ibid., 13.

10. Ibid., 13.

11. Trewhitt, 32.

12. Shapley, 17.

13. McNamara, 4–6.

14. Ibid., 6.

15. Alasdair MacIntyre, *After Virtue* (South Bend: Notre Dame Press, 1981), 76–78. See also Chapter 2 in this volume.

16. Shapley, 22.

17. Ibid., 23.

18. Ibid., 21.

19. Ibid.

20. Trewhitt, 36.

21. Ibid., 36.

22. Shapley, 30.

23. Shapley, 31–36.

24. Shapley, 31–33.

25. Ibid., 34.

26. Trewhitt, 38–39.

27. Shapley, 37.

28. Halberstam, 281.

29. John A. Byrne, *The Whiz Kids: The Founding Fathers of American Business and the Legacy They Left Us* (New York: Doubleday, 1993), 88.

30. Trewhitt, 43.

31. Shapley, 47.

32. Trewhitt, 44.

33. Shapley, 47–50.

34. Ibid., 48.

35. Byrne, 248.

36. Ibid., 254.

37. Shapley, 52. For his tendency to alter statistics to support his arguments, see also Byrne, 254.

38. Shapley, 85.

39. MacIntyre, 77.

40. For excellent discussions of McNamara's debating style see Byrne, 254. See also Shapley, 64–65, and Halberstam, 288–289.

41. Charles E. Sumner, "The Managerial Mind," in Robert Manley and Sean Manley, eds. *The Age of the Manager* (New York: Macmillan, 1962), 153–154.

42. Ibid., 97.

43. William W. Kaufmann, *The McNamara Strategy* (New York: Harper and Row, 1964), 69.

44. Shapley, 99.

45. Trewhitt, 86–87.

46. Ibid., 87–88.

47. Quoted in James M. Roherty, *Decisions of Robert McNamara: A Study of the Role of the Secretary of Defense* (Coral Gables, FL: University of Miami Press, 1970), 69.

48. Robert S. McNamara, *The Essence of Security: Reflections in Office* (New York: Harper and Row, 1968), 96.

49. McNamara, 22–23.

50. Ibid., 24.

51. McNamara memorandum to JFK, October 7, 1961, Papers of John F. Kennedy, JFK Library, Boston (hereafter JFK Papers), Department of Defense file, Box 270, 1.

52. Ibid., 2. For a good discussion of the fight over the B-70, see Shapley, 106–107.

53. Shapley, 114–115.

54. Trewhitt, 100–101.

55. Shapley, 117–118.

56. Minutes of National Security Council meeting, July 20, 1961, 3, JFK Papers, national security files, NSC minutes, Box 212.

57. Trewhitt, 102–103.

58. Shapley, 141–144.

59. Robert McNamara, "The Communist Design for World Conquest," reprinted in *Vital Speeches* 28 (March 1, 1962): 296–299.

60. Ibid., 297.

61. Ibid., 297–298.

62. For a good discussion of the influence of RAND corporation game theorists in the McNamara Pentagon see Lawrence Freedman, *The Evolution of Nuclear Strategy* (New York: St. Martin's Press, 1989), chs. 12–15.

63. McNamara, "Communist Design," 298. See also "Major National Security Problems Confronting the United States," speech delivered before the Economic Club of New York, November 18, 1963, reprinted in *Department of State Bulletin* (December 16, 1963): 914–921.

64. In an April 1961 speech to the Associated Press, McNamara disclosed a Pentagon regulation that he enacted "against statements of foreign policy or foreign affairs by officials of the Defense Department." See "National Defense Policies," reprinted in *Vital Speeches* (May 1961): 452–455. Obviously over time McNamara would come to disregard this gag rule, but it is significant that he began his career as secretary of defense under this self-imposed constraint.

65. McNamara testimony before the Armed Services Committee, February 18–24, reprinted in *Congressional Quarterly Weekly Report* (February 26, 1965): 313–315.

66. Shapley, 165–167.

67. Laurence Chang and Peter Kornbluh, *The Cuban Missile Crisis, 1962: A National Security Archive Documents Reader* (New York: New Press, 1992), 86.

68. Transcript of the first Executive Committee meeting, October 16, 1962, in Chang and Kornbluh, 89–91.

69. Shapley, 169–171.

70. Ibid., 169–170.

71. Transcript of the second Executive Committee meeting, October 16, 1962, in Chang and Kornbluh, 100–101.

72. Ibid., 101.

73. Shapley, 170–171.

74. Elie Abel, *The Missile Crisis* (New York: J. B. Lippincott, 1966), 81.

75. Trewhitt, 106–108.

76. Shapley, 176–178.

77. Ibid., 177.

78. Ibid., 178.

79. Ibid., 180.

80. Ibid., 185.

81. Fred Kaplan, *The Wizards of Armageddon* (New York: Simon and Schuster, 1983), 270–271.

82. Ibid., 271.

83. Shapley, 139.

84. Kaplan, 260.

85. Ibid.

86. Shapley, 139. For an excellent intellectual history of game theorizing at the RAND corporation and its impact on McNamara era nuclear strategy see Freedman, chs. 12–15.

87. Kaplan, 261–262.

88. Shapley, 140.

89. Ibid., 139.

90. Quoted in Kaufmann, 75.

91. Freedman, 209–210.

92. Shapley, 185.

93. Ibid., 188.

94. Freedman, 238–241.

95. Shapley, 191–192.

96. Ibid., 192.

97. Kaplan, 316–317.

98. Ibid., 317.

99. Shapley, 195. As Shapley points out, in order to rationalize the larger forces that were already in existence, McNamara simply argued that each leg of the strategic nuclear triad should be able to retain at least 400 megatons of retaliatory punch after a Soviet first strike. Thus the 400-megaton figure was actually multiplied by three.

100. Kaplan, 319.

101. Although MAD did replace counterforce as the Pentagon's official public nuclear doctrine, the counterforce strategy remained the guiding principle of the military's nuclear war fighting plan (SIOP) for many years after McNamara's official public adoption of MAD. See Shapley, 201.

102. Kaplan, 320–325.

103. Shapley, 191.

104. Ibid., 192.

105. Freedman, 248.

106. Halberstam, 209.

107. Shapley, 133.

108. *The Pentagon Papers: The Defense Department History of United States Decisionmaking on Vietnam*, Senator Gravel edition (Boston: Beacon Press, 1971), vol. 2, 107.

109. Ibid., 108.

110. Ibid.

111. Ibid.

112. Ibid., 109.

113. In his Vietnam memoirs, McNamara wrote that he began to have second thoughts about this memo to Kennedy within a day or two after he sent it. See McNamara, *In Retrospect*, 38–39.

114. Shapley, 133.

115. Abramson, 612–615.

116. Shapley, 256.

117. Halberstam, 314–315.

118. Shapley, 250.

119. Halberstam, 314–315.

120. Ibid., 314.

121. Ibid., 315.

122. MacIntyre, 76–77.

123. McNamara, *In Retrospect*, 48.

124. Ibid., 255–258.

125. Ibid., 54.

126. Memorandum of conference with President Kennedy, August 29, 1963, 1, JFK Papers, national security files, meetings and memos on Vietnam, Box 316.

127. Abramson, 624–625.

128. This was partly a function of the collapse of Diem's systematically biased military reporting system. With this reporting system no longer in place to artificially "brighten" the reports on the military situation in the South, accurate reports began to filter back to Washington, showing the true deterioration that had been occurring. See Shapley, 292.

129. *Pentagon Papers*, vol. 3, 30–31.

130. Ibid., 31.

131. McNamara, *In Retrospect*, 111.

132. Halberstam, 425–426.

133. *Pentagon Papers*, vol. 3, 151.

134. Halberstam, 426.

135. *Pentagon Papers*, vol. 3, 503.

136. Ibid., 504.

137. Shapley, 301.

138. Ibid., 302.

139. Kaplan, 330.

140. Ibid., 332–333.

141. Ibid., 333–334.

142. Shapley, 303.

143. Ibid.

144. Ibid., 305.

145. Due to a severe storm, the crews of the destroyers were never able to identify visually any attacking patrol boats; their radar and sonar equipment indicated that they were under torpedo attack. See Shapley, 306–307.

146. Halberstam, 500–503.

147. Ibid., 602–605.

148. Ibid., 604.

149. Shapley, 310–311.

150. Ibid., 313–318.

151. Halberstam, 607.

152. McNamara testimony before the House Armed Services Committee, February 18–24, 1965, reprinted in *Congressional Quarterly Weekly Report* (February 26, 1965), 313.

153. Ibid.

154. For other communications that contain these same themes see transcript of McNamara press conference, April 26, 1965, reprinted in *Department of State Bulletin* (May 17, 1965). See also transcript of McNamara testimony before the House Armed Services Committee, January 20–25, 1966, reprinted in *Congressional Quarterly Weekly Report* (February 26, 1966).

155. *Congressional Quarterly* (February 26, 1966), 628–629.

156. Shapley, 317.

157. Bundy-McNamara memo to LBJ, quoted in McNamara, *In Retrospect,* 168–169.

158. Ibid., 319.

159. *Pentagon Papers,* vol. 3, 302.

160. Ibid., 306.

161. Ibid., 308–311.

162. Ibid., 312–315.

163. Ibid., 313.

164. Ibid.

165. Ibid., 332–333.

166. Ibid., 705–706.

167. Quoted in Shapley, 323.

168. Shapley, 328.

169. Ibid., 338–339.

170. *Pentagon Papers,* vol. 4, 297.

171. McNamara, *In Retrospect,* 192.

172. Ibid., 299.

173. Ibid., 340–341.

174. Ibid., 355.

175. *Pentagon Papers,* vol. 4, 623.

176. Ibid.

177. McNamara, *In Retrospect,* 219–220.

178. Shapley, 364–365.

179. McNamara, *In Retrospect,* 236.

180. McNamara memo to Johnson, January 24, 1966, quoted in ibid., 237.

181. Ibid.

182. Ibid., 366–367.

183. Ibid., 367.

184. Shapley, 414–415.

185. Ibid., 417–419.

186. McNamara, *In Retrospect,* 273–274.

187. See McNamara, *In Retrospect,* 22–24, 203.

188. The managerial knowledge stock discussed by MacIntyre does, however, consist of lawlike generalizations. See MacIntyre, 76–77.

6

Assessing the Cultural Shaping Process

The city-on-the-hill, market, and pragmatic myths are metaphorical models of U.S. society and have filled important collective identity-generating and legitimation functions in this society. The Puritan, entrepreneur, pioneer, and manager representative characters have provided idealized identity and behavioral templates that correspond loosely to specific myths. For example, the market myth portrays American society as an idealized grand arena for individual economic competition, and the entrepreneur representative character provides an idealized model for individual behavior in this society.

The many symbolic structures that make up what is often portrayed as a monolithic and coherent U.S. culture are extremely complex, as are the relationships among them. This complexity is especially evident among the symbolic structures highlighted in this study. Narratives reflecting the city-on-the-hill, market, and pragmatic myths often contradict each other as to the meaning of the United States and what it means to be an American. The Puritan, entrepreneur, and manager representative characters often provide contradictory templates for individual social behavior.

That these symbolic structures infuse the American experience with quite different meanings has important significance for the analyst trying to discern how American culture influences individual policymakers and U.S. foreign policy as a whole. Taken together, the three biographical case studies in this book provide evidence to suggest that the worldviews, self-conceptions, and policymaking behavior of each statesman were significantly shaped by at least one myth or representative character (or a myth-character combination) and that this cultural shaping led in each case to a distinct Cold War outlook and diplomatic or policymaking style. The case studies also generate some other interesting insights and generalizations about the cultural shaping process, and it is to these that we now turn.

THE MYTH-WORLDVIEW-POLICY NEXUS OF INFLUENCE

The first type of culture-to-policy relationship examined in the case studies was between specific myths and worldviews and between those myth-influenced worldviews and policy preferences and policymaking behavior. In the Dulles and Harriman case studies there was strong evidence of mythical influence and of consistency between worldviews and policy preferences and policymaking behavior. In the McNamara case the evidence of mythical influence was less substantial because of the lack of actual mythical imagery in any of McNamara's statements. However, there was indirect evidence of mythical influence in the form of consistency between some of his beliefs and certain themes of the pragmatic myth.

The evidence for a particular myth influencing worldview, policy preferences, and policymaking behavior was strongest in the Dulles case study, particularly with regard to the city-on-the-hill myth.[1] Both philosophically and instrumentally, his beliefs regarding the relationship between morality and diplomacy and regarding the moral nature of the Cold War confrontation were consistent with this myth, and at times his arguments on this issue were justified using city-on-the-hill imagery. His beliefs regarding the most important sources of U.S. power in the Cold War (he emphasized moral and spiritual power resources) and the best strategy for dealing with the Soviets (he believed bargaining and compromise with communists to be immoral) were also consistent with this myth, and his arguments on these matters also contained imagery from the myth on occasion. Dulles's policy preferences and policymaking behavior were significantly consistent with these beliefs. Dulles nearly always opposed efforts to negotiate with the Soviets (as well as the communist Chinese and Vietminh). Sometimes his opposition was overridden by Eisenhower, but other times it was not (i.e., the 1954 Geneva conference). Nonetheless it represented a clear pattern of policy preferences and policy behavior that was consistent with his city-on-the-hill beliefs about the moral nature of Cold War confrontation and the immorality of compromising with the Soviets (or more generally the communists).

There was also significant consistency between his city-on-the-hill belief in the importance of moral power as a weapon in the Cold War and his frequent quasi-evangelistic efforts in writings and speeches at Alliance meetings (i.e., SEATO, CENTO) to create a spiritual bond within the anticommunist world. Dulles's early policy preferences and policy behavior in support of an active liberation policy aimed at the Eastern European satellites were also consistent with this city-on-the-hill–influenced belief about the potency of moral or spiritual power as a weapon in the Cold War.

The Harriman case study provides some evidence of myth-to-worldview-to-policy influence, but the evidence is not as strong as in the Dulles case study.[2] Although Harriman's Cold War worldview showed slight evidence (in one article) of city-on-the-hill myth influence, the predominant imagery was from the market myth. In the mid-1950s, Harriman began to conceptualize the Cold War as a competition between the United States and the Soviets to see who would provide the predominant model for social and economic development in the Third World. He thus began to focus on U.S. economic power (in both a material and an ideational sense) as a primary weapon to prevent Soviet (and more generally communist) expansion. In his articles from the mid-1950s and into the early 1960s he began to argue that the United States should answer "Khrushchev's challenge" for a competition of development models (although the United States would first have to make the Soviets cease their support of wars of national liberation so the modeling contest would be fought on a level playing field). His arguments along these lines were consistent with the market myth and also contained market myth imagery.

There was also consistency between this market myth–influenced belief and his policy preferences and policymaking behavior while working on Indochina policy in the Kennedy-Johnson administrations. In both Laos and South Vietnam he argued for U.S.- and Soviet-brokered neutralization settlements that would protect each country from communist insurgencies so that they could choose a development model without communist coercion (aided by U.S. bribery in the form of massive development assistance). Having persuaded Kennedy on the merits of this strategy, he actually achieved such a neutralization settlement in Laos, although it was short-lived. He also tried to persuade both Kennedy and later Johnson to follow a similar plan for South Vietnam, but he was unable to do so. Thus his policy preferences and policymaking behavior in this area showed significant consistency with his market myth–influenced belief in the potential of the American free-enterprise system as a model for development.

Each of the Dulles and Harriman case studies turned up imagery from at least two myths in the communications of the policymakers. McNamara's communications contained no imagery from any of the three myths. Perhaps it makes sense that someone who was as driven as McNamara to always remain objective and rational in his analysis would shun a conceptual device as imprecise and irrational as myth for explaining or justifying a belief or policy preference. Perhaps he felt that logic and "facts" were sufficient. This would certainly be consistent with his role conceptions and descriptions of his management philosophy and with others' accounts of his intellectual style. There is, however, indirect evidence of myth-to-worldview influence in the form of consistency between some of his beliefs and themes of the pragmatic myth. For example, his prevailing belief in the importance of preserving a wide range of response options in the face of possible Soviet aggression was consistent with the pragmatic myth's theme of American ingenuity and adaptability. Also, his implication that the United States was tactically disadvantaged in its Cold War struggle because of its adherence to moral principles is consistent with the pragmatic adage "whatever works is good." McNamara's belief in adaptability and modulation of military force to promote rational behavior was consistent with his policy preferences and policy behavior.

The case study evidence that individual worldviews, policy preferences, and policymaking behavior were influenced by specific myths may be used to construct a heuristic model of this process. In the three biographical case studies (especially in the Dulles and Harriman cases) there is evidence that key beliefs within the policymaker's worldview were colored or shaped by a specific myth. In both the Dulles and Harriman cases, statements of certain key beliefs even contained actual imagery from the city-on-the-hill and market myths, respectively. This suggests that a significant "nexus of influence" existed between specific myths and individual worldviews. This myth-to-worldview nexus of influence makes up the first half of the myth-influence model.

The second half of the myth-influence model posits a nexus of influence between the policymaker's worldview and his policy preferences and policymaking behavior. In all three cases (especially those of Dulles and Harriman) there was substantial evidence of stable policy preference and policymaking behavior patterns that were consistent with the highlighted myth-influenced components of the individual's worldview. This myth-to-worldview-to-policy model provides us with a useful heuristic for understanding the process by which myths shape the worldviews and behavior of policymakers.

THE REPRESENTATIVE CHARACTER NEXUS OF INFLUENCE

The second culture-to-policy relationship examined was that between specific representative characters and self- and role conceptions, policy preferences, and policymaking behavior. In all three case studies there were very solid patterns of policy preferences and policymaking behavior that were consistent with the paradigmatic modes of social action of the three representative characters.

The evidence that individual policy preferences and policy behavior are consistent with the profiles of the representative characters is greatly reinforced by evidence that the individual actually conceived of himself or his role in ways that are consistent with the representative character structures. This was the case in both the Dulles and McNamara case studies; examination of Harriman's communications during his diplomatic career failed to yield such a clear picture.

In the Dulles case study the role-conception evidence was very consistent with the moral and epistemological profile of the Puritan representative character. In describing his role as statesman Dulles both conveyed the Puritan's sense of divine annointedness and exhibited the moral and epistemological stances of the Puritan character. He likened any attempt to make foreign policy without heeding the moral law as revealed by God to trying to make foreign policy "in violation of the laws of physics." Missing from his role conceptions was a description of the paradigmatic mode of social action of the Puritan representative character. However, in some communications he did argue that the American people had a duty to spread their moral principles and political ideals in a conversion and mobilization campaign to build up the free world. This is in essence a collective version of the Puritan's paradigmatic mode of social action.

Definite patterns in Dulles's policy preferences and policymaking behavior were consistent with his role conceptions. Early in his tenure as secretary of state he argued for a liberation policy that is consistent with the conversion and mobilization process just described. Throughout his tenure as secretary of state he traveled around the world and made quasi-evangelistic speeches on building a moral and spiritual bond within the anticommunist coalitions.

During his wartime involvement with the Federal Council of Churches, Dulles exhibited the same approach to influencing world politics. This behavioral continuity across time and across formal roles provides additional support for the viability of the representative character concept.

The McNamara case study also provides solid evidence of representative character influence. In fact, the self- and role-conception evidence is significantly stronger because there is more of it. In his memoirs, McNamara reflected on his exposure to the rationalistic and scientistic milieu at Berkeley and his discovery of his analytical talents as profoundly shaping his identity and also on his role conceptions while secretary of defense. These statements reflect the manager character's paradigmatic mode of social action—quasi-experimental manipulation of bureaucratic resources in an attempt to find the optimal resource mix—and the manager character's myopic moral stance: whatever works is good. Other statements exhibit an epistemological and operational hubris that is consistent with what Alasdair MacIntyre describes as the manager character's knowledge- and effectiveness-based grounds for his claim to authority within the bureaucracy and society.[3]

There is also remarkable consistency between McNamara's role conceptions and his policy preferences and policymaking behavior. Throughout his tenure as secretary of defense his approach to Cold War confrontations (whether with the Soviets, the Chinese or the North Vietnamese) showed a consistent pattern. His steadfast assumption seemed to be that he could find the exact level or mixture of force application that would cause the adversary to behave "rationally." This is remarkably consistent with the manager representative character's paradigmatic mode of manipulating bureaucratic resources in a attempt to find the optimal mix.

Even though the Harriman case study does not provide direct evidence of representative character influence, it does provide some support for the viability of the representative character concept. His worldview, policy preferences, and policymaking behavior throughout his diplomatic career reflected a strong and stable belief in negotiations, and this belief and behavior pattern is consistent with the entrepreneur representative character: competition and negotiation in business deals. The persistence of this belief and behavior pattern across time and formal roles does lend some support to the viability of the representative character concept. Harriman's operating style as a businessman—he had a preference for dealmaking over administration of his extant businesses—was consistent with his "take me to your leader" style of diplomacy.

The case study evidence that these individuals' self- and role conceptions, policy preferences, and policymaking behavior were influenced by specific representative character structures allows for the construction of a second heuristic model of the cultural shaping process. This second model posits a "nexus of influence" between a specific representative character and an individual's self- and role conceptions and a further nexus of influence between these conceptions and policy preferences and policymaking behavior. Specifically, this model would lead one to expect to find stable patterns of policy preferences and policymaking behavior that are consistent with the individual's representative character–influenced self- and role conceptions. This was certainly the case with both Dulles and McNamara.

This representative character nexus-of-influence model thus supplements the myth nexus-of-influence model as a useful heuristic for understanding how societal-level symbolic structures shape policymakers and thereby policy. From the standpoint of comparative foreign policy analysis, these two models may serve as a useful starting point for exploring how societal-level symbolic structures influence policymakers and policy in other cultural contexts.

CULTURAL ANALYSIS AS A
COMPLEMENT TO OTHER APPROACHES

This book is not an argument for cultural determinism. Its overriding message is rather that culture must be considered an important variable in any analytical framework that seeks to explain foreign policy behavior.[4] This framework includes such individual psychological variables as personality and cognitive processes as well as such social-psychological variables as small-group dynamics and social identity processes. Other influences that have to be considered for any given bit of foreign policy making behavior are institutional factors (i.e., bureaucratic politics and organizational process), domestic politics, and international systemic factors. Although this list is certainly not exhaustive, it does give an indication of just how many different influences the analyst must examine in order to provide a complete explanation of a given foreign policy behavior.

Cultural shaping analysis—the study of socially transmitted symbolic structures and their influence on policymakers and policy— can be used to complement and strengthen these other approaches to understanding U.S. foreign policy behavior. This is the case particularly with the individual-level approaches based on personality or cognitive psychology. Personality and cognitive approaches tend to approach human behavior from a procedural angle; they focus on how the policymaker operates. Personality approaches highlight patterns in the way that policymakers deal emotionally with situations or people, and cognitive approaches highlight patterns in the way policymakers process information. Cultural analysis can supplement these procedural insights with substantive ones.

For example, a personality study may tell us that Woodrow Wilson's childhood relationship with his father left him unable to compromise with Senate leaders on the Versailles treaty.[5] The cultural approach may focus on similar aspects of Wilson's childhood in order to explain his crusading style of diplomacy (i.e., examining Wilson's father as a Puritan role model). The difference between the two approaches in this case is largely one of purpose. Whereas the personality analyst will examine Wilson's childhood in order to fully explain his behavior as a unique individual, the cultural analyst will use the representative character concept to explain Wilson as a recurring type of American statesman—the Puritan diplomat. By analyzing Wilson in the light of the Puritan representative character, we can then compare Wilson's identity and behavior patterns with those of other American statesmen (Dulles, for example) to establish shared patterns. Thus the cultural approach allows us to generalize across individuals in the making of U.S. foreign policy. Undertaken together, personality and cultural analyses not only yield a richer explanation of Wilson the individual but also allow us to begin to generalize about a recurring type of U.S. policymaker.

Cultural shaping analysis can strengthen a cognitive study by showing the cultural sources of the subject's core beliefs, self-conceptions, and role conceptions, all of which help determine what a given situation means to a subject. Whereas the cognitive approach tells us how the subject's beliefs filter incoming information, cultural shaping analysis—by exploring the cultural roots of those beliefs and of the self- and role conceptions of the policymaker—allows us to determine the extent to which certain beliefs and stable behavior patterns might be shared by other policymakers who were influenced by the same societal-level symbolic structures.

Thus in addition to complementing and strengthening other approaches to explaining foreign policy decisions, the cultural shaping approach allows the analyst to identify recurring belief and behavior patterns among policymakers within the same cultural system (e.g., Woodrow Wilson and John Foster Dulles as Puritan diplomats). Establishing such recurring belief and behavior patterns among policymakers with similar cultural backgrounds could even allow analysts to make loose predictions about how "culturally typed" policymakers would react given certain situations.

Although the symbolic structures studied here are transmitted throughout U.S. society (and may therefore be considered a societal phenomenon ontologically), the place they exert their influence on policymaking is in the minds of individual statesmen. The three case studies provide strong evidence that the worldviews, self- and role conceptions, policy preferences, and policy behavior of three very important cold warriors were substantially influenced and shaped by different symbolic structures.

More important, they show that it seems to matter a great deal (for helping to understand significant patterns of beliefs and behavior over time) exactly *which* symbolic structures predominately influenced each policymaker. This is a major contribution of the cultural shaping approach, since ultimately it is individuals who make policy.

NOTES

1. There was market myth imagery in some of Dulles's earlier writings on international relations but no evidence of market myth influence in later communications.

2. Part of the reason is that Harriman did not communicate his beliefs with the frequency that Dulles did. It seems that Dulles poured out his basic beliefs about the world almost every time he had an audience. Also, Harriman never addressed some of the basic philosophical questions (i.e., regarding the relationship between morality and diplomacy).

3. Alasdair MacIntyre, *After Virtue* (South Bend: Notre Dame Press, 1981), 76–77.

4. For an excellent example of such an analytical framework, see Eugene Wittkopf, ed., *The Domestic Sources of American Foreign Policy: Insights and Evidence* (New York: St. Martin's Press, 1994), 1–10.

5. For the personality argument on the Versailles episode, see Alexander George and Juliette George, *Woodrow Wilson and Colonel House: A Personality Study* (New York: Dover, 1956).

Selected Bibliography

BOOKS

Abel, Elie. *The Missile Crisis.* New York: J. B. Lippincott, 1966.

Abramson, Rudy. *Spanning the Century: The Life and Times of W. Averell Harriman, 1891–1986.* New York: William Morrow, 1992.

Alexander, Jeffrey, ed. *Durkheimian Sociology: Cultural Studies.* Cambridge: Cambridge University Press, 1988.

Ambrose, Stephen. *Eisenhower: The President and Elder Statesman.* New York: Simon and Schuster, 1984.

Baker, Ray S., and Dodd, William E., eds. *The Public Papers of Woodrow Wilson, 1917–1924.* 2 vols. New York: Harper, 1927.

Baldwin, L. D. *The Meaning of America: Essays Toward and Understanding of the American Spirit.* Pittsburgh: University of Pittsburgh Press, 1976.

Baritz, Loren. *City on a Hill: A History of Ideas and Myths in America.* New York: John Wiley, 1964.

———. *Backfire: A History of How American Culture Led Us into Vietnam and Made Us Fight the Way We Did.* New York: Morrow, 1985.

Bellah, Robert. *Beyond Belief: Essays on Religion in a PostTraditional World.* New York: Harper and Row, 1970.

———. *The Broken Covenant: American Civil Religion in a Time of Trial.* Chicago: University of Chicago Press, 1992.

Bellah, Robert, Madsen, Richard, Sullivan, William, Swidler, Ann, and Tipton, Steven. *Habits of the Heart: Individualism and Commitment in American Life.* Berkeley: University of California Press, 1985.

Berger, Peter, and Luckmann, Thomas. *The Social Construction of Reality: A Treatise in the Sociology of Knowledge.* New York: Anchor Press, 1966.

Boorstin, Daniel. *The Genius of American Politics.* Chicago: University of Chicago Press, 1953.

Brown, Seyom. *The Faces of Power: United States Foreign Policy from Truman to Clinton.* New York: Columbia University Press, 1994.

Burns, Edward M. *The American Idea of Mission: Concepts of National Purpose and Destiny.* New Brunswick: Rutgers University Press, 1957.

Byrne, John A. *The Whiz Kids: The Founding Fathers of American Business and the Legacy They Left Us.* New York: Doubleday, 1993.

Chang, Laurence, and Kornbluh, Peter. *The Cuban Missile Crisis, 1962: A National Security Archive Documents Reader.* New York: New Press, 1992.

Commager, Henry S. *The American Mind: An Interpretation of American Thought and Character Since the 1880s.* New Haven: Yale University Press, 1950.

De Tocqueville, Alexis. *Democracy in America.* 2 vols. New York: Vintage Books, 1990.

Dewey, John. *Reconstruction in Philosophy*. Boston: Beacon Press, 1920.
———. *Human Nature and Conduct*. New York: Henry Holt, 1922.
Diggins, John. *The Promise of Pragmatism: Modernity and the Crisis of Knowledge and Authority*. Chicago: University of Chicago Press, 1994.
Dreiser, Theodore. *The Financier*. New York: Harper, 1912.
Drucker, Peter. *The Effective Executive*. New York: Harper and Row, 1966.
Dulles, John F. *War, Peace, and Change*. New York: Harper, 1939.
Durkheim, Émile. *The Rules of the Sociological Method*, 8th ed. Translated by Sarah Solajay and John Meuller. Glencoe, IL: Free Press, 1966.
———. *Sociology and Philosophy*. Translated by D. F. Pocock. Glencoe, IL: Free Press, 1953.
———. *The Elementary Forms of the Religious Life*. New York: Collier Books, 1961.
Eisenhower, Dwight D. *Waging Peace*. New York: Doubleday, 1965.
Ewing, David. *The Managerial Mind*. New York: Free Press, 1962.
Franklin, Benjamin. *The Autobiography and Other Writings*. New York: Penguin Books, 1986.
Freedman, Lawrence. *The Evolution of Nuclear Strategy*. New York: St. Martin's Press, 1989.
Geertz, Clifford. *The Interpretation of Cultures*. New York: Basic Books, 1973.
George, Alexander, and George, Juliette. *Woodrow Wilson and Colonel House: A Personality Study*. New York: Dover, 1956.
Greenstein, Fred. *The Hidden Hand Presidency: Eisenhower as Leader*. New York: Basic Books, 1982.
Guhin, Michael. *John Foster Dulles: A Statesman and His Times*. New York: Columbia University Press, 1972.
Haber, Samuel. *Efficiency and Uplift: Scientific Management in the Progressive Era, 1890–1920*. Chicago: University of Chicago Press, 1964.
Halberstam, David. *The Best and the Brightest*. New York: Random House, 1972.
Hall, Michael. *The Life of Increase Mather*. Middleton: Wesleyan University Press, 1984.
Hamilton, Alexander, Madison, James, and Jay, John. *The Federalist Papers*. New York: Bantam Books, 1982.
Harriman, W. Averell, and Abel, Elie. *Special Envoy to Churchill and Stalin: 1941–1946*. New York: Random House, 1975.
Hawthorne, Nathaniel. *The Scarlet Letter*. New York: W. W. Norton, 1978.
Hillsman, Roger. *To Move a Nation: The Politics of Foreign Policy in the Administration of John F. Kennedy*. New York: Dell Books, 1968.
Hofstadler, Richard. *The Age of Reform*. New York: Vintage Books, 1955.
Hoopes, Townsend. *The Devil and John Foster Dulles*. Boston: Little, Brown, 1973.
Howells, W. D. *The Rise and Fall of Silas Lapham*. Bloomington: University of Indiana Press, 1971.
Hughes, Emmett J. *The Ordeal of Power: A Political Memoir of the Eisenhower Years*. New York: Atheneum, 1963.
Hunt, Michael. *Ideology and U.S. Foreign Policy*. New Haven: Yale University Press, 1987.
Huntington, Samuel. *American Politics: The Promise of Disharmony*. Cambridge: Harvard University Press, 1981.
Isaacson, Walter, and Thomas, Evan. *The Wise Men: Six Friends and the World They Made*. New York: Simon and Schuster, 1986.

James, William. *The Will to Believe.* New York: Longmans, Green, 1896.
————. *A Pluralistic Universe.* New York: Longmans, Green, 1909.
Jervis, Robert. *Perception and Misperception in International Politics.* Princeton: Princeton University Press, 1976.
Johnson, Thomas, and Miller, Perry, eds. *The Puritans.* New York: Harper and Row, 1938.
Kaplan, Fred. *The Wizards of Armageddon.* New York: Simon and Schuster, 1983.
Kaufmann, William. *The McNamara Strategy.* New York: Harper and Row, 1964.
Kennan, George. *Memoirs: 1925–1950.* Boston: Little, Brown, 1967.
Kroeber, A. L., and Kluckhohn, Clyde. *Culture: A Critical Review of Concepts and Definitions.* New York: Random House, 1952.
Leites, Nathan. *The Operational Code of the Politburo.* New York: McGraw Hill, 1951.
Lerner, Max. *America as a Civilization.* New York: Simon and Schuster, 1957.
MacIntyre, Alasdair. *After Virtue.* South Bend: University of Notre Dame Press, 1981.
May, Ernest, and Neustadt, Richard. *Thinking in Time: The Use of History for Decision Makers.* New York: Free Press, 1986.
Maurer, Herrymon. *Great Enterprise: Growth and Behavior of the Big Corporation.* New York: Macmillan, 1955.
McCullough, David. *Truman.* New York: Simon and Schuster, 1992.
McNamara, Robert. *The Essence of Security: Reflections in Office.* New York: Harper and Row, 1968.
————. *In Retrospect: The Tragedy and Lessons of Vietnam.* New York: Times Books, 1995.
Mercer, Lloyd. *E. H. Harriman: Master Railroader.* Boston: Twayne Books, 1985.
Miller, Perry. *Errand in the Wilderness.* Cambridge: Harvard University Press, 1964.
————. *The Life of the Mind in America: From the Revolution to the Civil War.* New York: Harcourt Brace, 1965.
Morgan, Edmond. *The Puritan Dilemma: The Story of John Winthrop.* Boston: Little, Brown, 1958.
The Pentagon Papers: The Defense Department History of United States' Decision-making in Vietnam. Senator Gravel edition, 5 vols. Boston: Beacon Press, 1972.
Perry, Ralph B. *Puritanism and Democracy.* New York: Vanguard Press, 1944.
Pruessen, Ronald. *John Foster Dulles: The Road to Power.* New York: Free Press, 1973.
Randle, Robert F. *Geneva 1954: The Settlement of the Indochinese War.* Princeton: Princeton University Press, 1969.
Richardson, J. D., ed. *A Compilation of the Messages and Papers of the Presidents: 1789–1902.* Washington, DC: Bureau of National Literature and Art, 1903.
Rischen, Moses, ed. *The American Gospel of Success.* New York: Quadrangle Books, 1965.
Robertson, James O. *American Myth, American Reality.* New York: Hill and Wang, 1980.
Roherty, James M. *The Decisions of Robert McNamara: A Study of the Role of the Secretary of Defense.* Coral Gables: University of Miami Press, 1970.

Rosati, Jerel. *The Politics of United States Foreign Policy.* Fort Worth: Harcourt Brace, 1993.

Schlesinger, Arthur Jr. *The Cycles of American History.* New York: Houghton Mifflin, 1986.

Shapley, Deborah. *Promise and Power: The Life and Times of Robert McNamara.* Boston: Little, Brown, 1993.

Smelser, Neil. *Karl Marx on Society and Social Change.* Chicago: University of Chicago Press, 1973.

Starr, Harvey. *Henry Kissinger: Perceptions of International Politics.* Lexington: University of Kentucky Press, 1984.

Toulouse, Mark. *The Transformation of John Foster Dulles: From Prophet of Realism to Priest of Nationalism.* Macon, GA: Mercer University Press, 1985.

Tudor, Henry. *Political Myth.* New York: Praeger, 1972.

Trewhitt, Henry. *McNamara.* New York: Harper and Row, 1971.

Van Dusen, Henry, ed. *The Spiritual Legacy of John Foster Dulles: Selections from His Articles and Addresses.* Philadelphia: Westminster Press, 1960.

Williams, William A. *The Tragedy of American Diplomacy.* New York: Dell, 1959.

———. *The Contours of American History.* Chicago: University of Chicago Press, 1966.

Weber, Max. *The Methodology of the Social Sciences.* New York: Free Press, 1949.

———. *The Protestant Ethic and the Spirit of Capitalism.* New York: Charles Scribner's Sons, 1958.

Welter, Rush. *The Mind of America: 1820–1860.* New York: Columbia University Press, 1975.

Wuthnow, Robert. *Meaning and Moral Order: Explorations in Cultural Analysis.* Berkeley: University of California Press, 1984.

Wyllie, Irvin. *The Self-Made Man in America: The Myth of Rags to Riches.* New York: Free Press, 1954.

Yergin, Daniel. *Shattered Peace: The Origins of the Cold War and the National Security State.* Boston: Houghton Mifflin, 1977.

ARTICLES

Dulles, John F. "The Allied War Debts." *Foreign Affairs* 1 (September 15, 1922): 115–132.

———. "The Road to Peace." *Atlantic Monthly* 156 (October 1935): 492–499.

Forbes, B. C. "New Business Star: Harriman II." *Forbes* (October 30, 1920): 5–15.

George, Alexander. "The Operational Code: A Neglected Approach to the Study of Political Leaders and Decision Making." *International Studies Quarterly* 23 (1969): 190–222.

Glad, Betty. "Black and White Thinking: Ronald Reagan's Approach to Foreign Policy." *Political Psychology* 4, 1 (1983).

Halberstam, David. "Dead Wrong" (Review of Robert McNamara, *In Retrospect: The Tragedy and Lessons of Vietnam*). *Los Angeles Times,* Book Review Section, April 14, 1995.

Harriman, W. Averell. "Our Primary Task: A Healthy Economy." *Commercial and Financial Chronicle* (May 8, 1947): 5–41.

———. "U.S. Task in Promoting World Peace." *Commercial and Financial Chronicle* (August 28, 1947): 31–33.

———. "Leadership in World Affairs." *Foreign Affairs* (July 1954): 525–539.

———. "Danger Unrecognized: The Soviet Challenge and American Policy." *Atlantic Monthly* (April 1956): 42–47.

———. "My Alarming Interview with Krushchev." *Life Magazine* (July 1959): 14–18.

———. "The United States and the Far East." *Annals of the American Academy of Political and Social Science* 342 (July 1962): 90–95.

Iden, V. G. "W. A. Harriman Seeks and Wins Front Rank in Marine Field." *Marine Review* (March 1921): 119–125.

Loving, Rush. "W. Averell Harriman Remembers Life with Father." *Fortune* (May 8, 1978): 197–201.

Walker, Stephen. "The Evolution of Operational Code Analysis." *Political Psychology* 11, 2 (1990): 403–418.

ARCHIVAL COLLECTIONS

Defense Department correspondence of Robert McNamara. John F. Kennedy Presidential Library, Boston, MA.

John Foster Dulles Papers. Princeton University, Princeton, NJ.

W. Averell Harriman Papers. Library of Congress, Washington, DC.

Index

About the Book

In what ways does national culture influence the direction of U.S. foreign policy? What are the mechanisms through which culture shapes policy outcomes? Stephen Twing's thoughtful analysis illustrates precisely how certain cultural elements influenced the policy preferences and policymaking behaviors of three Cold War–era statesmen: John Foster Dulles, Averell Harriman, and Robert McNamara.

Drawing on a wealth of primary source materials, Twing traces the evolution of each statesman's thoughts about world politics. His study lucidly demonstrates that each was powerfully shaped by at least one central U.S. myth or "representative character"—and that all three men behaved in the policymaking arena in ways highly consistent with their culturally influenced worldviews.

Stephen W. Twing is visiting assistant professor of political science at Virginia Polytechnic Institute.